Structural Analysis and the Process of Economic Development

Economic development is full of discontinuities. Mainstream economists perceive these as external disturbances to a natural state of equilibrium, but this book argues that much of the discontinuities are part of economic development, suggesting that patterns can be understood with structural analysis.

Structural Analysis and the Process of Economic Development presents a detailed analysis of the trajectory of Swedish economic change since the nineteenth century. The emergence of structural analysis in economic research is reviewed, as well as a chapter devoted to development blocks, a key concept that was outlined in the 1940s and that has much in common with the more recent notions 'techno-economic paradigms' and 'general-purpose technologies'. Structural analysis and the major contributions by Schön are introduced in this book. Also highlighted is Sweden's integration into the international economy via the nineteenth-century capital markets, along with structural analysis as a tool for understanding climate change. The recent technique of wavelet analysis and its potential for structural analysis is demonstrated in a non-technical chapter.

This book is suitable for those who are interested in and study political economy, economic history and European history.

Jonas Ljungberg is a Professor in Economic History at Lund University, Sweden.

Routledge Frontiers of Political Economy

For a complete list of titles in this series please visit www.routledge.com/books/series/SE0345

151. Capitalist Diversity and Diversity within Capitalism
Edited by Geoffrey T. Wood and Christel Lane

152. The Consumer, Credit and Neoliberalism
Governing the modern economy
Christopher Payne

153. Order and Control in American Socio-Economic Thought
Social scientists and Progressive-Era reform
Charles McCann

154. The Irreconcilable Inconsistencies of Neoclassical Macroeconomics
A false paradigm
John Weeks

155. The Political Economy of Putin's Russia
Pekka Sutela

156. Facts, Values and Objectivity in Economics
José Castro Caldas and Vítor Neves

157. Economic Growth and the High Wage Economy
Choices, constraints and opportunities in the market economy
Morris Altman

158. Social Costs Today
Institutional analyses of the present crises
Edited by Wolfram Elsner, Pietro Frigato and Paolo Ramazzotti

159. Economics, Sustainability and Democracy
Economics in the era of climate change
Christopher Nobbs

160. Organizations, Individualism and Economic Theory
Maria Brouwer

161. Economic Models for Policy Making
Principles and designs revisited
S.I. Cohen

162. Reconstructing Keynesian Macroeconomics, Volume 2
Integrated approaches
Carl Chiarella, Peter Flaschel and Willi Semmler

163. Architectures of Economic Subjectivity
The philosophical foundations of the subject in the history of economic thought
Sonya Marie Scott

164. Support-Bargaining, Economics and Society
A social species
Patrick Spread

165. Inherited Wealth, Justice and Equality
Edited by Guido Erreygers and John Cunliffe

166. The Charismatic Principle in Social Life
Edited by Luigino Bruni and Barbara Sena

167. Ownership Economics
On the foundations of interest, money, markets, business cycles and economic development
Gunnar Heinsohn and Otto Steiger; translated and edited with comments and additions by Frank Decker

168. Urban and Regional Development Trajectories in Contemporary Capitalism
Edited by Flavia Martinelli, Frank Moulaert and Andreas Novy

169. Social Fairness and Economics
Economic essays in the spirit of Duncan Foley
Edited by Lance Taylor, Armon Rezai and Thomas Michl

170. Financial Crisis, Labour Markets and Institutions
Edited by Sebastiano Fadda and Pasquale Tridico

171. Marx and Living Labour
Laurent Baronian

172. A Political Economy of Contemporary Capitalism and its Crisis
Demystifying finance
Dimitris P. Sotiropoulos, John G. Milios and Spyros Lapatsioras

173. Against Utility-Based Economics
On a life-based approach
Anastasios Korkotsides

174. Economic Indeterminacy
The dance of the meta-axioms
Yanis Varoufakis

175. Freedom, Responsibility and Economics of the Person
Jérôme Ballet, Damien Bazin, Jean-Luc Dubois and François-Régis Mahieu

176. Reality and Accounting
Ontological explorations in the economic and social sciences
Richard Mattessich

177. Profitability and the Great Recession
The role of accumulation trends in the financial crisis
Ascension Mejorado and Manuel Roman

178. Institutions and Development After the Financial Crisis
Edited by Sebastiano Fadda and Pasquale Tridico

179. The Political Economy of Gunnar Myrdal
A reassessment in the post-2008 world
Örjan Appelqvist

180. Gender Perspectives and Gender Impacts of the Global Economic Crisis
Edited by Rania Antonopoulos

181. Hegel, Institutions, and Economics
Performing the social
Carsten Herrmann-Pillath and Ivan A. Boldyrev

182. Producer Cooperatives as a New Mode of Production
Bruno Jossa

183. Economic Policy and the Financial Crisis
Edited by Łukasz Mamica and Pasquale Tridico

184. Information Technology and Socialist Construction
The end of capital and the transition to socialism
Daniel E. Saros

185. Beyond Mainstream Explanations of the Financial Crisis
Parasitic finance capital
Ismael Hossein-zadeh

186. Greek Capitalism in Crisis
Marxist analyses
Stavros Mavroudeas

187. Of Synthetic Finance
Three essays of speculative materialism
Benjamin Lozano

188. The Political Economy and Media
Coverage of the European Economic
Crisis
The case of Ireland
Julien Mercille

189. Financial Cultures and Crisis
Dynamics
*Edited by Bon Jessop, Brigitte Young and
Christoph Scherrer*

190. Capitalism and the Political
Economy of Work Time
Christoph Hermann

191. The Responsible Economy
Jefferson Frank

192. Globalization and the Critique of
Political Economy
New insights from Marx's writings
Lucia Pradella

193. Exit from Globalization
Richard Westra

194. Reconstructing Keynesian
Macroeconomics, Volume III
Financial markets and banking
*Carl Chiarella, Peter Flaschel and
Willi Semmler*

195. The European Union and
Supranational Political Economy
*Edited by Riccardo Fiorentini and
Guido Montani*

196. The Future of Capitalism after the
Financial Crisis
The varieties of Capitalism debate in the
age of austerity
*Edited by Richard Westra, Dennis Badeen
and Robert Albritton*

197. Liberal Learning and the Art of
Self-Governance
Edited by Emily Chamlee-Wright

198. The Systemic Nature of the
Economic Crisis
The perspectives of heterodox economics
and psychoanalysis
Arturo Hermann

199. Economies of Death
Economic logics of killable life and
grievable death
*Edited by Patricia J. Lopez and
Kathryn A. Gillespie*

200. Civil Society, the Third Sector and
Social Enterprise
Governance and democracy
*Edited by Jean-Louis Laville, Dennis
Young and Philippe Eynaud*

201. Economics, Culture and
Development
Eiman O. Zein-Elabdin

202. Paradigms in Political Economy
Kavous Ardalan

203. The Economics of Voting
Studies of self-interest, bargaining, duty
and rights
Dan Usher

204. The Political Economy of Food and
Finance
Ted P. Schmidt

205. The Evolution of Economies
An alternative approach to money
bargaining
Patrick Spread

206. Representing Public Credit
Credible commitment, fiction, and the rise
of the financial subject
Natalie Roxburgh

207. The Rejuvenation of Political
Economy
*Edited by Nobuharu Yokokawa,
Kiichiro Yagi, Hiroyasu Uemura and
Richard Westra*

208. Macroeconomics After the
Financial Crisis
A Post-Keynesian Perspective
*Edited by Mogens Ove Madsen and
Finn Olesen*

209. Structural Analysis and the Process
of Economic Development
Edited by Jonas Ljungberg

Structural Analysis and the Process of Economic Development

Essays in memory of Lennart Schön

Edited by
Jonas Ljungberg

Routledge
Taylor & Francis Group

LONDON AND NEW YORK

First published 2016
by Routledge
2 Park Square, Milton Park, Abingdon, Oxon OX14 4RN

and by Routledge
52 Vanderbilt Avenue, New York, NY 10017

First issued in paperback 2020

Routledge is an imprint of the Taylor & Francis Group, an informa business

British Library Cataloguing in Publication Data
A catalogue record for this book is available from the British Library

Library of Congress Cataloging in Publication Data
Names: Ljungberg, Jonas, editor.
Title: Structural analysis and the process of economic development/edited by Jonas Ljungberg.
Description: New York : Routledge, 2016.
Identifiers: LCCN 2015046125| ISBN 9781138101302 (hardback) | ISBN 9781315657042 (ebook)
Subjects: LCSH: Economic development–Sweden. | Economic history.
Classification: LCC HC373 .S77 2016 | DDC 338.9485–dc23
LC record available at http://lccn.loc.gov/2015046125

ISBN 13: 978-0-367-66840-2 (pbk)
ISBN 13: 978-1-138-10130-2 (hbk)

Typeset in Times New Roman
by Deanta Global Publishing Services, Chennai, India

Contents

List of figures   ix
List of tables   xi
About the contributors   xiii
Preface   xv
Acknowledgement   xvii

1   Introduction: structural analysis and the process of
    economic development   1
    JONAS LJUNGBERG

2   How it all began: on structural periods   19
    OLLE KRANTZ AND CARL-AXEL NILSSON

3   Identifying and modelling cycles and long waves in
    economic time series   34
    FREDRIK N. G. ANDERSSON

4   Development blocks and structural analysis   56
    JOSEF TAALBI

5   The Gerschenkron effect, creative destruction and
    structural analysis   78
    JONAS LJUNGBERG

6   The gold standard and industrial breakthrough in Sweden   103
    HÅKAN LOBELL

7   The development of economic growth and inequality
    among the Swedish regions 1860–2010: evidence from
    regional national accounts   126
    KERSTIN ENFLO AND MARTIN HENNING

8 Regional analysis and the process of economic development: changes in growth, employment and income 149

MARTIN HENNING, KARL-JOHAN LUNDQUIST AND LARS-OLOF OLANDER

9 Economic environmental history: anything new under the sun? 174

ASTRID KANDER

Index 191

Figures

2.1	Swedish GDP per capita, 1560–2010	23
3.1	GDP growth: original data and wavelet transforms, 1902–2010	39
3.2	TFP growth: original data and wavelet transforms, 1902–2010	40
3.3	Inflation: original data and wavelet transforms, 1902–2010	41
4.1	A sequence of widening imbalances	62
4.2	The community of innovations centered on ICT technologies	71
4.3	Carrier industries in Sweden, 1970–2007	72
5.1	Ratio between Paasche and Laspeyres price indices for manufacturing, 1888–1992	80
5.2	Prices of machinery, electrical equipment and cars, relative to prices of all manufactures, 1888–1992	86
5.3	Prices of butchery and textiles, relative to prices of all manufactures, 1888–1992	89
5.4	Prices of mineral goods (building materials), relative to prices of all manufactures, 1888–1992	90
6.1	Sweden's capital imports, 1850–1913	104
6.2	Stockholm exchange rates of bills payable in Hamburg and London, monthly 1804–1914	107
6.3	Sweden's import and export of specie and bullion as per cent of GDP, 1836–1914	109
6.4a	Composition of money and specie reserves, 1834–1860	110
6.4b	Composition of money and specie reserves, 1860–1880	110
6.4c	Composition of money and specie reserves, 1880–1913	111
6.5	*Riksbank* official discount rate, 1850–1914	115
6.6	Exchange rates for Scandinavian bill of exchange in Hamburg compared with rates for Hamburg/Berlin bills in Stockholm, monthly 1882–1913	121
7.1	Location and names of the Swedish regions	133
7.2	Regional shares (%) of total national GDP in 1860 and 2007	134
7.3	Regional shares (%) of total national population in 1860 and 2007	135
7.4	Long-run Adjusted Geographic Concentration (AGC) index of population in Sweden, 1860–2010	136
7.5	Long-run Adjusted Geographic Concentration (AGC) index of population in European countries	136

7.6 GDP per capita in the regions, indexed to the nation (nation=100) in 1860   138

7.7 GDP per capita in the regions, indexed to the nation (nation=100) in 2007   139

7.8 Sweden's regional inequality: coefficient of variation of GDP per capita among regions, 1860–2000   140

7.9 Correlations between distributions of regional GDP, regional GDP per capita and population in the regional system   141

8.1 Classification of actor industries (manufacturing sector)   154

8.2 Classification of service industries   154

8.3 Most salient supply- and demand-driven industries   155

8.4 Growth indices of most salient supply- and demand-driven industries, and other industries, 1985–2008   156

8.5 Growth of value added in total market economy versus growth of employment in different tiers of regions, 1985–2008   166

8.6 Growth of value added in total market economy versus growth of total market income in different tiers of regions, 1985–2008   169

8.7 Regional growth rates in market income and total income, 1985–2008   169

Tables

3.1	Standard deviations, 1902–2010	42
3.2	Simulation results: two time horizons	47
3.3	Simulation results: three time horizons	49
3.4	Regression results inflation model: one time horizon	50
3.5	Regression results inflation model: three time horizons	51
A3.1	Data sources	55
4.1	Imbalances that spurred innovation activity, 1970–2007	70
5.1	Construction of a commodity price index from scattered observations	82
5.2	Average annual percentage rate of change in product prices relative to all manufactures, 1888–1992	93
5.3	Classification of industries according to change in relative prices, with sales volumes during five periods, 1888–1992	95
5.4	Typology of market forces for industries during different periods, 1888–1992	99
6.1	The number of banks and savings banks in Sweden, 1830–1910	118
7.1	Rank order correlations across Swedish counties, 1860–2000	140
7.2	Transformation matrix of regional GDPs, 1890–2000	141
7.3	Transformation matrix of regional GDP/capita, 1890–2000	142
8.1	Characteristics of transformation and rationalization	151
8.2	Growth in value added in most salient supply-driven, most demand-driven industries, and other industries, 1985–2008	157
8.3	Employment in most salient supply- and demand-driven industries, and other industries, 1985–2008	158
8.4	Population and number of industries within tiers in 2000	159
8.5	Regional growth rates and shares of value added in most salient supply- and demand-driven industries, and other industries, 1985–2008	160
8.6	Regional growth rates of value added: most salient supply-driven industries and total market economy, 1985–2008	162
8.7	Regional growth rates in value added: most salient demand-driven industries and total market economy, 1985–2008	163

8.8   Regional growth rates in value added: other industries and
       total market economy, 1985–2008   163
8.9   Regional growth rates of employment and value added
       of total market economy, 1985–2008   165
8.10   Regional growth rates of market income and total market
       economy value added, 1985–2008   168

Contributors

Fredrik N. G. Andersson is senior lecturer in economics at Lund University. His research combines the development of new wavelet methods for economic analysis with empirical applications of the methods to study long-run economic change.

Kerstin Enflo is associate professor in economic history at Lund University and a Wallenberg Academy Fellow. Her research is presently focused on long-run regional growth patterns in the Nordic countries.

Martin Henning is associate professor in economic geography at the University of Gothenburg. He is especially interested in regional growth and transformation in a historical perspective, and regional labour mobility.

Astrid Kander is professor in economic history at Lund University. Her research is focused on energy and sustainable growth in a historical perspective, in particular measurement issues related to climate change.

Olle Krantz is professor (emeritus) in economic history at Umeå University and previously had various positions at Lund University. His research has focused on economic growth and structural change on the basis of historical national accounts, as well as the Swedish household and ornamental glass industry.

Jonas Ljungberg is professor in economic history at Lund University. His research is presently focused on the exchange rate arrangements and their long-term impact on convergence and economic growth in Europe.

Håkan Lobell is assistant professor in economic history at Lund University. His main research interests lie in the fields of monetary and financial history, history of monetary thought, and economic growth and change.

Karl-Johan Lundquist is professor in economic geography and head of the Department of Human Geography at Lund University. His research is in evolutionary economic geography, focusing on different aspects of localization dynamics and the role of technology and its diffusion in time and space.

Carl-Axel Nilsson was associate professor in economic history at the University of Copenhagen, preceded by various positions at Lund University. His main field of research was economic growth and structural change based on Swedish and Danish historical national accounts. Nilsson passed away in September 2015.

Lars-Olof Olander is senior professor in human geography at Lund University. He is working on growth and long-term regional transformation in urban hierarchies and on problems concerning decarbonization of modern economies.

Josef Taalbi is postdoc in economic history at Lund University and is a holder of the prestigious Wallander Scholarship. His research interests are the economics of innovation and long-term economic change, labour market relations and the philosophy and history of economic thought.

Preface

The plan was that this volume should be subtitled *Essays in Honour of Lennart Schön* and come off the printing press some weeks before his 70th birthday, 29 June 2016. Regrettably, that will not happen. Lennart, who was our mentor, source of inspiration and colleague, passed away in early January. We knew that he was seriously ill, but his optimism, fighting spirit and humour kept him going. He still gave his lectures last autumn and continued with research until the Christmas holidays.

This continuously restless work has also left its mark on this volume. The aim has been to focus on his most pointed contribution, the structural analysis approach, and how this has inspired and guided our own work. The Introduction is an effort to review this approach, and how it has developed through Lennart's works. Reflecting on the whole content, we obviously miss a bibliography that would have more comprehensively shown the contributions of Lennart Schön. A few remarks, however, should be added here in highlighting areas and issues where Lennart has left his mark.

In his doctoral dissertation (1979) about the emergence of the factory system in Swedish cotton textiles, Lennart uncovered that this took place before the surge in exports of sawn timber and iron. This finding laid a basis for his emphasis, in several publications throughout his life, of the internal factors in Swedish and Scandinavian industrialization. However, with this emphasis he did not deny the importance and influence of the international economy. On the contrary, industrialization as well as the further development of the Swedish economy was seen by Lennart as an interaction between internal and external factors. A decade after his doctoral dissertation, Lennart, in a project headed by Erik Dahmén and financed by the Swedish Debt Office, again uncovered evidence that changed conventional wisdom. It was the magnitude of the Swedish foreign debt before the First World War that had been underestimated by previous historians. The finding meant that capital imports were an important contribution to Swedish industrialization and this, moreover, corroborated Lennart's previous emphasis of the domestic market.

It was not long before another important publication, about Swedish electrification, was released by Lennart, in 1990. Here, the key notion of 'development blocks', originating from Erik Dahmén, was applied and elaborated. The complementarities accentuated by development blocks are also crucial for the idea about general-purpose technologies (GPTs) which gained currency in the literature in the 1990s. Lennart saw the connections and adopted GPT along with development blocks in his analyses. One may say that while not all development blocks constitute a GPT, all GPTs form development blocks.

In those years, from his dissertation up to the early 1990s, much of Lennart's efforts were directed toward extending Swedish Historical National Accounts back to 1800. The Bank of Sweden Tercentenary Foundation financed these research projects which Lennart and Olle Krantz pursued. There was a sort of division of labour, with Lennart covering commodity production and Olle services, with others working on construction and prices. Even if there were previous estimates back to 1861, and official data from 1950, a large amount of data for almost two centuries were presented in a consistent way. Much of this work was pioneering not least in an international context and it provided the basis for Lennart's interpretation of Sweden's economic history as a series of structural cycles, similar to the classical long waves. Outlines of the structural cycles had been presented before but were fully developed in *Omvandling och obalans* (*Transformation and Imbalance*) in 1994, as an appendix to the government's *Long-Term Survey of the Swedish Economy*. This grew into Lennart's now classic book, with its first Swedish edition in 2000, *An Economic History of Modern Sweden: Growth and Transformation during Two Centuries*. If any single work can be seen as a source of inspiration for the present volume, it is Lennart's book, so rich in scope and deep in analysis. He was, consequently, awarded the Swedish Pro Lingua prize in 2007 for this book, together with his shorter though incisive *Thoughts about Cycles* (still only in Swedish). Lennart's brilliance as an author was due, not least, to his ability to explain complex relations in very easy and plain language. These successes whet his appetite and the next project resulted in *An Economic History of the World* (in Swedish) in 2010, dealing with the industrial era which followed a first volume, by Johan Söderberg, on pre-industrial times. Hopefully, we will soon see an English edition since Lennart managed, shortly before his passing away, to complete the translation of this sizeable book.

Lennart's occupation with the global context was also reflected in recent research papers and unfinished work on differences in purchasing power parities (PPPs) and structural change. In recent years, moreover, his collaboration with Olle Krantz was revived and resulted not only in updates to the historical national accounts series since 1800, but also to their extension back to the reign of Gustavus Vasa.

Despite Lennart's impressive record of important and work-intensive contributions to research, when we met he was always calm, even in the midst of a stressful atmosphere. Relaxed, he almost always had time for a discussion. Nevertheless, as an academic, Lennart was not limited to research. He was also an appreciated teacher and supervisor, for a period the vice dean of the Lund University School of Economics and Management, a co-founder of CIRCLE (Centre for Innovation, Research and Competence in the Learning Economy) and president of EHES (European Historical Economics Society), to mention but a few of his activities.

We hope that this volume will inspire students, colleagues and other readers to further explore the works and thoughts of Lennart Schön.

The authors
Lund, January 2016

Acknowledgement

Support from the Bank of Sweden Tercentenary Foundation for the preparation of this book is gratefully acknowledged.

Lennart Schön, photo by Mats Brangstrup

Tabula Honoraria in Memoriam Lennart Schön

Göran Ahlström
Lilie-Anne Aldman
Claes-Göran Alvstam
Fredrik N.G. Andersson
Martin Andersson
Fredrik Andersson
Lena Andersson-Skog
Håkan Arvidsson & Ingrid Giselsson
Tobias Axelsson
Joerg Baten
Stefano Battilossi
Marie-Louise & Tommy Bengtsson
Mats Benner & Åsa Lundqvist
Bengt Åke Berg
Lennart & Gun-Britt Berntson
Olof Björnberg
Kristina Björnberg & Fritz Larsson
Göran Blomqvist
Jan Bohlin
Magnus Bohman
Jutta Bolt
Stephen Broadberry
Dan Bäcklund
Benny Carlson
Bo Carlsson
Eric & Cecilia Clark
Fernando Collantes
Herman de Jong
Göran Djurfeldt
Martin Dribe
Richard Easterlin
Kerstin Enflo & Erik Wengström
Susanna Fellman
Rainer Fremdling
Carl Benedikt Frey
Lars Fälting

Ben P.A. Gales
Karl Gratzer
Erik Green
Christer Gunnarsson & Agneta Franssen
Martin Gustavsson
Per Hallén
Christina Hamrin
Ylva Hasselberg
Neelambar Hatti & Rajni Hatti Kaul
Peter Hedberg
Sakari Heikkinen
Sven Hellroth
Martin Henning
Ingrid Henriksen
Rolf Henriksson
Ellen Hillbom
Riitta & Reino Hjerppe
Ursula Hård
Ann Ighe & Staffan Granér
Maths Isacson
Inger Jonsson & Göran Rydén
Pernilla Jonsson
Christina & Lars Jonung
Hans Jörgensen
Niels Kærgård
Astrid Kander
Tobias Karlsson
Birgit Karlsson
Olle Krantz
Hans Kryger Larsen
Tom Kärrlander
Hans Landström
Kristina Lilja
Håkan Lindgren
Magnus Lindmark
Ann-Marie & Jonas Ljungberg

Avdelningen för ekonomisk historia, Institutionen för ekonomi och samhälle, Göteborgs universitet (Unit for Economic History, The Department of Economy and Society, University of Gothenburg).

Ekonomisk-historiska institutionen, Lunds universitet (Department of Economic History, Lund University).

Ekonomisk-historiska institutionen, Stockholms universitet (Department of Economic History, Stockholm University).

Ekonomisk-historiska institutionen, Uppsala universitet (Department of Economic History, Uppsala University).

Enheten för Ekonomisk historia Umeå universitet (Unit for Economic History, The Department of Geography and Economic History, Umeå University).

Stiftelsen Riksbankens Jubileumsfond (The Swedish Foundation for Humanities and Social Sciences).

1 Introduction

Structural analysis and the process of economic development

Jonas Ljungberg

The aim of this book is to present, to a wider audience, the foundations and applications of an approach that has been elaborated over several decades at Lund University. It is only natural that such a book should be dedicated to Lennart Schön, who has been the main architect and given this approach its prominence, in particular in Swedish public debate but also in the international profession of economic historians. His magnum opus, *An Economic History of Modern Sweden*, which first appeared in 2000 in Swedish,[1] demonstrates the relevance and viability of this approach, denoted as structural analysis, which is general and not limited to Sweden. Consequently, when the late Lars Herlitz (2002), in a rich review article, commented on Schön's work, he began by placing it on a par with the doyen of Swedish economic history, Eli Heckscher. However, Schön's more coherent interpretations were also seen as opposed to the rather fragmented views of Heckscher. Herlitz went on to place Schön in the international discourse on long waves and economic growth, and this is the point of departure for the discussion that follows.

Hence, this introduction begins with a discussion of long waves and 'structural cycles', the latter being a principal notion in Schön's work. The structural cycles have been derived from the tools of structural analysis, and this connection is scrutinized. As demonstrated by Schön's many publications, structural analysis is a sharp tool and the approach has inspired the contributions to this volume. The final part of this introduction gives an overview of the following chapters.

Structural cycles

Lennart Schön's work might be more associated with 'structural cycles' than 'structural analysis', which is a concept that has gained currency in science or physics. However, to arrive at the notion of structural cycles, Schön had to apply the approach or methodology of structural analysis, which in the 1970s was adopted in research in economic history at Lund. There were predecessors to this approach, of course, but as a more coherent approach structural analysis was developed in the work with historical national accounts, a field where Sweden, around 1990, demonstrated unique detail of the nineteenth and twentieth centuries.[2] Among the predecessors to, or the inspiratory sources for, structural analysis in economic history were scholars such as Alexander Gerschenkron,

Walt Rostow, Johan Åkerman, Erik Dahmén and Lennart Jörberg. The last three had a connection with Lund: Åkerman held the chair in economics at Lund from 1940 to 1961 (see Hegeland, 1961; Mjöset, 2009), Dahmén was a student of Åkerman but then held a chair at Stockholm School of Economics, and Jörberg held the chair in economic history at Lund between 1972 and 1992 and was then succeeded by Lennart Schön. Further references to these scholars are given in the following chapters, which is why no particular details are given here except their similarity with Joseph Schumpeter, notably in their distrust of general equilibrium as a description of the economy or as a starting point for analysis.[3]

For Lennart Schön, another similarity to Schumpeter is well known: Kondratieff's 'Long Waves', usually labelled 'structural cycles' by Schön. The existence of long waves in the economy has been the subject of controversy for about a century. Lennart Schön has often made the connection between 'structural cycles' and 'long waves', or used the terms synonymously. However, whereas much of the literature has looked for evidence of long waves in the rates of economic growth and similar aggregates, Schön has focused on underlying mechanisms and the characteristics of economic growth. This is precisely what structural analysis is, and through its application to the Swedish economy Schön arrived at the interpretation of a long-term process of structural cycles. Through structural analysis the interplay between actors, markets and institutions over time is quantitatively examined. A crucial concept in this interplay is the 'development block', which emerges from innovations and encompasses complementarity between different actors (discussed further in Chapter 4). One topic of interest in structural analysis is, of course, structural change, which on a very general level concerns the reallocation of resources and output from agriculture to industry to services, which, however, can be broken down to lower levels and other aspects. One usual method for the study of structural change is shift-share analysis, which is a widely used technique for the decomposition of a process of change into contributing factors, for example decomposing aggregate productivity growth into one part that is due to reallocation of resources between sectors and another part due to changes within sectors.[4]

Hence, structural cycles are a generalization describing Swedish economic history and are not necessarily valid for other countries. Of course, Swedish structural cycles have a crucial relation with the international economy. The long pulsations of the international economy are very much present in *An Economic History of Modern Sweden* and the three Industrial Revolutions are clearly important, though not the only, driving forces.[5] However, the structural cycles have domestic mechanisms, and whether structural cycles exist, or what they look like in other countries, is a matter for further research. An objection to the use of 'structural' and 'cycles' is that they imply determinism; the illusion of a perfect model of the future. Remarkably, the same criticism can be directed towards Schumpeter, who saw the process of economic development as recurrent phases of cycles of different lengths. However, Schumpeter was also the instigator of the 'entrepreneur', a concept that highlights the importance of the actors. For Schumpeter, the long waves were driven by the uneven generation of innovations by entrepreneurs.

Kuznets (1940), in his classic review of Schumpeter's *Business Cycles* (1939), saw the clustering of innovation as a hypothesis in need of evidence or a rationale.[6] Whereas Schumpeter thought the discontinuous, yet repetitive, behaviour of entrepreneurs/innovators constitutes the cause of the long waves, Schön finds the mechanism of the cycles in the dynamics of the structure. A critique demands that endogenously generated cycles should be of exactly the same length. Basically this critique could be returned as monocausal in only recognizing exogenous factors as occasional disturbances of a perennial equilibrium. If we think of endogenous factors not only as generating return to an equilibrium, but also as generating dynamic phases of change, as with Schumpeter's 'creative destruction', then there is still room for exogenous factors that influence the timing and intensity of the cycles. For Schön, the length and actual outcome of the structural cycles are modified by the involved actors.[7] As a model of the future, the structural cycles are hence conditional on actors and furthermore that the economy retains basic traits of the industrial epoch.[8]

Structural analysis and patterns of growth

A key to the characteristics of economic growth is found in investments. Broadly, investments could be of different kinds, oriented towards novelty or oriented towards efficiency. While the former kinds of investments result in growth with structural change, the latter result in growth within the existing structure. In neoclassical theory, these different kinds of investment should ensue simultaneously and their effects be mixed up with no particular variations over time. However, in the research for the construction of the Swedish Historical National Accounts, a periodical pattern was uncovered over the nineteenth and twentieth centuries as regards the relative importance of the different kinds of investments. This finding was one of the cornerstones in the building of the theory about structural cycles.[9] The periods when investments in novelty were more important are labelled 'transformations', whilst periods with more investments in efficiency are labelled 'rationalizations'. Both transformations and rationalizations have lasted about 20 years each, and a 'structural crisis' has ended the rationalizations and started the next transformation.

These structural cycles are traced back at least to the crisis in the late 1840s, which was followed by a surge of industrialization along new paths that in the 1870s and 1880s had expanded to big staple export industries based on natural resources. The role of these export industries in sawn timber, iron and oats motivates a digression in Swedish economic historiography. The response to the British opening up with free trade could easily be overestimated, as argued by Lennart Schön in his doctoral dissertation (1979). In his work, Schön investigated the nineteenth-century development of the Swedish textile industry, notably in cotton. The size and importance of this industry had been rather neglected, although its output by the middle of the century was larger than the much-acclaimed sawmill industry. Schön employed Gerschenkron's method of changing weight bases in index calculations as a way to explore the transformation of the cotton industry from an exclusive, high-quality production to a large-scale production for a broader market. This way of using the index problem became a tool in structural analysis, and is treated in some detail in Chapters 2 and 5 in this volume.[10] The importance of the cotton industry and the rise of mass consumption (even if modest by later standards) led Schön to oppose the received view of Swedish industrialization – which he labelled 'the export model' – with 'the domestic market model'.[11] The point was not to deny the role of the export industries, which actually included agriculture with the swift growth of exports of oats, besides wood and iron. However, the emphasis lay on the preceding early nineteenth-century development, and the rise of domestic consumption, which contradicted a Lewis model view where cheap surplus labour made up the basis for Swedish industrialization. This new interpretation was later corroborated by the uncovering of the huge Swedish capital imports from the middle of the century up to shortly before the First World War (Schön, 1989; see also Chapter 6 in this volume). Capital imports balanced commodity imports, which were actually larger than the exports, and meant that investments were not made at the cost of consumption.[12] Hence, the growth of the export industries was part of a broader development.

Certainly the exports of primary, or slightly refined, products such as oats, wood and iron were crucial in the modernization of Sweden in the second half of the nineteenth century. However, in the 1880s the growth of these staple industries slowed down. After decades of rationalization the structural cycle turned into a structural crisis aggravated by the collapse of Baring Brothers. Baring Brothers was an investment bank in London, but its difficulties originated in Argentina. Financial turmoil followed in Europe, and in the wake of the crisis a transformation began. The Swedish 'old staple' industries were superseded, from the 1890s, by modern industries of the 'Second Industrial Revolution', such as electrical engineering, pulp and paper, and consumption industries. The emergence of new industries is typical of the transformation period and is reflected in the different kinds of investments mentioned on p. 3. This can also be seen in the ratio of investments in construction to investments in machinery, which increases. Other characteristics of the transformation period are found in productivity and foreign trade. It is primarily the nature of productivity change that is affected, not the growth rate. Productivity change can be decomposed, by shift-share analysis, into change within sectors and change due to reallocation between sectors or structural change. During transformations the latter kind of productivity change increases. Similarly with foreign trade: for the new and emerging industries, typically the domestic market is most important and therefore exports decline relative to imports. These recurrent patterns were found in the analysis of historical national accounts.

The Great Depression in the early 1930s marked the next structural crisis, despite hitting Sweden comparatively mildly and unleashing another transformation centred around infrastructure, automotive and large-scale engineering industries. It has often been argued that Sweden could benefit from its advantage of not being a belligerent nation and had a running start in exports after the war compared to the rest of Europe. However, this advantage had already been realized during the war, and the transformation starting in the 1930s fostered positive and high growth rates after 1941. In this cycle, Sweden substantially caught up with international top-income levels but the success story was interrupted by the crisis of the 1970s. The transformation that came with the 'Third Industrial Revolution' over the following decades, however, fundamentally changed the structure of Swedish industry, and in the 1990s small enterprises and services were major forces in the resurfacing growth. However, in the period from the mid-1970s to the early 1990s Sweden lagged behind with stagnating growth and showcased as 'eurosclerosis', or how institutional rigidity undermined a success story (Olson, 1990, 1996; see also Lindbeck, 1983; Henrekson *et al.*, 1996). Some authors also found that the illness had a 'particularly pernicious variant', notably 'Suedosclerosis' (Ståhl and Wickman, 1995). Schön (1993) disputed this view and saw the slowdown as an illustration of the Solow Productivity Paradox,[13] which prepared for a new surge in Swedish economic growth. The surge in Swedish economic growth that came after 1993 lends support to Schön's interpretation, whereas the proponents of the 'sclerosis' view, a decade after the turn of the trend, continued to complain about the Swedish failure.[14] From the perspective of structural cycles, the Great Recession came as no surprise but signifies a new structural crisis, for which the solution would not be 'more of the same' but rather innovation opening up for a more sustainable development.

The reader might be struck by the coincidence of the Swedish structural crises with big international or global crises: 1848, the year of 'The Communist Manifesto' and unrest in Europe; the Baring Crisis and its transatlantic repercussions in the early 1890s; the New York stock exchange crash in 1929 followed by the Great Depression of the 1930s; OPEC I and II in 1973 and 1979 with the spectacular distress of steel, shipbuilding and other major industries; and the recent Global Recession sparked off by the Lehman Brothers crash in September 2008. The coincidence of big international crises with the structural crises raises a question about the relation between Sweden and the international economy, and also the particular nature of the structural crises.

First, have these international crises driven the Swedish structural cycle? To some extent, yes, but basically the mechanism for the cycle has been in the structural composition of the Swedish economy, which has matched international trends remarkably well. This is not to suggest that the international economy has passed through the same structural cycles as the Swedish economy, and the aim of structural analysis is not to find the same patterns everywhere. The correspondence with the international economy, however, is highlighted by a comparison with the 'trend periods' in Rostow (1978). Rostow avoids talking about 'cycles' but the 'trend periods' are recurrent fluctuations in relative prices in the world economy.[15] Up to the 1970s, the end of Rostow's study, Schön's periods of transformation broadly correspond to trend periods with a fall in the ratio of world market prices of manufactures to prices of primary products, while there were periods of rationalization in Sweden when that ratio of prices rose in the world market. For Rostow (1978, p. 299), the trend variations could be explained by 'two major variables: the relative abundance or scarcity of various foodstuffs and raw materials; and the character of the leading sectors in the major economies'. Even so, these global trend periods are all the more important for a given country, the more integrated in the international economy the country is. The extent and nature of the integration, however, is largely a question of the internal structure of the country in question.

A closer reading of Schön (2012a) would even suggest the interpretation that the Swedish structural cycles have been driven by the international development. One should then say that the international development has been a necessary though not sufficient condition. The crucial, sufficient, condition of the story is that the Swedish economy has been fairly well integrated with the international economy, both as regards institutions (as suggested by Chapter 6) and the structural composition of industry. In recent publications, Schön (2009, 2012b) further developed the international context of the structural cycles. The moving forces are the 'secular waves' of innovation, originating in the three industrial revolutions of leading countries. These secular innovation waves have in turn contained their imbalances, preparing for the structural crises, which in the Swedish case have generated two structural cycles per wave.[16]

Second, what distinguishes the structural crises from other major crises, for example in 1872, 1907, 1921 or 1992? The sequel of these crises was 'more of the same' whereas the structural crises were connected with technological shifts and the new directions of the development. Hence, could it not be argued that the 'structural crises' have typically been caused by particular events – shocks such as the Lehman Brothers crash in 2008, the oil crises, 1973 and 1979, the Wall Street crash, 1929, or the Baring Brothers crash, 1890? And are these shocks not exogenous to normal economic life, which is broadly followed by a return to normality? The structural analysis approach does not share this idea of shocks and normality but views the crises as a normal outcome of an economy that encompasses periods with changing characteristics and is driven by imbalances. For example, more than OPEC I and II lay behind the difficulties of the 1970s and nowhere in western Europe was there a return to the 'normality' of the 1950s and 1960s, when steel and other traditional, large-scale industries were major factors in economic growth. As Houpt *et al.* (2010, p. 345) note: 'In industry, big was no longer beautiful: the "visible hand", as Chandler had termed the progressive replacement of market allocation mechanisms by large firm management, suffered a serious setback.' It is not convincing to account the oil crises for all of the ubiquitous divide that is associated with the crisis of the 1970s, and it is reasonable to search for more endogenous causes in the economy. To that end we can return to where this review of the structural analysis began: investments and the Swedish economy. Schön has highlighted that the structural crises are connected with troughs and lower turning points in the ratio of investments to GDP. The investment ratio has displayed a secular growth since the nineteenth century, although with a high volatility in the shorter term. Yet, there is also a swing-like pattern around the secular trend, and whereas lower turning points occur in the structural crises, the upper turning points have often coincided with outbursts of crisis. Cases in point are those mentioned earlier in the Introduction: 1872, 1907 together with 1921 and 1992. These are 'crises of transformation' or 'crises of culmination' in the model of structural cycles (Schön, 2012a, pp. 15–16, 336). The upper turning point in the 1950s is not connected with any such blatant crisis, which arguably was due to the regulated capital market of the Bretton Woods regime. The fluctuations that actually occurred in the real economy were not reinforced by any financial crisis, which in the 1960s contributed to a widespread belief in the death of the business cycle. Yet, as pointed to in Chapter 5 on p. 100, the early 1950s clearly experienced a crisis.

The issue of turning points in the structural cycle motivates a look at the similarities and differences between Lennart Schön's structural cycles and Carlota Perez's techno-economic paradigms. The very concept of 'techno-economic paradigms' will be considered later in the Introduction, together with the similar concepts of 'general-purpose technologies' and 'development blocks' (see also Chapter 4). Perez (2002) prefers, for different reasons, the label 'successive great surges of development' instead of long waves or cycles but their length of about half a century is the same. Further, there is a clear similarity between her 'installation' and 'deployment' periods, and Schön's 'transformation' and 'rationalization', respectively. Installation signifies the emergence of innovations and new technology, just as with transformation, while deployment is when the new technology has become general. However, for Perez the turning points between installation and deployment come with a crash or crisis such as the Great Depression of the 1930s, and a new turning point is expected with the Dotcom Crisis (Perez, 2002) or the Great Recession (Kattel *et al.*, 2011). The start of each great surge comes with a 'big bang', a radical innovation, such as the microprocessor in 1971, making its appearance about halfway between the turning points. Clearly, the successive great surges and the structural cycles are out of rhythm. For Perez, there are no structural crises but turning points instigated by a financial crash, following a bubble. Schön also recognizes the usual bubbles, created by the frenzied investments in infrastructure during the transformations, such as in the early 1990s or back in 1907. The difference is in the perception of the structural crises, which, according to Schön, both end a cycle that has come to maturity and start a new one by opening opportunities for innovation. Innovations, or inventions, are held back by the old industries, and when these face difficulties, in the structural crisis, the new technology is unleashed (Schön, 1998, 2009, 2012). The technical change is thus more endogenous in the economy than with the 'big bang'. However, given the methodological differences between Schön and Perez, it is rather the broad similarities than the differences that are striking. The structural cycles are based on a close examination of, primarily, quantitative data for one country, Sweden. The successive great surges are derived from a broader interpretation – 'reasoned history' as proposed by Freeman and Louçã (2001, pp. 123ff.) or 'contextual history' as Mjöset (2009) suggests – of vaguely defined 'core countries'. This type of intuitive discourse is fruitful for generating hypotheses but provides too flexible a framework for explanation.[17]

In structural analysis, a search for relations or causal mechanisms is crucial and consequently endogeneity is seen less as a problem than a reality. As suggested on p. 6, the crisis of the 1970s had more structural causes than soaring oil prices. Moreover, even the hike in oil prices could be seen as an endogenous response to two decades of decreasing relative prices of oil, which opened for the decisions by OPEC. The structural changes in the international economy, shifting away from heavy industry to services, however, worked against the sustainability of OPEC's price policy. Instead of being the ultimate cause of the crisis of the 1970s, the oil price turbulence was itself a consequence of changes in economic structure and international power relations (Schön, 2012a, p. 279f.).

Besides scepticism concerning the exogeneity of shocks, structural analysis also differs from the mainstream neoclassical view on the exogeneity of institutional change. Schön emphasizes institutional change as a part of the transformation while the rationalization period broadly faces institutional stability. For example, the breakthrough of democracy and the modern press occurred in Sweden during the transformation after the structural crisis of the 1890s. The famous 'Swedish model' for the labour market emerged in the period after the Great Depression, which also saw an international paradigm shift in economic policy with the rise of Keynesianism paralleled in Sweden by the Stockholm School with Gunnar Myrdal, Bertil Ohlin and others. The break-up of Keynesianism, and of the 'Swedish model', came with the rise of neo-liberal privatization and deregulation after the structural crisis of the 1970s. Hence institutions are more effects than causes during transformations, but by framing the rules they become more causal during rationalizations.

Over recent decades, a literature on endogenous institutional change has grown.[18] Nelson (2011) struggles with the issue of direction of change in an appraisal of Perez's view on institutional change as a necessary element of the deployment phase. Clearly, there is a risk of a *post hoc ergo propter hoc* argument in treating institutions as endogenous. This is the case when the actual institutions are simply explained by their function, or seen as optimal in their context.[19] Institutional change as part of the transformation in the structural cycle does not predict that solutions become optimal, just that change is prompted by new conditions in the economy. Schön discusses, for example, the First World War as an outcome of a failure to build integration in Europe in a period of rapid growth and globalization (2012, p. 206). A game theoretical approach to endogenous institutional change is definitely compatible with the structural cycle.

Neoclassical analysis is built on the assumption of equilibrium and that the economy tends to return to equilibrium. By contrast, structural analysis perceives imbalances as a major cause of change in the economy. The imbalance between different kinds of investment has generated the periods of transformation and rationalization in the Swedish economy. If the same pattern is not displayed by other countries, with the same timing and lengths of period, it does not mean that imbalances of this sort are absent. There are probably such imbalances but national idiosyncrasies contribute to more or less modifying the structural cycle. The same reservation could be made regarding historical modifications over time and this is a reason why the Swedish structural cycle has not been repeated with exact regularity. Finding national patterns and related idiosyncrasies is part of the research programme of structural analysis, rather than looking for the same waves everywhere.

It is something of an irony that some Schumpeterian and evolutionary economists have begun to shun the idea of long waves or cycles in the economy, while some of a neoclassical breed are open to such long-term patterns. Evolutionary economists struggling to frame the economy in models find it difficult to formalize the persistence of disequilibrium, and choose to avoid the disturbing waves (Silverberg and Verspagen, 2003). The concept of general-purpose technologies (GPT), on the other hand, has motivated economists from the mainstream to think in terms of periodical variations and complementarities (Bresnahan and Trajtenberg, 1992). A GPT is a path-breaking technology that is pervasive; that is, it is used in a lot of activities and eventually influences the whole economy and society. Microprocessor-based ICT, electricity and the steam engine are major GPTs. Complementarity is an important aspect of a GPT, meaning that its utility increases in combination with certain other activities. One could see the concept of GPT as a response to the neglect, by neoclassical economics, of complementarity and its fixation with substitution, implying that in the end everything can be reduced to a question of price. The emergence and even precedence, over the last few decades, of concepts synonymous with, or closely related to, GPT, such as technological paradigms, trajectories or styles (Dosi, 1982; Perez, 1983; Freeman and Perez, 1988), as well as the previously mentioned techno-economic paradigm, should indicate that there is something of more fundamental importance in the economy than what is incorporated in the production function. In Lipsey, Carlaw and Bekar (2005), GPT is further developed to a comprehensive view or framework, acknowledged as 'structuralist-evolutionary' and partly opposed to the neoclassical. The latter's assumption that general equilibrium is a point of departure and return is seen as unrealistic and herein the structuralist-evolutionary view cannot be distinguished from the approach of structural analysis. Similarly, the notion of 'path dependence', which emphasizes friction and resistance to change in technology and institutions (David, 1985; Arthur, 1990) and which has gained wide currency in the social sciences, can be seen as a reaction to the unrealism of assumptions with rational expectations. Path dependence demonstrates why there is continuity in history but also explains why change, when it comes, is often turbulent and contributes to the appearance of distinct periods. The tension between stability and change is central to Schön's work, and in much of good economic history it could be added, why 'path dependence' more or less conceptualized what was empirically widely recognized. However, this is another example where structural analysis matches with heterodox solutions to problems in mainstream thinking.

Interestingly, there is a key concept in structural analysis, notably the 'development block', which captures much the same, or at least to some extent overlaps with notions about technological paradigms and GPT. The 'development block' was elaborated by Erik Dahmén and is useful for understanding the structural cycle.[20] A development block emerges around a radical or significant innovation, and downstream and upstream connections develop with other firms and industries. Their complementarities give rise to externalities, both positive and negative, which are important in the process of economic growth. The emphasis on complementarity remains in contrast to traditional neoclassical theory with its focus on substitution and substitutability, which cannot explain externalities. Typically, a development block passes through a life cycle and comes into maturity during the rationalization period. Its complementarities, implying flexibility at a young age but expanding rigidity with higher age, might now become a constraint on change. However, the development block must transform and adapt to new circumstances in order not to stagnate or even disappear. The theoretical importance of a development block is that it captures complementarity and time. It does not, however, like GPT and technological paradigms, classify and pertain to a particular technology, nor does it require that the actual technology becomes pervasive or determinant for the whole economy. Yet, development blocks can be used to describe and analyse what is also seen as a GPT, as demonstrated by examinations of the role of electricity in Swedish long-term development (Schön, 1990, 1991; Kander *et al.*, 2007). Arguably, 'development blocks' are more instrumental in the analysis of industrial development and can be tracked, for example, in network relations (Enflo *et al.*, 2008; Taalbi 2014). The concepts are not excludable, however, and in Lennart Schön's works (e.g., 2007 together with Kander and Enflo, and 2009) both 'GPT' and other concepts are found to be useful for the effective communication of a rich research.

The creation of new development blocks, or the transformation of old ones, has typically come in the wake of structural crises. This can be explained by an application of the notion of 'transformation pressure', which originates from Dahmén and compounds both negative factors with problems created by or faced in production, and positive factors such as opportunities opened up by new circumstances. The fact that the emergence of development blocks is concentrated in time might, together with the life-cycle trajectories of the single development blocks, suggest an explanation for the time pattern of the structural cycles or why the structural crises have broadly occurred with 40-year intervals. This is certainly a central question for the structural analytical research programme that is still waiting for an answer. Of course, there are several other questions to be tackled with the toolbox of structural analysis and the following chapters provide some examples, and it is left to the reader to assess, and be inspired.

Contributions

'How it all began' is the slightly equivocal title of Chapter 2, by Olle Krantz and Carl-Axel Nilsson. While the contemplated 'beginning' is the application of structural analysis in economic history at Lund in the 1970s, the chapter also makes a broad survey of the emergence of economic history as an independent discipline in Swedish universities. The roots of structural analysis, however, are essentially traced in the works by the economist Johan Åkerman. Åkerman's distinction between 'calculus models' and 'causal analysis' motivated his search for, in today's vocabulary, structural breaks. The calculus models could be applied to periods between the structural breaks, or structural limits in the vocabulary of

Åkerman, which is also used by Krantz and Nilsson. Structural limits actually mean something more than structural breaks, as should be clear from their discussion and the longer excerpt from their (1978) paper reprinted in the chapter. A similar distinction between calculus models and causal analysis was made by Angus Maddison (1987), with 'proximate' versus 'ultimate causes'. The beginning of structural analysis, as it were, did not only grow out of local roots but was highly inspired by Alexander Gerschenkron and Simon Kuznets, as Chapter 2 and the rest of this volume will highlight.

'Identifying and modelling cycles and long waves in economic time series' is the title of Chapter 3, by Fredrik N. G. Andersson. The way of modelling long waves raised disagreement already between Kuznets (1940) and Schumpeter (1939). Kuznets was far from convinced by Schumpeter's estimation of the 'inflection points', which determined the frequency of the cycles and how the long waves were related to shorter cycles such as Juglars and Kitchins. Schumpeter was impressed by Ragnar Frisch, a pioneer in econometrics, but he preferred 'a simplified free-hand adaptation of Professor Ragnar Frisch's method' (Schumpeter, 1939, p. 469) instead of the statistical analysis. The method was more intuitive than transparent, but as explained by Andersson later efforts to econometrically delineate long waves have not been any more successful. The usual methods are designed to capture either the long- or the short-term variations. As a consequence, information between annual changes and the long-term is ignored. Moreover, the long-term analysis of trends is constrained by the (often tacit) assumption about an equilibrium to which the economy returns. However, by applying wavelet analysis, Andersson is able to decompose a time series into a set of cycles ranging from short cycles lasting only a few time periods to long cycles lasting several time periods, and thereby relaxing the assumption of only a short-run and a long-run and the assumption of a stable long-run equilibrium. From the point of view of structural analysis, cycles appear in the underlying growth factors but not necessarily in aggregate series such as GDP. Yet, with wavelet analysis, Andersson shows long-cyclical patterns in GDP per capita, total factor productivity (TFP), and inflation for Sweden, Australia and the USA over the twentieth century. All the more interesting will it be for future research to apply wavelet analysis on series that today underpin the conception of the structural cycles, such as investment ratios, wage shares, export ratios, and relative prices.

'Development blocks and structural analysis' is the title of Chapter 4, by Josef Taalbi. The notion of development blocks is a key tool in structural analysis and has been briefly introduced in the preceding pages. Its origin in a paper by Erik Dahmén back in the early 1940s is highlighted by Taalbi. A remarkable feature with the notion of 'development blocks' is that its inception preceded other similar or partly overlapping concepts such as 'technological systems', 'techno-economic paradigms', and general-purpose technologies with several decades. The increasing popularity in recent decades of concepts which capture complementarities in the economy responds to a gap in the mainstream toolbox. Just like spill-over effects and externalities, complementarities are difficult to assess with precision and the treatment in the literature is mostly qualitative. The chapter also discusses these empirical issues and briefly presents Taalbi's own contribution in combining qualitative data and statistical techniques for a so-called technology flow matrix, which enables the identification of development blocks and interdependencies in Swedish manufacturing since 1970. Besides a few studies, development blocks have so far not been comprehensively mapped across time. The notion has mostly been used for the analysis of a delimited context or broad outlines. As a research agenda, one could think about the economic history of manufacturing as the emergence, maturing and transformation of industries with their interrelations, framed as a history of development blocks.

'The Gerschenkron effect, creative destruction and structural analysis' is the title of Chapter 5, by the present author. The empirical context is relative prices and sales volumes of manufacturing industries over the 'antedated twentieth century' 1888–1992. The basic arguments are that relative prices change not only in the short term but also over trend periods that in some cases are secular, and that new products (innovations) typically have falling relative prices and growing volumes while the opposite holds for old or obsolete products. Arguably, the movement of relative prices is broadly consistent with Schön's periods of transformation and rationalization, and structural cycles.

'The gold standard and industrial breakthrough in Sweden' is the title of Chapter 6, by Håkan Lobell. The relation between the international economy and the industrialization of Sweden has been the subject of some controversy, as discussed on p. 5. Of course, there was a close connection with the outside world! The traditional view is that British free trade by mid-century triggered Swedish export industries and created a dual economy, where low wages could generate high profits that drove investments and further industrialization. However, this view has become much contested. First, it was argued that commercialization of agriculture and the growth of a domestic market in the first half of the nineteenth century, as is evident in the growth of a vigorous textile industry, had prepared the response to the opportunity provided by British free trade. Second, it was shown that previous estimates of capital imports had been far too low. Hence, even if exports were thriving, imports were even larger which is why both consumption and investments could grow. Lobell adds considerable depth to this picture by uncovering the development of Swedish monetary policy and financial markets, which must be seen as a *sine qua non* for the efficacious management of capital imports. The chapter is also a significant contribution to the literature about international capital markets in the nineteenth century, both before and during the gold standard.

'The development of economic growth and inequality among the Swedish regions 1860–2010' is the title of Chapter 7, by Kerstin Enflo and Martin Henning. The chapter draws on research that is part of a larger collaborative project on historical GDPs for regions in Europe. Regional agglomeration and clusters is a long-established field of research while the recently emerging research in historical geography traces the spatial disparities back across time. Enflo and Henning use the Swedish counties, 24 in all, as the regional units. These are basically administrative units and do not necessarily constitute economic regions but nevertheless uncover the contours of a Swedish regional system, as shown by the authors.

The distribution between counties of population, GDP, and GDP per capita are examined in the chapter. In contrast to what was typical for industrialization in other countries, the population became more decentralized during this process in Sweden. After 1930 the concentration of the population increased, in particular due to the growth of the three metropolitan cities: Stockholm, Gothenburg and Malmö. Also from a comparative perspective, the inequality between regions has remained lower than in other European countries. During the industrialization up to the early twentieth century there was a divergence in income, after which followed a convergence between counties until about 1975, when again divergence increased. Enflo and Henning relate these alterations to the role of natural resources versus human capital in the different industrial cycles since the mid-nineteenth century.

'Regional analysis and the process of economic development', is the title of Chapter 8, by Martin Henning, Karl-Johan Lundquist, and Lars-Olof Olander. Like the previous chapter it has a regional perspective. However, while the previous chapter makes a broader survey of regional patterns over 150 years, Chapter 8 analyses the effects of the Third Industrial Revolution on regional growth and employment. The analysis is based on a meticulous examination of regional data for industries in both manufacturing and (private) services down to a very low level of aggregation. The results are remarkable, yet should not be surprising for someone familiar with structural cycles. The reader should keep in mind, from the introductory section, that the story told is very much about general-purpose technologies as well as development blocks. These are transmitters of the complementary relations that constitute the different categories of industries and create the regional patterns across time and space. Hence, the regional divergence over recent decades is driven by new development blocks that in the early and late phases of transformation are concentrated in the metropolitan regions, in particular Stockholm. In the rationalization phase, from the turn of the millennium, the divergence slows down when the new technologies diffuse regionally. Also, the effects on gross and disposable incomes are scrutinized and it is discovered that social transfer payments had a deliberate levelling effect on regional income disparities during transformation. However, during the rationalization, transfers amazingly had the reverse effect and aggravated the disparities. The chapter demonstrates the strength and potential of structural analysis in the application of geography, which the authors call a 'systemic approach'. This is partly opposed, partly complementary, to the now well established 'New Economic Geography' and the focus on clusters, which search for the particular advantages instead of the evolving regional system.

'Economic environmental history. Anything new under the sun?' is the title of the last chapter, by Astrid Kander. This is an essay in reflection, looking back on the research ventures by the author and her growing international network of collaborators. The starting point is how free or independent a scholar is in relation to previous research and tutors. As a PhD student of Lennart Schön, Kander was trained in structural analysis and from there developed a new field that places the environment, and in particular the issue of climate change, in an economic historical context. This has shed new light on the interrelations of energy and economic growth and also challenged some of the current day gloomy interpretations of the effect that globalization has on national environmental performance. The reader gets a summary of the emerging field of environmental economics, with emphasis on the conceptual and methodological approaches employed. The essay could be read, and is intended, as advice for young researchers who want to make a difference.

Notes

1 An English translation with the title *Sweden's Road to Modernity* came off the press from SNS Förlag (Stockholm) in 2010, and with the original title from Routledge in 2012, which is the edition referred to in this volume. The English editions have been enlarged and elaborated in some aspects.

2 For a contemporary state of the art, see van Ark (1995), and a retrospect on Swedish historical national accounts, Bohlin (2003). The publication of the aggregate GDP series had to wait until Krantz and Schön (2007), even though preliminary versions were accessible in Maddison (1995, 2001). Edvinsson (2005) also published an aggregate GDP series for Sweden, very much building upon the sectorial accounts of the project at Lund (Krantz, 1986, 1987a, 1987b, 1991; Schön, 1988, 1995; Pettersson, 1987; Ljungberg, 1988). The accounts of Swedish foreign trade were eventually published (Schön, 2015) but had been generously circulated for decades! Krantz and Schön (2007) has been updated, and extends back to 1560, in Schön and Krantz (2012a, b).

3 Although Schumpeter had a remarkable ambivalence toward equilibrium economics in his appraisal of the Walrasian system, as discussed by Freeman (2011).

4 Invented by Fabricant (1942), and used by, for example, Nordhaus (1972) and Broadberry (1998). Schön applied shift-share analysis in his dissertation on the textile industry in the nineteenth century (1979) and in his examination of the electrification of Sweden (1990; 1991; 2012).

5 The theory of structural cycles is presented and put into context in the book which had its first, Swedish edition in 2000. Early outlines appeared long before, as mentioned in Chapter 2 (endnote 13 and references therein). In personal communication (October 2015) Lennart saw his extensive paper for a public investigation, printed as a separate volume (1994) as the first elaborated version. Yet, a shorter presentation came the year before in a journal article (1993), and in English in a book chapter (1998).

6 The issue stirred a still ongoing controversy. See, for example, Kleinknecht *et al.* (1992), Silverberg (2003) and Metz (2011) as well as Chapter 3 in this volume.

7 This is at least implicitly clear in his publications and has been underlined several times in personal communication.

8 Yet, predictions are possible even if conditional. In 1992 the newspaper *Dagens Industri*, stirred by the sharp decline in real estate prices and a banking crisis, had a feature article about Lennart Schön and the structural cycle. The newspaper extrapolated the historical generalization and predicted the next severe crisis to occur in 2010 (*Dagens Industri*, 1992).

9 Logically 'structural cycles' are a generalization from a historical pattern and, it might be argued, not strictly a theory. However, for the interpretation of Swedish economic history, it is a theory that has to stand up to the facts.

10 It should be noted, though, that Schön was not the first to take up Gerschenkron's method. In their analysis of (an earlier generation of the) historical national accounts, Olle Krantz and Carl-Axel Nilsson (1975) discussed the effects of shifting weight bases.

11 Similar views were expressed by Fridholm, Isacson and Magnusson (1976) and the interpretation has remained an issue in the *Scandinavian Economic History Review*. See, for example, Hodne (1994), Schön (1997), Ljungberg (1996, 1997), Ljungberg and Schön (2013).

12 Corresponding scenarios were later highlighted for the other Nordic countries (Ljungberg and Schön, 2013). These, like Sweden, were sources of mass emigration,

and the significant capital imports qualify the simplification that 'capital chases after labor' in the transatlantic economy (Williamson, 1996, p. 294).
13 'You can see the computer age everywhere but in the productivity statistics,' remarked Robert Solow (1987) in a book review.
14 '... particularly in Sweden has the long-term economic growth been especially weak *over the past three decades*' argued Assar Lindbeck in a newspaper article before the Swedish referendum about the euro (Lindbeck, 2003; translation JL, italics added).
15 See, however, Rostow (1975) where an 'appropriate theory of long waves' is demanded, and outlined.
16 It could furthermore be noticed that the index problem is again innovatively employed as an analytical tool in Schön (2012b). Thus, for an international comparison of the nature or composition of economic growth, GDP levels are re-weighted with different purchasing power parity (PPP) benchmarks.
17 Perez's (2002, p. 62) agnosticism when it comes to quantitative data takes on post-modernist dimensions: 'It would in fact be justified to assert that long-term aggregate series, truly long-term ones, attempting to span two or three paradigms in terms of money, are senseless'.
18 See, for example, Harley (1991), Greif and Laitin (2004); and, for the Swedish labour market and the structural cycle, Svensson (2004).
19 Compare the critical article by Sheilagh Ogilvie (2007), succinctly titled 'Whatever is, is right?'
20 See, for example, Dahmén (1988) and Schön (1991); the origin of 'development block' and related concepts are treated more in detail in Chapter 4 in this volume.

References

Arthur, W. B. (1990), 'Positive feedbacks in the economy', *Scientific American*, vol. 262, pp. 92–9.
Bohlin, J. (2003), 'Swedish historical national accounts: the fifth generation', *European Review of Economic History*, vol. 7, pp. 73–97.
Bresnahan, T. and Trajtenberg, M. (1992), 'General purpose technologies: engines of growth?' *NBER Working Paper 4148*.
Broadberry, S. N. (1998), 'How did the United States and Germany overtake Britain? A sectoral analysis of comparative productivity levels, 1870–1990', *Journal of Economic History*, vol. 58, pp. 375–407.
Dagens Industri (1992), 'Kriskarusellen', 27 October.
Dahmén, E. (1988), '"Development blocks" in industrial economics', *Scandinavian Economic History Review*, vol. 36, pp. 3–14.
David, P. (1985), 'Clio and the economics of QWERTY', *American Economic Review*, vol. 75, pp. 332–7.
Dosi, G. (1982), 'Technological paradigms and technological trajectories: a suggested interpretation of the determinants and directions of technical change', *Research Policy*, vol. 26, pp. 147–62.
Edvinsson, R. (2005), *Growth, Accumulation, Crisis: with New Macroeconomic Data for Sweden 1800–2000*. Stockholm: Almqvist & Wiksell International.
Enflo, K., Kander, A. and Schön, L. (2008), 'Identifying development blocks – a new methodology', *Journal of Evolutionary Economics*, vol. 18, pp. 57–76.
Fabricant, S. (1942), *Employment in Manufacturing, 1899–1939: an Analysis of its Relation to the Volume of Production*. New York: NBER Books.
Freeman, C. (2011), 'Schumpeter's business cycles and techno-economic paradigms'. In Drechsler, W., Kattel, R. and Reinert, E. S. (eds) *Techno-Economic Paradigms. Essays in Honour of Carlota Perez*. London: Anthem Press.

16   *Jonas Ljungberg*

Freeman, C. and Louçã, F. (2001), *As Time Goes By. From the Industrial Revolutions to the Information Revolution*. Oxford: Oxford University Press.

Freeman, C. and Perez, C. (1988), 'Structural crises of adjustment, business cycles and investment behavior'. In Dosi, G., Freeman, C., Nelson R., Silverberg, G. and Soete L. (eds) *Technical Change and Economic Theory*. London: Pinter Publishers.

Fridholm, M., Isacson, M. and Magnusson, L. (1976), *Industrialismens rötter*. Stockholm: Prisma.

Greif, A. and Laitin, D. D. (2004), 'A theory of endogenous institutional change', *American Political Science Review*, vol. 98, pp. 633–52.

Harley, C. K. (1991), 'Substitution for prerequisites: endogenous institutions and comparative economic history'. In Sylla, R. and Toniolo, G. (eds) *Patterns of European Industrialization. The Nineteenth Century*. London: Routledge.

Hegeland, H. (ed.) (1961), *Money, Growth, and Methodology and Other Essays in Economics: in Honor of Johan Åkerman*. Lund: Gleerup.

Henrekson, M., Jonung, L. and Stymne, J. (1996), 'Economic growth and the Swedish model'. In N. Crafts and G. Toniolo (eds) *Economic Growth in Europe Since 1945*. Cambridge: Cambridge University Press.

Herlitz, L. (2002), 'Analytisk historia om tillväxt – reflektioner kring Lennart Schöns *En modern svensk ekonomisk historia*', *Historisk tidskrift*, pp. 605–26.

Hodne, F. (1994), 'Export-led growth or export specialization?' *Scandinavian Economic History Review*, vol. 42, pp. 296–310.

Houpt, S., Lains, P. and Schön. L. (2010), 'Sectoral developments, 1945–2000'. In Broadberry, S. and O'Rourke, K. H. (eds) *The Cambridge Economic History of Modern Europe*, vol. 2. Cambridge: Cambridge University Press.

Kander, A., Enflo, K. and Schön, L. (2007), 'In defense of electricity as a general purpose technology', *CIRCLE Working Paper 2007/06*.

Kattel, R. (2011), 'Small States, innovation and techno-economic paradigms'. In Drechsler, W., Kattel, R. and Reinert, E. S. (eds) *Techno-Economic Paradigms. Essays in Honour of Carlota Perez*. London: Anthem Press.

Kattel, R., Drechsler, W. and Reinert, E. S. (2011), 'Introduction: Carlota Perez and evolutionary economics'. In Drechsler, W., Kattel, R. and Reinert, E. S. (eds) *Techno-Economic Paradigms. Essays in Honour of Carlota Perez*. London: Anthem Press.

Kleinknecht, A., Mandel, E. and Wallerstein, I. M. (eds) (1992), *New Findings in Long-wave Research*. New York: St. Martin's Press.

Krantz, O. (1986), *Transporter och kommunikationer 1800–1980*. Lund: Ekonomisk-historiska föreningen.

Krantz, O. (1987a), *Husligt arbete 1800–1980*. Lund: Ekonomisk-historiska föreningen.

Krantz, O. (1987b), *Offentlig verksamhet 1800–1980*. Lund: Ekonomisk-historiska föreningen.

Krantz, O. (1991), *Privata tjänster 1800–1980*. Lund: Ekonomisk-historiska föreningen.

Krantz, O. and Nilsson, C.-A. (1975), *Swedish National Product 1861–1970. New Aspects on Methods and Measurement*. Kristianstad: CWK Gleerup.

Krantz, O. and Schön, L. (2007), *Swedish Historical National Accounts, 1800–2000*. Lund Studies in Economic History 41.

Kuznets, S. (1940), 'Schumpeter's business cycles', *American Economic Review*, vol. 30, pp. 257–71.

Lindbeck, A. (1983), 'The recent slowdown of productivity growth', *Economic Journal*, vol. 93, pp. 13–34.

Lindbeck, A. (2003), 'Oklokt att bli fripassagerare i EMU', *Dagens Nyheter*, 30 July 2003.

Lipsey, R. G., Carlaw, K. I. and Bekar, C. T. (2005), *Economic Transformations. General Purpose Technologies and Long Term Economic Growth*. Oxford: Oxford University Press.

Ljungberg, J. (1988), *Deflatorer för industriproduktionen 1888–1955*. Lund: Ekonomiskhistoriska föreningen.

Ljungberg, J. (1996), 'Catch-up and static equilibrium. A critique of the convergence model', *Scandinavian Economic History Review*, vol. 44, pp. 265–75.

Ljungberg, J. (1997), 'The impact of the great emigration on the Swedish economy', *Scandinavian Economic History Review*, vol. 45, pp. 159–89.

Ljungberg, J. and Schön, L. (2013), 'Domestic markets and international integration: paths to industrialisation in the Nordic countries', *Scandinavian Economic History Review*, vol. 61, pp. 101–21.

Maddison, A. (1987), 'Ultimate and proximate growth causality: a critique of Mancur Olson on the rise and decline of nations', *Scandinavian Economic History Review*, vol. 36, pp. 25–9.

Maddison, A. (1995), *Monitoring the World Economy, 1820–1992*. Paris: OECD.

Maddison, A. (2001), *The World Economy. A Millennial Perspective*. Paris: OECD.

Metz, R. (2011), 'Do Kondratieff waves exist? How time series techniques can help solve the problem', *Cliometrica*, vol. 5, pp. 205–38.

Mjöset, L. (2009), 'The contextualist approach to social science methodology'. In Byrne, D. and Ragin, C. (eds) *The Sage Handbook of Case-based Methods*. London: Sage.

Nelson, R. R. (2011), 'Technology, institutions and economic development'. In Drechsler, W., Kattel, R. and Reinert, E. S. (eds.), *Techno-Economic Paradigms. Essays in Honour of Carlota Perez*. London: Anthem Press.

Nordhaus, W. D., (1972), 'The recent productivity slowdown,' *Brookings Papers on Economic Activity*, pp. 493–536.

Ogilvie, S. (2007), '"Whatever is, is right"? Economic institutions in pre-industrial Europe', *Economic History Review*, vol. 60, pp. 649–84.

Olson, M. (1990), *How Bright are the Northern Lights? Some Questions About Sweden*. Lund University Press.

Olson, M. (1996). 'The varieties of eurosclerosis: the rise and decline of nations since 1982'. In Crafts, N. and Toniolo, G. (eds.), *Economic Growth in Europe Since 1945*. Cambridge University Press.

Perez, C. (1983), 'Structural change and assimilation of new technologies in the economic and social systems', *Futures*, vol. 15, pp. 357–76.

Perez, C. (2002), *Technological Revolutions and Financial Capital. The Dynamics of Bubbles and Golden Ages*. Cheltenham: Edward Elgar.

Pettersson, L. (1987), *Byggnads- och anläggningsverksamhet 1800–1980*. Lund: Ekonomisk-historiska föreningen.

Rostow, W. W. (1975), 'Kondratieff, Schumpeter, and Kuznets: trend periods revisited', *Journal of Economic History*, vol. 35, pp. 719–53.

Rostow, W. W. (1978), *The World Economy. History & Prospects*. Austin: University of Texas Press.

Schön, L. (1979), *Från hantverk till fabriksindustri. Svensk textiltillverkning 1820–1870*. Kristianstad: Arkiv (diss.).

Schön, L. (1988), *Industri och hantverk 1800–1980*. Lund: Ekonomisk-historiska föreningen.

Schön, L. (1989), 'Kapitalimport, kreditmarknad och industrialisering 1840–1905'. In Dahmén E. (ed.) *Upplåning och utveckling. Riksgäldskontoret 1789–1989*. Stockholm: Riksgäldskontoret.

Schön, L. (1990), *Elektricitetens betydelse för svensk industriell utveckling*. Vällingby: Vattenfall.

Schön, L. (1991), 'Development blocks and transformation pressure in a macro-economic perspective – a model of long-term cyclical change', *Skandinaviska Enskilda Banken Quarterly Review*, vol. 20(3–4), pp. 67–76.

Schön, L. (1993), '40-årskriser, 20-årskriser och dagens ekonomiska politik', *Ekonomisk debatt*, vol. 21(1), pp. 7–18.

Schön, L. (1994), *Omvandling och obalans. Bilaga 3 till Långtidsutredningen 1994*. Stockholm: Finansdepartementet.

Schön. L. (1995), *Jordbruk med binäringar 1800–1980*. Lund: Ekonomisk-historiska föreningen.

Schön, L. (1997), 'Internal and external factors in Swedish industrialization', *Scandinavian Economic History Review*, vol. 45, pp. 209–23.

Schön, L. (1998), 'Industrial crises in a model of long cycles: Sweden in an international perspective'. In T. Myllyntaus (ed.) *Economic Crises and Restructuring in History. Experiences of Small Countries*. Katharinen: Scripta Mercaturae.

Schön, L. (2009), 'Technological waves and economic growth. Sweden in an international perspective, 1850–2000', *CIRCLE Working Paper 2009/06*.

Schön, L. (2012a), *An Economic History of Modern Sweden*. Oxon: Routledge.

Schön, L. (2012b), 'Long-term innovation waves and the potential dissonance between Europe and Asia'. In Oxelheim, L. (ed.) *EU-Asia and the Re-Polarization of the Global Economic Arena*. Singapore: World Scientific.

Schön, L. (2015), *Utrikeshandel 1800–1870*. Lund: Ekonomisk-historiska föreningen.

Schön, L. and Krantz, O. (2012a), 'Swedish Historical National Accounts, 1560–2010', *Lund Papers in Economic History 123*.

Schön, L. and Krantz, O. (2012b), 'The Swedish economy in the early modern period: constructing historical national accounts', *European Review of Economic History*, vol. 16, pp. 529–49.

Schumpeter, J. A. (1939), *Business Cycles. A Theoretical, Historical, and Statistical Analysis of the Capitalist Process*. New York: McGraw-Hill.

Silverberg, G. (2003), 'Long waves: conceptual, empirical and modelling issues', UNU-MERIT Research Memoranda 15.

Silverberg, G. and Verspagen, B. (2003), 'Breaking the waves: a Poisson regression approach to Schumpeterian clustering of basic innovations', *Cambridge Journal of Economics*, vol. 27, pp. 671–93.

Solow, R. M. (1987), 'We'd better watch out', *New York Times Book Review*, 12 July 1987.

Ståhl, I. and Wickman, K. (1995), *Suedosclerosis: the Problems of Swedish Economy: Excerpts*. Stockholm: Timbro.

Svensson, L. (2004), 'Technology shifts, industrial dynamics and labour market institutions in Sweden, 1920–1995'. In Ljungberg, J. and Smits, J.-P. (eds) *Technology and Human Capital in Historical Perspective*. Basingstoke: Palgrave Macmillan.

Taalbi, J. (2014), *Innovation as Creative Response: Determinants of Innovation in the Swedish Manufacturing Industry, 1970-2007*. Lund studies in economic history, 67 (diss.).

van Ark, B. (1995), 'Towards European historical national accounts', *Scandinavian Economic History Review*, vol. 43, pp. 3–16.

Williamson, J. G. (1996), 'Globalization, convergence, and history', *Journal of Economic History*, vol. 56, pp. 277–306.

2 How it all began

On structural periods

Olle Krantz and Carl-Axel Nilsson

Economic history became a discipline of its own in Sweden with Eli F. Heckscher (1879–1952). He was an economist by education and professor in economics at the privately owned Stockholm School of Economics. In 1929 his professorship was changed to economic history, which, actually, had been his major interest for a long time. In his approach he applied economic theory – neoclassical – and well-thought-out quantification to the economic-historical analysis.[1] Heckscher was not alone in working with historical issues of an economic kind in Sweden in the early twentieth century. Some historians also studied such issues, and this was sometimes called economic history. However, it could best be characterized as applying historical methods to economic sources.[2] Economic-historical questions were also studied by economists.

The discipline, however, was not established at Swedish universities until the 1940s. Then, after assiduous work by Heckscher and others, economic history was introduced at all Swedish universities and soon professorships were established. Historians were appointed to the chairs with one exception: Oscar Bjurling at Lund University. He was educated as an economist, but to be considered qualified for a position in economic history he had to take his doctoral degree in history.[3]

Hence, there was a certain difference between the economic-historical departments at Lund and the other universities concerning methodological approach. At Lund, after some years, economic history was practised by a young generation of researchers who employed modern thoughts and methods. Early examples are the theses of Gunnar Fridlizius (1957) and Lennart Jörberg (1961). In the 1960s, the methodological thoughts developed, among other things with inspiration from the then popular and much discussed 'New Economic History', also called 'Cliometrics', which emanated from the USA.[4] New Economic History was characterized by a systematic application of neoclassical economic theory and quantification, which meant a qualified work with data, among other things through the use of econometric techniques. Furthermore, explicit hypotheses could be used as well as counterfactual methods. Some work of this kind was made at Lund, but new economic history was mostly not received uncritically. Rather, it stimulated interest in various theoretical approaches including Marxist theory, as this happened in the 'revolutionary' 1960s and 70s. Scholars like

Alexander Gerschenkron and Simon Kuznets were important and their work was much discussed. Inspiration also came from others such as Joseph Schumpeter and the Swedish economists Johan Åkerman and Erik Dahmén. What is dealt with here is one of the main research fields that developed at the economic history department at Lund: economic growth and structural analysis.

Gerschenkron's (1904–1979) approach or model of economic change was developed for Europe in the nineteenth and early twentieth centuries and, thus, it did not comprise the rest of the world. The model was an attempt to combine uniformity of industrialization with historical uniqueness, and it started with two observations: 'The map of Europe in the nineteenth century showed a motley picture of countries varying with regard to the degree of their economic backwardness. At the same time, processes of rapid industrialization started in several of those countries from very different levels of economic backwardness.'[5] In the model based on these observations one important implication was that the more backward a country's economy was, the more probable that its industrialization started with a sudden 'great spurt' in industrial output.

To study these processes Gerschenkron employed various methods, of which especially one aroused great interest among economic historians at Lund. It was the use of the so-called index number problem as a methodological tool in the analysis. In volume or price series a difference almost always arises between Laspeyres and Paasche indices, i.e. base year weighted and given year weighted indices. Weights pertaining to an early base year tend to give higher values to the indices than weights from a late one. This difference was often considered as a complication, even a nuisance, by economists but this was contrary to Gerscenkron's view. He meant that it could be used to study structural change and to delimit periods with different structures. The difference between the indices is often called the Gerschenkron effect.[6]

Kuznets' (1901–1985) importance was twofold. He started his career by studying long-term movements in economic variables. One important contribution was his tracing of long-term regularities in the economy. However, it was not a question of long waves of a Kondratieff type, i.e. *c*. 50 years. Instead, he identified so-called long swings, or Kuznets swings as they were also labelled. The length of these were around 20 years.[7] Kuznets' interest was also directed towards historical national accounts which formed the basis for studies of economic growth and structural change, i.e. shifts in proportions between sectors and branches of the economy. Kuznets collected historical GDP and other series for as many countries as possible and, hence, in this respect he was a forerunner of Angus Maddison.[8]

Joseph Schumpeter's (1883–1950) theory of technical change[9] is often included in long wave analysis with emphasis on the shifts between cycles. Production methods as well as goods, after having had great importance for economic growth, become successively less and less important and demanded. After some time they become victims of creative destruction and, thus, give way to new methods and goods. This means a renewal of the economy. The main actors in these processes are the entrepreneurs who exploit the new ideas in innovation processes.

The thinking and empirical research of the Swedish economist Johan Åkerman (1896–1982) was also of importance, as previously mentioned and further shown below in the extract from the report on structural limits. He made a difference between what he called causal analysis, i.e. analysis of the long-term economic performance, and calculus models which in practice are mainstream economic models. In causal analysis, driving forces, cycles and structures play a fundamental role, as does periodization of the economic development. This means identification of homogeneous periods in the economic performance of a country. Another Swedish economist of importance was Erik Dahmén (1916–2005). He was a student of Åkerman and was much inspired by him. Furthermore, Schumpeter exerted great influence on Dahmén especially concerning the theory of innovation and entrepreneurs. Periodization, on the other hand, was less important for Dahmén. Instead, he chose his research periods in advance, not mainly considering the long-term economic performance. Nevertheless, his thoughts worked as inspiration for researchers at the department of economic history at Lund.

Hence, one inheritance from Kuznets was delimiting homogeneous structural periods in the long-run economic performance. Their origin and character could then be analysed with the help of the theories of Schumpeter, Åkerman and Dahmén. The periods could be traced with the help of historical national accounts, the use of which was also an inheritance from Kuznets. The national accounts approach also fitted a tradition in Sweden. Constructing historical accounts of this kind started with a great research programme pursued at Stockholm University in the interwar period.[10] Erik Lindahl and associates did a great job of estimating series for a large number of sectors and branches, and GDP 1861–1930; actually, this was one of the first attempts in the world to construct comprehensive historical national accounts. An effort was also made to arrive at series in constant prices with the use of the cost-of-living indices constructed in the same programme. Later, new historical GDP series, based on the earlier estimates and with various improvements, were published.[11]

However, since the methods used so far in historical national accounting were taken from contemporary national accounts, the special problems of historical series in current as well as constant prices were not discussed, which was also true internationally. When work on Swedish historical national accounts was taken up at Lund in the early 1970s one of the aims was to come to terms with this. New estimates were published in 1975[12] with inspiration from the scholars mentioned earlier in this chapter. Gerschenkron's insistence on carefully constructed deflators and on using the index number problem as a tool in the analysis was crucial, not least since it could be used in identifying and characterizing structurally homogenous periods. One way to delimit such periods was to depart from the different composition of different series in the historical national accounts pertaining in principle to the same item, i.e. GDP calculated on the production and expenditure side. This is discussed in the extract below. In the accounts from 1975 deflation was made using periods of around twenty years where Laspeyres and Paasche indices were employed. However, in recent Swedish historical accounts deflation with chain indices is often used.

Another tool for periodisation was to employ ratios between variables pertaining to the historical national accounts, for instance investment and export ratios. Then the character and origin of the periods were analysed using the ideas of Schumpeter, Åkerman, and Dahmén. This method in particular was used by Lennart Schön in developing the long cycle analysis.

Swedish historical national accounts: a new generation

Lennart Schön's research and analyses of long cycles[13] is presented at length in other parts of this book and hence it will not be dealt with here. However, since an important basis for his work is the Swedish historical national accounts and since he has actively participated in improving and extending them, a short overview is appropriate.

After the first attempt, mentioned earlier in this chapter, at the department of economic history at Lund to develop the historical accounts for the period 1861–1970, a large project was launched by Lennart Schön and Olle Krantz aimed at improving the existing series and estimating new ones from 1800 onwards. The research resulted in nine books published since 1984.[14] In these books, estimates of the different sectors and branches were described in detail. However, for various reasons[15] the data were not for a long time brought together to a complete set of historical national accounts but preliminary GDP series were presented.[16]

This situation changed in 2007 when the historical national accounts were finally completed and published.[17] Then chain index deflation was used and, furthermore, for the first time also, double deflation. However, a number of scholars rightly argued that this created problems with international comparisons since the accounts for other countries due to limited availability of data were not constructed in this way. Therefore, in a later version the Swedish historical accounts were revised and deflated by single deflation and these new data were published in 2012.[18]

The work was also continued in another direction, namely back in time, and entirely new series for GDP and the main sectors for the period 1560–1800 were published.[19] This was in line with international research where series for the early modern period and even further back in time were constructed for a number of countries. The reasons for this were the debate about the Great Divergence, i.e. the long-time difference in economic growth between Asia and Europe, and a desire to get a better understanding of the Industrial Revolution and its origin. One of the outcomes of this estimation work was an annual series for Sweden's GDP per capita in constant prices for the whole period 1560–2010. This series is shown in Figure 2.1.

The performance of the Swedish GDP per capita shows a cyclical pattern, which is briefly analysed in Schön and Krantz (2012a). From the beginning of the seventeenth century economic growth is visible lasting practically the whole century. This was also a century of intensive warfare and patriotic historians have named it the period of the Swedish empire. These efforts brought about strong economic activity, especially in the iron and copper industries and in sectors associated with

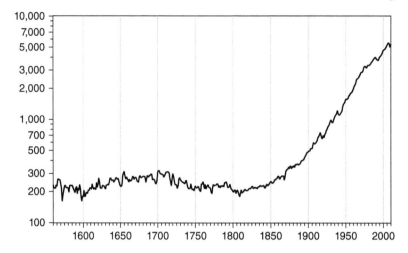

Figure 2.1 Swedish GDP per capita, 1560–2010: in constant kronor prices of 1910/12.

Source: Schön and Krantz (2012b); see also www.ekh.lu.se/en/research/economic-history-data/shna 1560-2010.

the war activities. Around the year 1700 things changed and the first decades of the eighteenth century were characterised by great economic problems of various kinds, including unsuccessful wars. The rest of the eighteenth century showed stagnation, even a decrease of GDP per capita. The governmental authorities worried about this and tried to counteract the tendencies through agricultural reforms, particularly enclosures, and by supporting industrial ventures. However, the stagnation lasted until the early nineteenth century when a turn towards economic growth took place, at first rather slow and then accelerating. This acceleration was due to a domestically initiated industrial growth, in combination with demand from abroad especially in wood, iron and oats.

Thus, a long-term cyclical pattern is visible. Maybe shorter pre-industrial patterns also exist. This remains to be studied and the national accounts provide a good foundation for such studies. Furthermore, the methods described earlier in this chapter – weight base changes and relating various series from the accounts to each other – could be used and refined in various ways, particularly since computer technology offers new and fascinating possibilities.

Krantz and Nilsson (1978)

The historical national accounts and the method of using the index number problem as a tool for periodization were crucial for the development of the long cycle analysis at the department of economic history at Lund. Therefore, an extract from Krantz and Nilsson (1978) is published here. It was originally written in Swedish and the reader will perhaps notice a style of the times. The report was an elaboration of certain ideas in a preceding book, Krantz and Nilsson (1975), and it is the theoretical and methodological part that has been extracted.[20]

The following is an extract from pp. 1–10 of 'On structural limits in the Swedish economy, 1861–1975. A method for the use of national accounts in the analysis of economic-historical change':

Introduction

Among those who work professionally with national accounts, two fields of application are common: 1) a basis for policy formulations with a relatively short-term perspective and 2) a framework for analysis based on economic production theory.[21] The technique for constructing data in current as well as constant prices has also largely been adapted for these uses.

With a few exceptions, however, national accounts have not been used in a systematic way by economic historians. Instead, they have worked with conventional series without worrying about their design and whether or not they are appropriate for historical analysis. In other words, historians have usually taken the series for granted and as unchangeable, like any other historical observation, for example the death date of a particular king.

But by relying on series constructed by non-historically trained statisticians, historians have left an important research field unnoticed. However, there are exceptions, such as Gerschenkron and Kuznets.[22] Like them, we mean that economic historians can employ GDP estimates as a basis for studies of variations in relatively long-term patterns of change, meaning periods of at least 15 to 20 years. When the series are used in this way, they should be elaborated in a relevant manner with regard to the aim of the study. The purpose of this report is to describe such a construction.

The next section presents the theoretical points of departure that have guided our work. Then a section follows that discusses our national accounts design and principles of deflation, the latter perhaps the most significant.

Theoretical and methodological points of departure

In our work with historical national accounts a method of empirical analysis of patterns of economic-historical change is applied. Of course, as a starting point there is a theoretical conception of how the studied economy works and changes.

In a market economy it is assumed that prices are formed by competition and that they are instruments of allocation, i.e. that they govern the economic decision-makers in their choice of products, technology and, not least, quantities produced. A major determinant of price formation in the Swedish economy is that it is integrated in an international market. From the mid-nineteenth century, integration has increased gradually since the modern parts of the economy have expanded in international competition.

Fundamental to our method of analysing economic change is the fluctuations in prices and quantities, which are the essential elements of economic decision-making. It is mainly the long-term patterns of change that become the subject of analysis. It is a question of characterizing homogeneous periods and establishing transitions between them.

Economic decisions can be assumed to be made on the basis of historical experience. Hence, they have a conservative character, which prevents continuous adaptation to changing expansion mechanisms. Crises associated with structural limits are consequences and, thus, periods with different patterns of expansion can be distinguished.

In this economic-historical perspective, neoclassical or Keynesian theory cannot constitute a methodical basis[23] since they are short-term theories, or rather theories with an 'imaginary' time perspective.

Our starting points are partly consistent with what Johan Åkerman – an economist outside the mainstream of Swedish economic science – pleaded for. A basic idea was that the theory of an existent society is dualistic. 'One has, on the one hand, calculus models, i.e. rationalizations of the plans of the relevant groups in a given time-localized society; on the other hand, a reconstructing causal analysis of the economic performance in a given time period.'

The former – the calculus models – are instruments for action, which 'have to be separated from the course of events both as to reality and to the scientific rationalization to make it possible to be designed as a logical cause-effect relationship'. Causal analysis, on the other hand, is the researcher's attempt to grasp and try to understand the total process, which continuously alters the context of these instruments for action and, thus, also these instruments. This causal analysis 'is directly based on the time series; its reconstruction is based on the observed and discussed causal context within given time periods'. This also provides different time scales: 'on the one hand the calculus model's imaginary 'time'– or reference scale, /.../ and on the other hand the actual calendar time scale of the causal analysis'.[24]

Certain concepts play a central role in the causal analysis, as Åkerman understood it. A central one is structure, which he dealt with extensively. Structural differences distinguish various periods in the economic process and these differences are linked to the driving forces – another one of the basic concepts of causal analysis. Åkerman defined a number of structural concepts[25] and then highlighted four that are relevant to causal analysis: 1) economic-political structure, which is the relationship between state and private business, 2) production structure, which concerns the relationship between various parts of the economy, i.e. branches and sectors, 3) monetary structure, which highlights a country's transition to a monetary economy, and 4) income structure, which shows the relationship between the various income groups in a society.[26]

The structural conditions can be measured by structural indicators, i.e. indicators of the elements defined in the structure. They are material for 'statistical analysis, whereby a systematization of overall tendencies and perhaps periodicities can appear.'[27] Thus, structure can mean 'one, within specified time limits, *the structural boundaries*, relatively unchanged economic mechanism, whereby the unchangeable character is established through study of the relationship of different variables during rising and falling economic activity.'[28]

Åkerman's strength is primarily on the theoretical level. His consistent separation of calculus models and causal analyses demonstrates the limitations of the conventional economic theory – the calculus models – as research tools in economic-historical studies.[29] On the other hand, his way of applying the causal analysis could be criticized.[30] He often chose easily accessible series on production, prices, population, etc. and related them to each other where appropriate. These data can indeed provide certain information, but the technique has limitations, because the series are not always constructed in a way that is relevant to the research problem.[31]

Thus, it is Åkerman's theoretical conceptions rather than his empirical studies that are of importance for our work. We mean that one cannot readily rely on existing statistical series and treat them as if they are historical facts. Instead, data should in principle be processed in such a way that the resulting series become directly adapted in time and space to the given course of events. This means that the theoretical approach should contain criteria for the empirical constructions.[32]

Against this background it is natural in economic-historical studies of long-term patterns of change to elaborate other – unconventional – constructions of national product series than those used in forecasting and production theory. The deflation problem obtains further significance. The historian has to pay special attention to the task of achieving comparability over long periods during which shifts, sometimes of a major kind, take place in the price and quantity structures. This implies special importance concerning choice of base periods, weight systems, etc.

In current prices, national accounts can of course be perceived as a coherent system, and series of domestic product as identical totals, irrespective of whether they are constructed on the expenditure or the production side. In analyses with a long-term perspective it is, however, fruitful to drop this approach and instead work with different domestic product totals, although they represent an identity in current prices. But sometimes they have very different patterns of change in their composition of goods and services. In constant prices, therefore, these totals can differ significantly.

It is also possible to select, treat and deflate separately subseries from the national accounts. Then, because of the changes in the composition of goods they can not be part of a coherent system. They can, however, be related to each other in different ways; with a terminology from Åkerman they can form composite structural indicators. These can then be included as important elements in analyses of economic transformation.

With this theoretical framework as a background, one can argue that elaboration of national accounts series is different from mechanical calculation work. Instead, at a high level of abstraction, the task is to summarize the results of the price and quantity changes, which govern and are consequences of the large number of decisions that constitute the historical transformation process. These predominantly short-term decisions can therefore be said to be the basic elements of the long-term patterns of change.

Method of analysis

Consequently, a concrete historical analysis based on national accounts data does not imply an uncritical acceptance of these data as they are presented, for example in official publications. On the contrary, it is in many respects an essential task to process the data in such a way that the purpose of the analysis is attained. Generally, our theoretical framework provides a more flexible view of the possibilities of dealing with national accounts data than is otherwise usually the case, and it makes it easier to develop unconventional methodological approaches to the analysis.

We agree, however, with the current perception of what the national accounts series should cover, namely 'goods or services, which are the result of a production process'. Furthermore, a purchase or other acquisition of a product (service) should only relate to something that 'can actually be produced'.[33]

Basically, we also concur with the usual groupings of national accounts in various sub-aggregates. In our classification we work with two totals: Domestic Supply (DS), i.e. domestic consumption and domestic investment, and Domestic Product (DP), i.e. total domestic production for export and for the home market.

Our primary purpose is to bring about series that allow analysis of long-term historical patterns of change. This does not mean that we have to cover the overall economy with *all* flows of goods and services. We consider it possible to form certain aggregates from the total collection of goods and services.

The total economic system is conventionally summarized in an expenditure approach:

$$GDP = C_p + C_m + I_p + I_m + E - M,$$

where C is consumption, I investments, E export and M import. Subscripts p and m denote domestically produced and produced abroad, respectively.

DS is used for the following elements in the expenditure approach:

$$C_p + C_m + I_p + I_m. \tag{2.1}$$

Thus, 2.1 includes the goods and services used in the country in question in a given year for final consumption and investment.

On the production side the aggregate *DP* is as follows:

$$C_p + I_p + E_p - F_m, \tag{2.2}$$

where F denotes intermediate goods.

In a given year, the goods and services that are produced within the country for final use in this country, or for export, are thus not included in its full value. The part that is produced abroad and added to the domestic production by imports of raw materials and semi-manufactured goods is deducted.

In current prices, (2.1) = (2.2) when $E = M$, provided, of course, that the values in both cases are expressed in the same type of prices, for example market prices. But it is easily understood that it must be an extreme case if identity arises in the volume calculation, because DS contains the elements C_m and I_m, while DP contains the element $(E_p - F_m)$. Only C_p and I_p are common elements.[34]

It is conventional in the expenditure approach to form sub-aggregates called private consumption of goods, private services consumption, investment including changes in stocks, and public consumption. We believe, however, that from the point of view of analysis it is unfortunate to treat public consumption in this way. Partly, this aggregate contains public activities of a collective nature, i.e. public administration, police, etc. It is questionable whether these activities should be seen as consumption or investment. Such a discussion would probably lead to confusion. Therefore, we consider this part of public consumption – for example public administration, etc. – as a particular sub-category. Another part of public consumption is activities of a fundamentally different nature: education, health care, social welfare, etc. These services are certainly collectively produced but they are subject to individual consumption. Services of the same kind are also produced privately, and then they are registered as private consumption. Therefore, we consider this type of public activity as private service consumption, which in turn is divided into privately produced and publicly produced parts.[35]

We also make a distinction from the conventional classification principles concerning inventory changes. Any change in stock affects the magnitude of DP in the year that the change actually occurs. But it should not be registered in DS this year when it is a question of an inventory increase. If this registration occurs there will be double counting because the increase will come forward as consumption or investment in a subsequent year,[36] and then of course will be registered in DS. An inventory reduction, however, immediately has a counterpart in increased consumption or investment in DS.

As for deflation, we mean that in principle base year weighted Laspeyres volume indices – or conversely Paasche price indices – are to be preferred over other indices.[37] The entire period of investigation was divided into a number of sub-periods called deflation periods. These were delimited in such a way that they could be expected to have different price structures. It seemed reasonable to use deflation periods of a length that fit the concept of Kuznets' cycles, i.e. periods of 15 to 25 years.

As period limits, boom years were selected. It can be assumed that major price shifts between products and groups of product primarily take place during the years of recession that immediately follow the marked economic boom years.

Within each sub-period Laspeyres indices were constructed containing as many individual products (services), or in some cases groups of goods (services), as possible. The aggregation was done with weights pertaining to the recession years at the beginning of the deflation periods. The different sub-periods – six for a 110-year time-span – were then linked to form continuous series.[38] The number of years in the base periods varied according to the specific conditions in each deflation period: at least two and at most four. Separate deflators were constructed for *DP* and *DS*. Since the various aggregates to a great extent are formed by different elements in the expenditure approach they also differ in the commodity composition. In principle, separate deflations using price series for all goods with the same base years normally give different volume indices for the different aggregates.

Thus, the essentials of our method have been introduced. We can relate the two separate totals – *DP* and *DS* – or relevant sub-totals to each other. Both sum up one and the same economy but may nevertheless show different volume growth over time, and these differences may be subject to analysis. Furthermore, each of the aggregates is weighted together and includes parts, all uniformly constructed with the same base years in each sub-period. The weight bases can be shifted and used for the construction of deflators referring to earlier or later periods. New volume series are then obtained which can be compared with the original ones and, in this case too, differences can be subject to analysis.

This methodical approach enables another type of analysis to that which is possible when national accounts are used more conventionally. It is possible to decide where boundaries should be drawn between homogenous periods and to analyse qualitative shifts in the economy. Thus, starting points for deeper analyses are obtained.

In order to clarify the use of the weight base shifts, the concept of Gerschenkron effects can be used. This term describes strong structural shifts, which means that some parts of an economy, particularly within the industrial and transport sectors, are growing very fast, at the same time as relatively decreasing costs, reflected in relatively falling market prices, make themselves felt. The mirror image is the existence of traditional production, which is driven back since its cost situation makes it less competitive.

We analyse Gerschenkron effects in the Swedish economy by comparing the values of two separate deflator calculations for each of the sub-periods.[39] One value originates from the initial estimate and the other one is calculated by using a new weight base, namely that of the subsequent period. Strong elements of Gerschenkron effects give lower values for the new deflator series than the original.

Weight base shifts, however, are not the only methodological approach that is made possible by our principles of deflation, as already mentioned. By relating the separate volume series *DP* and *DS* to each other, it is possible to perform an appropriate periodization of Swedish economic history.

The differences that arise in the *DP/DS* relation are due to the fact that *DP* contains export goods, while *DS* contains import goods. It is obviously not patterns of change in the trade balance that give rise to the differences. It is, instead, differences in the deflator changes that in a crucial way govern the emergence of the patterns.

It is also possible to construct special deflator series only for the kind of production within *DP* that can be subject to export and the type of product in *DS* that can be subject to import. The relationship between these new deflator series – *MPDP/MPDS*[40] – provides a terms-of-trade expression of a new type. It differs from common terms-of-trade concepts because it is not measured at the level of trade and does not include all goods crossing the country's borders. Instead, it is changes in the real impact of external trade on the country's economy that are measured.

All export is included in *MPDP* but in *MPDS* only those parts of imports that are goods for direct domestic consumption and investment. Other parts of the import, i.e. various types of inputs, including fuel, used in domestic production are not directly included.

Notes

1 For information on Heckscher's life and work, see for instance Hasselberg (2007) and Carlson (1988). It should be added that there are plenty of books and articles on this pioneer.
2 This was Johan Åkerman's view of economic history. According to him economic history consisted of narrations while analyses of economic change with application of theory belonged to economics.
3 On the birth of the discipline in Sweden, see for example Hettne (1980) and Hasselberg (2007).
4 Jörberg (1967) introduced new economic history to the Swedish audience.
5 Gerschenkron (1962), p. 353.
6 Later this was studied by, for example, Ljungberg (1990).
7 Kuznets (1930).
8 See, for example, Kuznets (1966). Maddison published his collections of series in a number of books, for example, Maddison (2007).
9 See, for example, Schumpeter (1934).
10 The programme *Wages, Cost of Living and National Income of Sweden 1860–1930* was led by Professor Gösta Bagge. A number of important contributions were published and the one of main interest here is Lindahl *et al.* (1937). For a study of this, see Carlson (1982).
11 Lindahl (1956) and Johansson (1967).
12 Krantz and Nilsson (1975).
13 Early attempts to develop these views are found in Schön and Nilsson (1978), Schön (1982) and Krantz and Schön (1983).
14 1) Schön (1995), 2) Schön (1988), 3) Pettersson (1987), 4) Krantz (1986), 5) Krantz (1991), 6) Krantz, (1987a), 7) Krantz (1987b), 8) Schön (1984), 9) Ljungberg (1988).
15 The reasons are briefly described in Krantz and Schön (2007), p. 3.
16 The data collected in the project were also used by Edvinsson (2005).
17 Krantz and Schön (2007). All data are also available at www.ekh.lu.se/en/research/economic-history-data/shna1560-2010.
18 www.ekh.lu.se/en/research/economic-history-data/shna1560-2010.
19 Schön and Krantz (2012a, b).
20 It should be remembered when reading that it was written in the 1970s.
21 See, for example, Statistiska Centralbyrån, NR-PM 1976:2, *Principer och riktlinjer för fastprisberäkningar av offentlig verksamhet.*

22 Kuznets (1966) and Gerschenkron (1962).
23 Our methodological view is also seen in a debate in the journal *Scandia*: Krantz and Nilsson (1976), Gustafsson *et al.* (1977) and Krantz and Nilsson (1977).
24 Åkerman (1942), p. 5 (translated in this book).
25 Åkerman (1939), p. 261ff.
26 Åkerman (1944), p. 23f.
27 Åkerman (1939), p. 272 (translated in this book).
28 Åkerman (1949), p. 1 (translated in this book; Åkerman's italics).
29 On these limitations, see also our articles in the debate referred to in footnote 23.
30 Erik Dahmén (1950) applied causal analysis to a limited research field, Sweden's industrial performance 1919–1939. As an empirical study with a consequent and firm framework it is excellent, but the time period of the analysis was not chosen from any points of departure, theoretical or empirical, that made it homogenous.
31 As a matter of curiosity it can be noted that Åkerman considered both causal analysis and calculus models as belonging to economic theory and, thus, economics. Economic history in his view is 'in principle non-causal and founded on studies of the sources', 'a chronicle as complete as possible, which is supposed to show what has really happened' Åkerman (1939), p. 262f.
32 A difference between Åkerman's and our theoretical framework is that we do not emphasize 'exogenous' driving forces to the same extent.
33 SCB, NR-PM 1976:2 (translated in this book).
34 An example of the consequences of using an arrangement based on the expenditure approach is found in the official Norwegian historical national accounts, which cover about a 100 years. There, in some cases even very large current account surpluses in current values are turned to the opposite, very large deficits, at the constant price calculation. (*Nasjonalregnskab 1865–1960*, Norges Officielle Statistikk XII, 1963) This is of course not surprising from a mathematical point of view, because – with this arrangement – it is a question of series with different commodity contents. But it cannot possibly be a reasonable effect associated with the kind of historical analysis that it is our purpose to pursue. This implicitly means that part of the value added which is produced within the country is turned into imports at constant price calculations.
35 We are aware of the difficulties in making a precise definition of the public services in the available statistical material. Above all, the fraction that we attribute to private consumption contains parts that should have been assigned to the aggregate public administration, etc.
36 An inventory increase may also appear in *DP* in a later year as exports. This is no problem as far as calculation is concerned because a corresponding stock decrease is taking place within the same aggregate.
37 SCB NR-PM 1976:2. See also Gerschenkron, 'Problems in Measuring Long-Term Growth in Income and Wealth', in Gerschenkron (1962), p. 437. There is also the possibility of using chain indices, sometimes called Divisia indices, which could sometimes be preferable, for instance with regard to analyses based on production theory.
38 Actually, the base year(s) could have been chosen from other parts of the deflation periods and probably the results would not have been very different.
39 The empirical part of this report is not reproduced here. See, however, Chapter 5 in Krantz and Nilsson (1975), and in this volume, an examination of Gerschenkron effects in price indices.
40 'Material Products' in *DP* and *DS*, respectively.

References

Åkerman, J. (1939), *Ekonomisk teori* I. Lund: C.W.K. Gleerups förlag.
Åkerman, J. (1942), 'Ekonomisk kalkyl och kausalanalys', *Ekonomisk tidskrift*, vol. 44, pp. 3–22.
Åkerman, J. (1944), *Ekonomisk teori* II, Lund: C.W.K. Gleerups förlag.

Åkerman, J. (1949), 'Strukturgränser i svensk industrialism', *Ekonomisk tidskrift*, vol. 51, pp. 1–18.

Carlson, B. (1982), *Bagge, Lindahl och nationalinkomsten: om* 'National Income of Sweden 1861–1930'. Lund: Ekonomisk-historiska institutionen.

Carlson, B. (1988), *Staten som monster: Gustav Cassels och Eli F Heckschers syn på statens roll och tillväxt*. Lund: Skrifter utgivna av Ekonomisk-historiska föreningen vol. LXI.

Dahmén, E. (1950), *Svensk industriell företagarverksamhet. Kausalanalys av den industriella utvecklingen 1919–1939*. Stockholm: IUI.

Edvinsson, R. (2005), *Growth, Accumulation, Crisis: with New Macroeconomic Data for Sweden 1800–2000*. Stockholm: Almqvist & Wiksell International.

Fridlizius, G. (1957), *Swedish Corn Export in the Free Trade Era: Patterns in the Oats Trade 1850–1880*. Lund: Gleerups.

Gerschenkron, A. (1962), *Economic Backwardness in Historical Perspective*. New York: Praeger.

Gustafsson, B., Odén, B., Ohlsson, R. and Olsson, C.-A. (1977), 'Modeller som tvångströja, repliker', *Scandia*, 1, pp. 88–108.

Hasselberg, Y. (2007), *Industrisamhällets förkunnare: Eli Heckscher, Arthur Montgomery, Bertil Boëthius och svensk ekonomisk historia 1920–1950*. Hedemora/Möklinta: Gidlunds förlag.

Hettne, B. (1980), *Ekonomisk historia i Sverige: en översikt av institutionell utveckling, forskningsinriktning och vetenskaplig produktion*. Lund: Historiska institutionen.

Johansson, Ö. (1967), *The Gross Domestic Product of Sweden and its Composition 1861– 1955*. Stockholm: Almqvist & Wiksell.

Jörberg, L. (1961), *Growth and Fluctuations of Swedish Industry 1869–1912: Studies in the Process of Industrialisation*. Stockholm: Almqvist & Wiksell.

Jörberg, L. (1967), 'Ekonomisk historia, jordbruksstatistik och depression', *Historisk Tidskrift*, (1), pp. 92–115.

Krantz, O. (1986), *Transporter och kommunikationer 1800–1980*. Lund: Ekonomisk-historiska föreningen.

Krantz, O. (1987a), *Husligt arbete 1800–1980*. Lund: Ekonomisk-historiska föreningen.

Krantz, O. (1987b), *Offentlig verksamhet 1800–1980*. Lund: Ekonomisk-historiska föreningen.

Krantz, O. (1991), *Privata tjänster 1800–1980*. Lund: Ekonomisk-historiska föreningen.

Krantz, O. and Nilsson, C.-A. (1975), *Swedish National Product 1861–1970. New Aspects on Method and Measurement*. Lund: LiberLäromedel/Gleerup.

Krantz, O. and Nilsson, C.-A. (1976), 'Modeller från ekonomisk teori i historisk forskning. Fruktbar forskningsstrategi eller tvångströja', *Scandia* 2, pp. 260–282.

Krantz, O. and Nilsson, C.-A. (1977), 'Genmäle', *Scandia* 1, pp. 109–115

Krantz, O. and Nilsson, C.-A. (1978), 'Om strukturgränser i svensk ekonomi 1861–1975. En metod att använda nationalproduktserier i analys av ekonomisk-historisk förändring', *Meddelande från ekonomisk-historiska institutionen, Lunds universitet* 1978:2.

Krantz, O. and Schön, L. (1983), 'Den svenska krisen i långsiktigt perspektiv', *Ekonomisk debatt.*

Krantz, O. and Schön, L. (2007), *Swedish Historical National Accounts 1800-2000*, Stockholm: Almqvist & Wiksell International.

Kuznets, S. (1930), *Secular Movements in Production and Prices, their Nature and their Bearing upon Cyclical Fluctuations*. Boston: Houghton Mifflin.

Kuznets, S. (1966), *Modern Economic Growth: Rate, Structure and Spread*. Yale: Yale University Press.

Lindahl, O. (1956), *Sveriges nationalprodukt 1861–1951*. Stockholm: Konjunkturinstitutet.

Lindahl, E., Dahlgren, E. and Kock, K. (1937), *The National Income of Sweden*, I–II. London: P. S. King.

Ljungberg, J. (1988), *Deflatorer för industriproduktionen 1888–1955*. Lund: Ekonomisk-historiska föreningen.

Ljungberg, J. (1990), *Priser och marknadskrafter i Sverige 1885–1969. En prishistorisk studie*. Lund: Ekonomisk-historiska föreningen (diss.).

Maddison, A. (2007), *Contours of the World Economy 1–2030 AD. Essays in Macro-Economic History*. Oxford: Oxford University Press.

Nasjonalregnskab 1865–1960, *Norges Officielle Statistikk XII*. Oslo, 1963.

Pettersson, L. (1987), *Byggnads- och anläggningsverksamhet 1800–1980*. Lund: Ekonomisk-historiska föreningen.

Schumpeter, J. (1934), *The Theory of Economic Development: An Inquiry into Profits, Capital, Credit, Interest, and the Business Cycle*. Cambridge, Mass.: Harvard University Press.

Schön, L. (1982), 'Det förstenade kapitalet', *Zenit* 1982, pp. 17–26.

Schön, L. (1984), *Utrikeshandel 1800–1870*. Lund: Ekonomisk-historiska föreningen, revised and published 2015: Schön, L. (2015), *Utrikeshandel 1800-2000*, Lund: Ekonomisk-historiska föreningen.

Schön, L. (1988), *Industri och hantverk 1800–1980*. Lund: Ekonomisk-historiska föreningen.

Schön, L. (1995), *Jordbruk med binäringar 1800–1980*. Lund: Ekonomisk-historiska föreningen.

Schön, L. and Krantz, O. (2012a), 'The Swedish economy in the early modern period: constructing historical national accounts', *European Review of Economic History*, vol. 16(4), pp. 529–549.

Schön, L. and Krantz, O. (2012b), 'Swedish historical national accounts 1560–2010', *Lund Papers in Economic History* 123, Lund University.

Schön, L. and Nilsson, C.-A. (1978), 'Investeringsmönster och kris i svensk ekonomi', *Zenit* 1978, pp. 25–37.

Statistiska Centralbyrån, NR-PM 1976:2, *Principer och riktlinjer för fastprisberäkningar av offentlig verksamhet*.

3 Identifying and modelling cycles and long waves in economic time series

Fredrik N. G. Andersson

Whether cycles longer than the business cycle, for example Kondratieff waves (Kondratieff, 1926) or structural cycles (Schön, 2009, 2012), exist has been debated for a long time (see, for example, van Duijn, 1985; Metz, 2011). For example, a substantial part of the economic literature rejects any cycles beyond the traditional business cycle (see, for example, Garrison, 1989). In many cases the rejection of long cycles is explained by the econometric methods used to study the economy (Freeman and Louçã, 2001). Econometric methods are designed to model the economy and economic hypotheses (Kennedy, 2001). The evolution of econometric methods is therefore closely linked to the evolution of economic theories and models (see, for example, Mills, 2003). Mainstream economic theories rarely consider an economy with more than two time horizons: short-run business cycle fluctuations and long-run (equilibrium) developments (examples include Samuelson, 1955; Goodfriend and King, 1997; Woodford, 2003). Consequently, most econometric methods only distinguish between short-term effects and long-term effects. In other words, standard econometric methods are not designed to identify or model any other cycles than the business cycle.

Researchers interested in long cycles try to overcome the limitations of standard time series methods by using simple long-run averages (Islam, 2003) or frequency domain methods to filter out the longer cyclical movements (Freeman and Louçã, 2001). These methods have several weaknesses. Simple averages may generate artificial cycles (Slutsky, 1938; Percival and Walden, 2006) and frequency domain methods assume the economy is stationary and repeats itself over time. The stationarity assumption is unlikely to hold for economic time series and imposing it may cause spurious cycles and other econometric problems (Mankiw, 2008).

An alternative time approach is wavelet methods. Similar to the frequency domain methods, the wavelet transform decomposes a time series into a set of short and long cycles, making it possible to identify various cyclical movements in the economy. Unlike frequency domain methods, however, the wavelet transform does not assume the economy is stationary and allows the cycles to change phase and size over time (Percival and Walden, 2006). The wavelet transform is therefore suitable for studying short and long cycles in economic activity (Crowley, 2007; Andersson, 2008).

The wavelet transform was initially developed in mathematics by Haar (1910). In economics the use of wavelet methods was pioneered by Ramsey (1996) and Ramsey and Lampard (1998). Since its introduction the application of wavelets in economics has grown rapidly with both theoretical and empirical contributions (Crowley, 2007; Andersson *et al.*, 2013; Gallegati and Semmler, 2014; Andersson and Ljungberg, 2015). Examples of applications include multiresolution analysis (Crowley, 2007), band spectrum regressions (Andersson, 2011; Andersson and Karpestam, 2013), forecasting (Wong *et al.*, 2003), estimating the long memory parameters (Andersson, 2014), denoising (Bruzda, 2014) and testing for auto-correlation (Li and Andersson, 2013).

This chapter contains an elementary introduction to wavelet analysis, how it can be applied to studying short and long cycles, and how to model the causes and consequences of the respective cycles using a simple band spectrum regression. The chapter contains both a theoretical discussion and empirical examples of wavelet analysis. A complete account of wavelet analysis is available in Percival and Walden (2006) and introductions to wavelet analysis for economists are available in Crowley (2007) and Andersson (2008, 2011).

Modelling cycles and long waves using wavelet analysis

Business cycles are easy to detect in any economic time series given their high frequency and sizable impact on many economic time series. Longer cycles are more difficult to identify because the short-term volatility in a time series often masks these cycles, and because long time series are necessary to identify long cycles and such longitudinal data are not always available. A cycle that is 40 years long, for example, requires at least 40 yearly observations for one full cycle to be identified. Using high-frequency data, i.e. quarterly data or monthly data instead of yearly data, does not increase the number of long-run observations and consequently does not make it easier to identify long cycles. In fact, using monthly data instead of yearly data may make it even more difficult to detect long cycles because high-frequency cycles, such as seasonal variations, commonly mask the underlying trends.

Some time series methods, but far from all, allow separation between short-term effects and long-term effects. Various bandpass filters, for example the Hodrick and Prescott (1981) and the Baxter and King (1995) filters, decompose time series into two components: a business cycle component and a trend component. Regression models for non-stationary time series such as ARIMA models and cointegration analysis similarly contain only one model for the short run and one model for the long run. For stationary time series, models are often limited to considering only one time horizon, because it is difficult to identify the effect of additional time horizons in the time domain unless the data are non-stationary.

The limitations of the time domain make it unsuitable for any studies where the economy is assumed to contain more than two time horizons, or when the long run is assumed to follow a cyclical pattern. An alternative to time domain analysis is frequency domain analysis. From an economic point of view, the frequency domain can reveal several interesting features of a time series, which are not directly observable in the time domain (Granger, 1966). In the frequency domain, a time series is not represented by a certain value at a given point in time but by a certain value for a given frequency. Each frequency, f, represents a cycle that is $1/f$ time periods long. A frequency of 0.10 therefore equals a cycle that is 10 time observations long and a frequency of 0.05 equals a cycle that is 20 time observations long. Instead of having one observation for each time point, in the frequency domain the time observations are replaced by a set of amplitudes (i.e. size) of the respective cycles.

The Fourier transform is commonly employed to transform a time series from the time domain to the frequency domain, and several empirical studies of long waves in economics have used this method (Rasmussen *et al.*, 1989; Coccia, 2010; Metz, 2011). A weakness of the Fourier transform (and the frequency domain) is that it assumes the economy is stationary and repeats itself deterministically. At the end of one cycle of a given periodicity a new cycle begins with the same amplitude as the last cycle. It is unlikely that the economy will follow such a predictable and deterministic pattern, which makes frequency analysis unsuitable for studies of the economy.

The wavelet transform, on the other hand, relaxes the stationarity assumption by combining time and frequency resolution. This is achieved by allowing each cycle for a given frequency to have its own amplitude. The wavelet transform is therefore suitable for time series where the underlying process changes over time, and also contains outliers and structural changes (Percival and Walden, 2006).

For discrete data, two wavelet transforms are available: the discrete wavelet transform and the maximal overlap discrete wavelet transform. The discrete wavelet transform (DWT) imposes a restriction on the sample size: only time series with $T=2^J$ observations, where J is an integer, can be transformed. The maximal overlap discrete wavelet transform (MODWT) does not impose such restrictions on the sample size. The MODWT also has better small sample properties than the DWT. Most economic studies therefore use the MODWT, but there are cases when the DWT is used as well (see, for example, Andersson, 2008).

In the next section the wavelet transform is introduced in more detail. This section is followed by a discussion of how wavelet methods can be applied to identify cycles and plot these cycles' developments over time. Thereafter follows a discussion of how to estimate models when the economic process is assumed to contain more than one time horizon (a band spectrum regression). Each section contains an empirical example to illustrate the technique.

The wavelet transform

Applying the wavelet transform to a time series creates a set of transform coefficients, where each coefficient can be described as the rescaled amplitude of a given cycle and a given frequency. The transform coefficients are obtained by using a transform matrix. Let **W** be the transform matrix (see Percival and Walden, 2006, for a detailed description of how to construct the transform matrix).[1] The transform coefficients are obtained by multiplying the transform matrix by the vector containing the variable that is to be transformed, in this case y,

$$\boldsymbol{\omega}_y = \mathbf{W}y, \tag{3.1}$$

where $\boldsymbol{\omega}_y$ are the transform coefficients. The transform matrix and the transform coefficients can be partitioned as

$$\boldsymbol{\omega}_y = \begin{bmatrix} \boldsymbol{\omega}_{1y} \\ \boldsymbol{\omega}_{2y} \\ \vdots \\ \boldsymbol{\omega}_{Jy} \\ \mathbf{v}_{Jy} \end{bmatrix} = \begin{bmatrix} \mathbf{W}_1 \\ \mathbf{W}_2 \\ \vdots \\ \mathbf{W}_J \\ \mathbf{V}_J \end{bmatrix} \times \mathbf{y}, \tag{3.2}$$

where the transform coefficients $\boldsymbol{\omega}_{jy}$, $j=1,\ldots,J$, represent the frequency band $1/2^{j+1}$ to $1/2^j$, and the transform coefficients $\mathbf{v}_{Jy}$ represent the frequency 0 to $1/2^{J+1}$. The first set of transform coefficients is consequently the rescaled size of cycles that are between 2 and 4 time observations long. The second set of transform coefficients is the rescaled size of cycles that are between 4 and 8 time observations long and so on. Because each frequency band represents cycles of a different periodicity, they consequently also represent different time horizons. The number of cycles that a time series can be decomposed into depends on the length of the time series. The longer the series the more cycles can be obtained (i.e. higher J).

The wavelet transform is complete, meaning that none of the information in a time series is lost in the transformation. The transform simply allows us to analyse the series from the perspective of cycles rather than from the perspective of a given time point. The transform is also orthogonal, meaning that all transform coefficients representing a given frequency band are independent of the transform coefficients representing another frequency band. The completeness and orthogonality properties of the wavelet transform are important. First, the completeness property implies that any analysis carried out in the time domain can also be carried out in the wavelet domain. The orthogonality property implies that we can analyse each frequency band as independent of the other frequency bands. We can thus identify a cycle, for example a long structural cycle, and model its causes and consequences without considering the shorter cycles. The orthogonality assumption also implies that the variance of the time series is the sum of the variance for each frequency band, i.e.

$$\| \mathbf{y} \| = \| \boldsymbol{\omega}_{1y} \| + \| \boldsymbol{\omega}_{2y} \| + \cdots + \| \boldsymbol{\omega}_{Jy} \| + \| \mathbf{v}_{Jy} \| \tag{3.3}$$

By using equation (3.3) we can determine how much of the variation in our time series is caused by the respective cycles, and obtain a measure of how important each time horizon is in the economic process.

Multiresolution analysis

Using the transform matrix a series can always be transformed back from the wavelet domain to the time domain. Using the entire transform matrix and all the transform coefficients we obtain the original time series. But we can also only use a subset of transform coefficients instead of the entire time series, which allows us to study how a cycle of a particular periodicity changes over time. The latter limited transform where a specific cycle or cycles are analysed is called multiresolution analysis. Multiresolution analysis is purely descriptive and is commonly followed by some additional modelling, for example a band spectrum regression.

To perform the multiresolution analysis, we define a detail as

$$D_{jt} = \mathbf{W}_j' \boldsymbol{\omega}_{jy}, \tag{3.4}$$

which gives us a time series that we can plot over time representing frequency band $1/2^{j+1}$ to $1/2^j$. The trend we define as a smooth S_{Jt} (frequency 0 to $1/2^{J+1}$). Because the wavelet transform is complete we can recover the original time series by summing all the details and the smooth

$$y_t = D_{1t} + D_{2t} + \dots + D_{Jt} + S_{Jt}. \tag{3.5}$$

Naturally, it is not given that all details represent a unique time horizon and we may wish to combine D_1 and D_2 to a 2- to 8-period-long cycle rather than studying them separately. All details are fluctuations around the constant/trend and therefore they have a zero mean. Only the smooth has a non-zero mean by construction.

Example of multiresolution analysis: cycles in economic activity

As an illustration of multiresolution analysis we decompose three time series: GDP growth, total factor productivity growth (TFP) and consumer price inflation. We use data from three countries: the United States, Sweden and Australia, and the time period covers the period from 1902 to 2010, in total 109 yearly observations. These three countries have been chosen due to data availability and because the economies have not been destroyed during wartime. For simplicity we limit the analysis to consider three time horizons: the short run (2- to 8-year-long cycles), the medium run (8- to 32-year-long cycles) and the long run (32 years and beyond). The short run therefore corresponds approximately to cycles of the same periodicity as Kitchin cycles, the medium run corresponds approximately to cycles with the same periodicity as Juglar and Kuznets cycles and the long run corresponds approximately to Kondratieff cycles or structural cycles (Schön, 2006; Crowley, 2007). A detailed description of the data sources are given in the Appendix to this chapter.

GDP growth is illustrated in Figure 3.1, TFP growth is illustrated in Figure 3.2 and inflation is illustrated in Figure 3.3. The original series are shown in Panel A of the respective figures. The short-run cycles are shown in Panel B, the medium-run cycles in Panel C and the long-run cycles in Panel D. Summing the series in Panels B, C and D gives the original series in Panel A by definition (see Equation (3.5)).

All original growth rates are highly volatile with inflation being the most volatile, fluctuating between −18% and 47%. Most of this volatility is caused by the short-run cycles. The medium- and the long-run cycles are smaller but not negligible. Table 3.1 shows the standard deviation for the three variables and the three

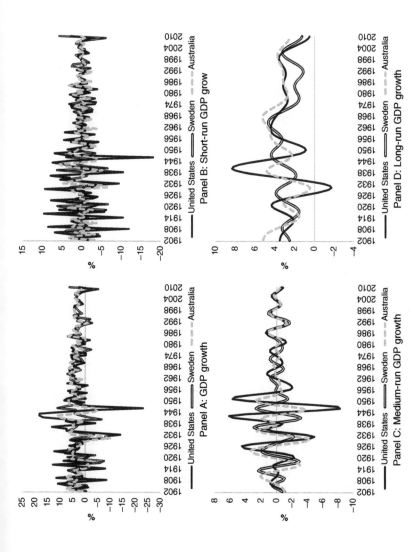

Figure 3.1 GDP growth: original data and wavelet transforms, 1902–2010.

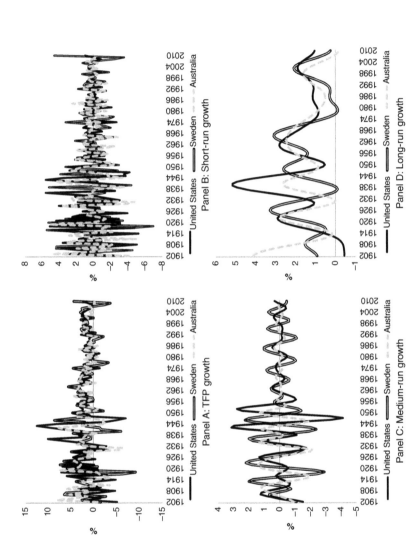

Figure 3.2 TFP growth: original data and wavelet transforms, 1902–2010.

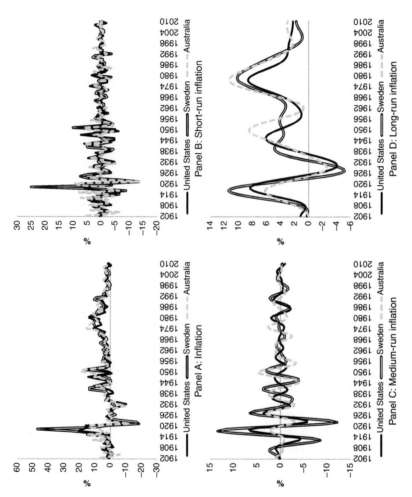

Figure 3.3 Inflation: original data and wavelet transforms, 1902–2010.

Table 3.1 Standard deviations, 1902–2010

	United States			Sweden			Australia		
	1902–2010	1902–1949	1950–2010	1902–2010	1902–1949	1950–2010	1902–2010	1902–1949	1950–2010
				GDP growth					
Short	4.2	5.9	2.0	2.6	3.3	1.9	2.1	2.7	1.5
Medium	2.3	3.0	1.5	1.2	1.7	0.7	1.5	2.1	0.7
Long	1.8	2.5	1.0	1.0	0.8	1.1	1.1	1.3	0.8
				TFP growth					
Short	2.2	3.1	1.0	2.2	2.8	1.5	1.8	2.5	1.2
Medium	1.0	1.4	0.7	1.0	1.4	0.6	0.8	1.1	0.3
Long	1.2	1.7	0.6	1.0	1.0	1.0	0.9	1.1	0.7
				Inflation					
Short	2.9	4.0	1.4	3.9	5.4	2.0	3.1	4.2	1.8
Medium	1.8	2.6	0.9	3.6	5.2	1.0	1.7	2.1	1.3
Long	3.0	3.7	2.3	3.7	4.4	2.9	3.5	3.3	3.3

time horizons. The short-run fluctuations are generally two to three times greater than the medium- or long-run volatility. The short-run volatility has declined over time while the medium- and long-run volatility has remained more or less constant. In any econometric analysis, in the time domain the short-term volatility would clearly mask any other cyclical movements in the series.

Although the medium- and long-run cycles are smaller than the short-run cycles they still have a measurable effect on the economy due to their persistence. The cumulative effect of the persistent movements in the economy can become relatively large. For example, compared to the average growth path, the long-run cycles in TFP growth cause a cumulative deviation from the growth path implied by the constant of +/–15%. For GDP growth the cumulative long-run growth effects are slightly smaller, but for inflation the long-run cumulative effects are even larger.

The economy has become more stable over time. The reduction in volatility is the largest for the short-run cycles and more modest for the medium run and the long run. As illustrated in Table 3.1, after 1950 volatility is reduced by almost half for the short run. The medium-run cycles and the long-run cycles also become smaller but the reduction is most pronounced for the short run. Not only does the size of the cycles change but their phase and length also vary. The long-run GDP and TFP cycles become longer after the mid-century.

In terms of harmonization we can see that for the short and medium run, all countries follow similar cycles that coincide in time after the 1970s. For the long-run GDP and TFP cycles, Australia and the United States become synchronized after the First World War. Sweden was lagging behind the United States by between 2 and 3 years prior to the Second World War but then synchronizes with the United States. The similarities across the countries clearly show that a large part of the developments are caused by common global causes.

The long-run cycles observed for GDP growth and TFP growth follow broadly the general classification of the long-run growth periods or growth waves suggested by, for example, van Duijn (1985), Devezas *et al.* (2005) and Schön (2012) for Sweden. For example, the structural growth crises, as defined by Schön, are clearly visible for Sweden with large declines in growth during the 1930s and the 1970s.

It is interesting to note that Perez (2002) and Schön (2012), among others, have argued that the long-run cycles are not necessarily visible in aggregate time series such as GDP growth or TFP growth. The respective growth waves they have identified have been derived using a wide set of non-econometric methods. Similarly, Freeman and Louçã (2001) question many of the statistical techniques that have traditionally been used to identify long-run cycles in economic time series as inappropriate and they argue for a non-statistical approach to identify long-run growth waves. However, when we use appropriate statistical methods, designed to identify long-run waves that are not stationary over time, we find long-run growth cycles in several economic time series. Moreover, the cycles we identify coincide with the long-run growth waves that van Duijn and Schön, among others, have identified. This indicates that multiresolution wavelet analysis is potentially a useful tool for identifying long-run growth waves. But multiresolution analysis in itself is never enough since it does not model the causes and consequences of the long-run growth cycles.

In summary, we can see that GDP growth, TFP growth and inflation all contain short-run, medium-run and long-run cycles. The short-run cycles have the largest amplitude but their effect on the economy is by definition only temporary. The medium-run cycles, but in particular the long-run cycles, are more persistent and their cumulative effect is relatively large and the medium- and long-run cycles are therefore not unimportant from an economic point of view. The cycles' properties, size and phase change over time, which is a sign of an economy constantly evolving.

Band spectrum regressions

Band spectrum regressions are a simple method to model relationships in the economy that vary depending on the time horizon (cycle). Introduced by Engle (1974) for the frequency domain, the estimator is easily modified to be used on the wavelet transform coefficients (Andersson, 2011).

In this section let us consider the case of stationary time series, in which case time series methods only allow for one time horizon. In the section on p. xx we will extend the traditional regression model to allow for several time horizons. In the section on p. xx we illustrate how traditional regression analysis is affected when the model consists of more than one time horizon by using a simulation study. Finally, the section on p. xx contains an empirical analysis where we consider the effect of growth on inflation using the data from the multiresolution analysis.

How to estimate a model using a band spectrum regression

The number of time horizons that we can consider is limited by the length of the time series. Similarly to the previous empirical example, let us consider three time horizons: short run, medium run and long run. In practice, the model can consist of either more or fewer time horizons.

$$y_t = a_0 + x_{SR,t}\beta_{SR} + x_{MR,t}\beta_{MR} + x_{LR,t}\beta_{LR} + \varepsilon_t, \tag{3.6}$$

where $x_{SR,t}$ are the short-run fluctuations, $x_{MR,t}$ are the medium-run fluctuations and $x_{LR,t}$ are the long-run fluctuations. By construction $x_t = x_{SR,t} + x_{MR,t} + x_{LR,t}$. To illustrate the effect on a traditional one time horizon model, assume the model in (3.6) is estimated using the common regression model,

$$y_t = x_t\beta + \eta_t, \tag{3.7}$$

where no consideration is taken of the possibility of multiple time horizons. Applying the ordinary least-squares (OLS) estimator to (3.7) we get

$$\hat{\beta} = (\mathbf{x'x})^{-1}\mathbf{x'y} = (\mathbf{x'x})^{-1}\mathbf{x'}(\mathbf{x}_{SR}\beta_{SR} + \mathbf{x}_{MR}\beta_{MR} + \mathbf{x}_{LR}\beta_{LR} + \varepsilon). \tag{3.8}$$

Because all frequencies are orthogonal to each other we get the expected value of the parameter estimate,

$$E\left[\hat{\beta}\right] = E\left[\left(\mathbf{x}'\mathbf{x}\right)^{-1}\mathbf{x}'\left(\mathbf{x}_{SR}\beta_{SR} + \mathbf{x}_{MR}\beta_{MR} + \mathbf{x}_{LR}\beta_{LR} + \boldsymbol{\varepsilon}\right)\right]$$

$$= \left(\mathbf{x}'\mathbf{x}\right)^{-1}\mathbf{x}'_{SR}\mathbf{x}_{SR}\beta_{SR} + \left(\mathbf{x}'\mathbf{x}\right)^{-1}\mathbf{x}'_{MR}\mathbf{x}_{MR}\beta_{MR} + \left(\mathbf{x}'\mathbf{x}\right)^{-1}\mathbf{x}'_{LR}\mathbf{x}_{LR}\beta_{LR} \quad (3.9)$$

As can be seen from (3.9), the expected value of the estimated parameter vector is a weighted average of short-run, medium-run and long-run parameters. The size of the weights $\left(\mathbf{x}'\mathbf{x}\right)^{-1}\mathbf{x}'_{SR}\mathbf{x}_{SR}$, $\left(\mathbf{x}'\mathbf{x}\right)^{-1}\mathbf{x}'_{MR}\mathbf{x}_{MR}$ and $\left(\mathbf{x}'\mathbf{x}\right)^{-1}\mathbf{x}'_{LR}\mathbf{x}_{LR}$ depends on the statistical properties of $\mathbf{x}$. For example, in a bivariate model with only one explanatory variable the weights in (3.9) are equal to the share of the variance in x_t explained by the long run, the medium run and the short run, respectively. If the long-run information dominates x_t, $\hat{\beta}$ is close to β_{LR}. If the short-run information dominates x_t, $\hat{\beta}$ is close to β_{SR}. For a non-stationary process the long-run information dominates asymptotically whereby we can expect the estimated parameter in a large sample to be close to the long-run value, but not necessarily in small samples, where the short-run fluctuations may still dominate.

It is not just the parameter estimates that are affected by estimating the miss-specified model in (3.7) instead of the correct model in (3.6); the variance estimation of the error term is also incorrect. The error term in (3.7) is equal to

$$\eta_t = \varepsilon_t + x_{SR,t}\left(\beta_{SR} - \beta\right) + x_{MR,t}\left(\beta_{MR} - \beta\right) + x_{LR,t}\left(\beta_{LR} - \beta\right). \quad (3.10)$$

As can be seen in (3.10), the disturbances in (3.8) include both the true disturbances (ε_t) and a miss-specification component: $x_{SR,t}\left(\beta_{SR} - \beta\right) + x_{MR,t}\left(\beta_{MR} - \beta\right) + x_{LR,t}\left(\beta_{LR} - \beta\right)$. Consequently,

$$var\left(\eta_t\right) = \sigma^2 + var\left(x_{SR,t}\right)\left(\beta_{SR} - \beta\right)^2 + var\left(x_{MR,t}\right)\left(\beta_{MR} - \beta\right)^2$$

$$+ var\left(x_{LR,t}\right)\left(\beta_{LR} - \beta\right)^2. \quad (3.11)$$

Because the estimated variance, with the common regression model in (3.7), is larger than the true variance we will reject a relationship between variables in the model too often.

For a correct estimate of the parameters it is necessary to apply a technique that allows us to split up the time series into its time horizon components. The band spectrum regression is similar to an ordinary regression; the only difference is that we estimate the model on a subset of all frequencies (time horizons) and not on the entire frequency band (all time horizons combined into one). We can choose to model all frequencies with either different variables or parameters or to focus on just a limited set of frequencies. For example, we may have a model that we expect will capture the long-run changes in the economy, but we do not have a good model for the short run. In this case we can then exclude the high frequencies from the analysis and only regress on the low frequencies.

Let us continue with our example that we have a model for all time horizons and the only difference across horizons is that the parameter values are different. The parameters in this model are estimated in two steps:

1) Decompose the explanatory variables into the various time horizons using the wavelet transform.
2) Estimate the parameters in the model using the decomposed data and an appropriate estimator such as an OLS. The parameters from the OLS will be both consistent and efficient given that all Gauss-Markov assumptions hold.

When the number of time horizons is uncertain we can decompose the series into as many cycles as possible and then test whether there are any statistically significant differences across the cycles. We can define a cycle as a unique time horizon if the parameters for that cycle are different compared to the other cycles. Similarly, we can define cycles as belonging to the same time horizon if there is no significant difference in the parameter estimates. This approach gives a data-driven method to define the number of time horizons and how long they last.

Simulations

How much the miss-specification of a mode affects the parameter estimates is illustrated in this section using two sets of simulations: one set with a model containing two time horizons and one set of simulations where the model contains three time horizons. The data we use are stationary, whereby we can only consider one time horizon with a traditional regression model. In the simulations we estimate the model using both an OLS and the band spectrum regression estimator.

First, consider the case of two time horizons: the short run and the long run. For simplicity we use a bivariate model with only one explanatory variable,

$$y_t = x_{LR,t}\beta_{LR} + x_{SR,t}\beta_{SR} + \varepsilon_t, \tag{3.12}$$

where we set $\beta_{LR} = 1$ and $\beta_{SR} = 0.2$, $\varepsilon_t \sim N(0,1)$, and we assume that the long run is defined by the frequencies 0 to 1/32 and the short run by the frequencies 1/32 to 1/2. In the case of monthly data, this would imply that the short run lasts up to 32 months and the long run 32 months and beyond. In the case of quarterly data, the short run would last up to 8 years and the long run from 8 years and beyond.

In this experiment we simulate x_t as an autoregressive process,

$$x_t = \rho x_{t-1} + \theta_t, \tag{3.13}$$

where we consider three choices of $\rho = \{0, 0.5, 1\}$, and we set $\theta_t \sim N(0,2)$. The greater the autoregressive parameter the more the long run influences x. Due to these variations between which component of x (short run or long run) dominates, depending on ρ, the expected value of β when estimating the model,

$$y_t = x_t\beta + \varepsilon_t, \tag{3.14}$$

varies as well. For example, the greater the value of ρ the closer $\hat{\beta}$ is to β_{LR}. Each experiment is carried out 1,000 times and the average estimated parameter and the standard error are presented in Table 3.2.[2]

As expected, the OLS parameter estimate from the traditional model with only one time horizon is biased. For smaller ρ, the high frequencies contain a larger proportion of the variance in x than the low frequencies do. The estimated parameter is therefore closer to the short-run parameter than the long-run parameter: the average estimate is 0.281. As ρ increases, the low frequencies become more influential and the estimated parameter comes closer to the long-run parameter. When $\rho=1$, x_t is a random walk and $\hat{\beta}$ should asymptotically approach β_{LR}. As can be seen in Table 3.2, when $T=100$ the estimated parameter is 0.916, but as T increases to 500, the average estimate is close to 1: the average estimate is 0.981 when $T=500$. Yet, there is still a small bias even for $T=500$.

The band spectrum regression estimates are on average unbiased and have smaller standard deviations. The variance of the residual is also correctly estimated by the band spectrum regression. The true value is 1 and the average

Table 3.2 Simulation results: two time horizons

T	Miss-specified model		Correctly specified model		
	$\hat{\beta}$	$\hat{\sigma}^2$	$\hat{\beta}_{LR}$	$\hat{\beta}_{SR}$	$\hat{\sigma}^2$
$\rho=0$					
100	0.281	1.124	1.017	0.199	0.980
	(0.061)	(0.174)	(0.211)	(0.056)	(0.147)
200	0.281	1.132	0.997	0.200	0.985
	(0.041)	(0.120)	(0.142)	(0.040)	(0.101)
500	0.281	1.146	0.995	0.200	0.995
	(0.025)	(0.081)	(0.085)	(0.024)	(0.064)
$\rho=0.5$					
100	0.412	1.362	1.000	0.200	0.975
	(0.076)	(0.229)	(0.107)	(0.054)	(0.138)
200	0.412	1.400	1.000	0.200	0.990
	(0.052)	(0.168)	(0.075)	(0.038)	(0.100)
500	0.416	1.425	1.000	0.200	0.995
	(0.035)	(0.109)	(0.045)	(0.025)	(0.063)
$\rho=1$					
100	0.916	4.728	1.000	0.200	0.980
	(0.065)	(2.819)	(0.013)	(0.044)	(0.138)
200	0.957	5.267	1.000	0.200	0.992
	(0.033)	(3.250)	(0.006)	(0.030)	(0.102)
500	0.981	5.454	1.000	0.200	0.999
	(0.016)	(3.176)	(0.002)	(0.019)	(0.064)

Note: The standard error of the parameter estimates are presented below the average parameter estimates. As a wavelet filter we use the Haar-wavelet.

estimate is, irrespective of p and T, within the interval 0.975 and 0.999. The estimate from the miss-specified model (3.10) is between 1.124 and 5.454, which is expected considering equation (3.11). The closer the parameter estimate is to the long-run parameter the greater the influence of the miss-specification component. The more $\hat{\beta}$ deviates from β_{SR} the higher the variance of the disturbance in the miss-specified model.

Next, we consider a case with three time horizons: the long run, the medium run and the short run. In this case, the miss-specified model will contain an additional third miss-specification component making the bias potentially even larger. As before, we let the frequencies 0 to 1/32 represent the long run, the medium run is represented by the frequencies 1/32 to 1/8 and the short run by the frequencies 1/8 to 1/2. Using monthly data, the short run is defined as cycles with a periodicity of 2 to 8 months, the medium run by cycles with a periodicity of 8 to 32 months and the long run as more persistent variations than 32 months. Using quarterly data, this definition of the time horizons implies that the short run lasts up to 2 years, the medium run 2 to 8 years and the long run is 8 years and beyond.

The data-generating process is given by

$$y_t = x_{SR,t}\beta_{SR} + x_{MR,t}\beta_{MR} + x_{LR,t}\beta_{LR} + \varepsilon_t, \tag{3.15}$$

where $x_{MR,t}$ is the medium-run variations in the explanatory variables and β_{MR} the medium-run parameter. In the simulations we set $\beta_{LR} = 1$, $\beta_{MR} = 0.5$ and $\beta_{SR} = 0.2$. As before, $\varepsilon_t \sim N(0,1)$ and x_t is simulated as an autoregressive process. The simulation results are presented in Table 3.3.

The results with three time horizons are similar to the results with two time horizons. The miss-specified model estimates a weighted average of the three time horizons and consequently the residuals include a miss-specification component. As indicated by the simulations, the closer the estimated parameter is to the long-run parameter, the greater the size of the miss-specification component.

The band spectrum regression is on average unbiased and more efficient than the miss-specified OLS estimator. One difference compared with the two time horizon models is that the standard error of the parameter estimates has increased. The increase is small for the long-run parameter and higher for the short-run parameter estimates. As for the two time horizon case, the estimates of the variance of the shocks are biased for the miss-specified model, but close to the true value for the band spectrum regression.

The results from the simulations clearly show the importance of considering estimation techniques that allow parameters to vary depending on the time horizon. Parameter estimates may otherwise become biased and cause us to draw the wrong conclusion about the nature of the relationships between different economic variables.

Empirical example: inflation and economic growth

As an illustration of a band spectrum regression we consider a simple regression model of consumer inflation. The relationship between inflation and economic

Table 3.3 Simulation results: three time horizons

T	Miss-specified model		Correctly specified model			
	$\hat{\beta}$	$\hat{\sigma}^2$	$\hat{\beta}_{LR}$	$\hat{\beta}_{MR}$	$\hat{\beta}_{SR}$	$\hat{\sigma}^2$
$\rho=0$						
100	0.326	1.151	1.018	0.499	0.199	0.971
	(0.062)	(0.177)	(0.222)	(0.235)	(0.066)	(0.146)
200	0.325	1.157	0.999	0.495	0.202	0.981
	(0.042)	(0.122)	(0.151)	(0.164)	(0.047)	(0.101)
500	0.325	1.170	0.995	0.500	0.200	0.992
	(0.026)	(0.082)	(0.091)	(0.104)	(0.029)	(0.064)
$\rho=0.5$						
100	0.485	1.361	1.004	0.496	0.202	0.965
	(0.072)	(0.215)	(0.114)	(0.169)	(0.079)	(0.137)
200	0.485	1.393	0.999	0.503	0.198	0.985
	(0.050)	(0.158)	(0.079)	(0.108)	(0.054)	(0.100)
500	0.490	1.411	1.000	0.501	0.202	0.994
	(0.033)	(0.096)	(0.044)	(0.072)	(0.036)	(0.062)
$\rho=1$						
100	0.934	3.690	1.000	0.496	0.202	0.971
	(0.052)	(2.006)	(0.014)	(0.092)	(0.075)	(0.137)
200	0.966	4.037	1.000	0.503	0.197	0.987
	(0.026)	(2.294)	(0.006)	(0.064)	(0.054)	(0.100)
500	0.985	4.143	1.000	0.500	0.200	0.997
	(0.012)	(2.223)	(0.003)	(0.041)	(0.036)	(0.064)

Note: The standard error of the parameter estimates are presented below the average parameter estimates. As a wavelet filter we use the Haar-wavelet.

growth is theoretically unclear. On the one hand, money neutrality implies that there should be no long-run relationship between inflation and economic growth if people behave rationally, while we may expect a short-run Phillips curve effect. Bordo *et al.* (2004), on the other hand, argue that technological improvements may also affect inflation over the long run. To test the relationship between economic activity and inflation, we estimate the following model with three time horizons following the multiresolution analysis,

$$\pi_{it} = a_i + \rho_i \pi_{it-1} + L^{SR}_{it-1}\beta_{Lji} + L^{MR}_{it-1}\gamma_{Li} + L^{LR}_{it-1}\delta_{Li} + C^{SR}_{it-1}\beta_{Cji} + C^{MR}_{it-1}\gamma_{Ci}$$

$$+ C^{LR}_{it-1}\delta_{Ci} + TFP^{SR}_{it-1}\beta_{TFPji} + TFP^{MR}_{it-1}\gamma_{TFPi} + TFP^{LR}_{it-1}\delta_{TFPi} + \varepsilon_{it}, \qquad (3.16)$$

where π_{it} is inflation, i denotes country (United States, Sweden, Australia), t denotes time, L is employment growth, C is real capital growth, a, ρ, β, γ, δ are the parameters to be estimated and ε_{it} is the error term. The lag of inflation is commonly used to model expected inflation. The inflation lag and the short-run measures of economic activity therefore represent the neoclassical Phillips curve (see, for example, Andersson and Jonung, 2014). Assuming that money neutrality holds, we expect no medium-run or long-run correlation between the real economy and inflation. If Bordo *et al.* (2004) are correct, we can expect a long-run relationship between inflation and TFP growth.

As a comparison, we also estimate a simple regression model using the original data and only one time horizon:

$$\pi_{it} = a_i + \rho_i \pi_{it-1} + L_{it-1}\beta_{Li} + C_{it-1}\beta_{Ci} + TFP_{it-1}\beta_{TFPi} + \varepsilon_{it} \,. \tag{3.17}$$

Because the data are stationary, we expect the results from the traditional regression model to be similar to the results for the short-run results from the band spectrum regression. The results from the original regression model are presented in Table 3.4 and the results from the band spectrum regression are presented in Table 3.5.

The results from the traditional regression model show support for the neoclassical Phillips curve (see Table 3.4). The lag of inflation (inflation expectations) is significant and so are TFP growth and labour growth. A higher rate of economic activity leads to higher inflation irrespective of whether growth is caused by intensive or extensive factors. This result holds for all three countries.

Once we split the data into three time horizons our conclusions partly change. Similarly to the traditional regression model, we find that TFP and labour growth has a significant and positive effect on inflation, but only for the short run and not for the other two time horizons. There is only a trade-off between inflation and labour growth for the short run. For the long run we find that TFP growth has a negative effect, supporting the claim by Bordo *et al.* (2004) that long-run

Table 3.4 Regression results inflation model: one time horizon

	United States	*Sweden*	*Australia*
Constant	−1.03	0.16	1.64
	(1.19)	(1.08)	(1.14)
Inflation$_{t-1}$	**0.67***	**0.74***	**0.86***
	(0.10)	**(0.12)**	**(0.07)**
TFP$_{t-1}$	0.06	**0.51****	**0.69***
	(0.25)	**(0.24)**	**(0.22)**
Capital$_{t-1}$	0.62	0.12	−0.12
	(0.40)	(0.29)	(0.24)
Labour$_{t-1}$	**0.28****	0.46*	**0.61****
	(0.12)	**(0.25)**	**(0.23)**
Adjusted R²	0.64	0.49	0.73
DWT	1.76	2.04	1.52

Note: ***, ** and * denote statistically significant at the 1%, 5% and 10% level, respectively. All significant parameters at the 5% significance level are in bold. Standard errors are presented in parenthesis below each parameter estimate.

Table 3.5 Regression results inflation model: three time horizons

		United States	Sweden	Australia
	Constant	−2.5	0.11	3.58
		(1.60)	(1.38)	(6.30)
Inflation$_{t-1}$	—	**0.40*****	**0.44*****	**0.82*****
		(0.14)	**(0.14)**	**(0.09)**
TFP$_{t-1}$	Short run	0.37	**0.95***	**0.90*****
		(0.28)	**(0.50)**	**(0.32)**
	Medium run	−0.81	−1.0	0.67
		(0.67)	(1.47)	(2.12)
	Long run	**−2.00*****	**−1.70*****	**−1.09*****
		(0.65)	**(0.67)**	**(0.40)**
Capital$_{t-1}$	Short run	1.65	−1.5	−0.14
		(1.45)	(2.55)	(0.51)
	Medium run	−2.1	2.60	−0.47
		(1.50)	(1.65)	(0.95)
	Long run	**3.1*****	**1.20*****	−0.58
		(0.86)	**(0.41)**	(1.19)
Labour$_{t-1}$	Short run	**0.35*****	**0.53***	**0.93****
		(0.13)	**(0.3)**	**(0.35)**
	Medium run	0.45	−0.45	0.38
		(0.34)	(0.81)	(0.97)
	Long run	1.00	1.7	−0.30
		(1.10)	(1.35)	(1.38)
	Adjusted R²	0.70	0.57	0.73
	DW	2.0	1.93	1.75

Note: ***, ** and * denote statistically significant at the 1%, 5% and 10% level, respectively. All significant parameters at the 5% significance level are in bold. Standard errors are presented in parenthesis below each parameter estimate. As a wavelet filter we use the Haar-wavelet.

productivity growth may cause negative long-run inflation impulses. The sign of the parameter, in other words, changes from positive in the short run to negative in the long run. We also find that capital growth has a positive long-run effect on inflation. For the short run we found no significant relationship between inflation and capital growth.

In the long run, TFP growth and capital growth are negatively correlated (−0.34). As the relative importance of the capital growth and TFP growth varies over time, the inflation impulses also vary according to our results. This obviously shows the complex challenge for monetary policy to control inflation as the infla-tion impulses vary over time. Because these are long-term changes (32 years and beyond), relatively long periods may appear as stable before the change in growth factors changes the inflation impulses and creates a period which, at the time, may appear unstable. Our results clearly show the importance of considering not just the business cycle's inflation impulses but also the long-run cycle's inflation impulses.

No parameter is significant for the medium run. This is potentially an indication that these cycles are less important in the economy, or at least in the inflation processes. It is important to note that these cycles are not part of the short run or the long run according to our results and therefore should not be merged by any of those two time horizons. Inflation does not revert to the long-run pattern once the short-run cycles are over. Instead, the inflation continues to fluctuate over the medium term, but we cannot explain those fluctuations using the variables we have in our model.

The parameter for the lag of inflation is higher for the traditional regression model with one time horizon than for the three time horizon model because the model does not adequately capture the long-run cycles in the economy. The autoregressive parameter therefore becomes larger because the model is miss-specified.

Summary

Traditional time series methods are designed to model at most two time horizons: short-run business cycle fluctuations and long-run equilibrium. And very often econometric techniques only consider the effect of one time horizon. In this chapter we have demonstrated how wavelet analysis can be employed to identify short and long cycles, and how it can be used to perform band spectrum regressions where the effect is allowed to vary across several time horizons. Empirical examples show that growth and inflation suggest the existence of long-run cycles and that the inflation processes vary depending on the time horizon.

Notes

1 The DWT and the MODWT can be applied using different wavelet filters. A wider filter yields more accurate frequency decomposition, but it also yields more boundary coefficients, which may affect the statistical analysis. For more information on how to choose a wavelet filter, see Percival and Walden (2006) and Andersson (2008).
2 As a wavelet filter we use the Haar wavelet.

References

Andersson, F. N. G. (2008), *Wavelet Analysis of Economic Time Series*. Lund Economic Studies 149 (diss.).
Andersson, F. N. G. (2011), 'Bandspectrum Regressions using Wavelet Analysis', *Department of Economics Lund University Working Paper* 2011:22.
Andersson, F. N. G. and Karpestam, P. (2013), 'CO_2 Emissions and Economic Activity: Short- and Long-Run Economic Determinants of Scale Energy Intensity and Carbon Intensity', *Energy Policy*, vol. 61, pp. 1285–94.
Andersson, F. N. G. and Ljungberg, J. (2015), 'Grain Market Integration in the Baltic Sea Region in the 19th Century', *Journal of Economic History*, vol. 75(3), pp. 749–90.
Andersson, F. N. G. and Jonung, L. (2014), 'The Return of the Original Phillips Curve? An Assessment of Lars E. O. Svensson's Critique of the Riksbank's Inflation Targeting 1997–2012', *Department of Economics Lund University Working Paper* 2014:28.

Andersson, F. N. G., Edgerton, D. L. and Opper, S. (2013), 'A Matter of Time. Revisiting Growth Convergence in China', *World Development*, vol. 45, pp. 239–51.

Baxter, M. and King, R. G. (1995), 'Measuring Business Cycles. Approximate Band Pass Filters for Economic Time Series', *NBER Working Paper Series 5022.*

Bordo, M., Lane, L. J. and Redish, A. (2004), 'Good and Bad Deflation', *NBER Working Paper 10329.*

Bruzda, K. (2014), 'Forecasting via Wavelet Denoising: The Random Signal Case'. In Gallegati, M. and Semmler, W. (eds) *Wavelet Applications in Economics and Finance.* London: Springer.

Butlin, N. G. (1962), *Australian Domestic Product Investment and Foreign Borrowing 1861–1938/39.* Cambridge: Cambridge University Press.

Coccia, M. (2010), 'The Asymmetric Path of Economic Long Waves', *Technological Forecasting and Social Change*, vol. 77, pp. 730–8.

Crowley, P. M. (2007), 'A Guide to Wavelets for Economists', *Journal of Economic Surveys*, vol. 21, pp. 207–67.

Devezas, T. C., Linstone, H. and Santos, H. J. S. (2005), 'The Growth Dynamics of the Internet and the Long Wave Theory', *Technological Forecasting and Social Change*, vol. 72(8), pp. 913–35.

Engle, R. F. (1974), 'Bandspectrum Regression', *International Economic Review*, vol. 15(1), pp. 1–11.

Freeman, C. and Louçã, F. (2001), *As Time Goes By*. Oxford: Oxford University Press.

Friedman, M. and Kuznets, S. (1954), *Income from Independent Professional Practice.* New York: National Bureau of Economic Research.

Gallegati, M. and Semmler, W. (eds) (2014), *Wavelet Applications in Economics and Finance.* London: Springer.

Garrison, R. (1989), 'The Austrian Theory of the Business Cycle in the Light of Modern Macroeconomics', *Review of Austrian Economics*, vol. 3, pp. 3–29.

Goodfriend, M. and King, R. C. (1997), 'The New Neoclassical Synthesis and the Role of Monetary Policy', *NBER Macroeconomics Annual*, vol. 12, pp. 231–83.

Granger, C. W. J. (1966), 'The Typical Spectral Shape of an Economic Variable', *Econometrica*, vol. 34(1), pp. 150–161.

Haar, A. (1910), 'Zur theorie der orthogonalen funktionensysteme', *Matematische Annalen*, vol. 69(3), pp. 331–71.

Haig, B. (2001), 'New Estimates of Australian GDP 1861–1948/49', *Australian Economic History Review*, vol. 41(1), pp. 1–34.

Hodrick, E. C. and Prescott, R. J. (1981), 'Post-War U. S. Business Cycles: An Empirical Investigation', *Northwestern University Centre for Mathematical Studies in Economics and Management Science Discussion Paper 451.*

Huberman M. (2005), 'Hours of Work in Old and New Worlds: the Long View 1870–2000', *IIIS Discussion Paper 95.*

Islam, N. (2003), 'What Have we Learnt from the Convergence Debate?' *Journal of Economic Surveys*, vol. 17(3), pp. 309–56.

Kennedy, P. (2001), *A Guide to Econometrics*. 4th Edition. Oxford: Blackwell Publisher.

Kondratieff, N. D. (1926), 'Die langen Wellen der Konjunktur', *Archiv für Sozialwissenschaft und Sozialpolitik*, vol. 56, pp. 573–609.

Li, Y. and Andersson, F. N. G. (2013), 'A Simple Wavelet Based Method in Testing a Wide Range of Serial Correlations in Panel Data', *Department of Economics Lund University Working Paper 2013:39.*

Maddison, A. (1994), *Standardised Estimates of Fixed Capital Stock: A Six Country Comparison*. Groeningen Growth and Development Centre: Research memorandum 570.

Mankiw, N. (2008), *Principles of economics*. 5th Edition. Mason: South-Western.

Metz, R. (2011), 'Do Kondratieff Waves Exist? How Time Series Techniques Can Help Solve the Problem', *Cliometrica*, vol. 5, pp. 205–38.

Mills. T. C. (2003), *Modelling Trends and Cycles in Economic Time-Series*. New York: Palgrave.

Percival, D. and Walden, T. (2006), *Wavelet Methods for Time Series Analysis*. Cambridge: Cambridge University Press.

Perez, C. (2002), *Technological Revolutions and Financial Capital*. Cheltenham: Edward Elgar Publishing.

Ramsey, J. B. (1996), 'The Contribution of Wavelet to the Analysis of Economic and Financial Data', *Philosophical Transactions of the Royal Society*, vol. A 357, pp. 2593–606.

Ramsey, J. B. and Lampart, C. (1998), 'Decomposition of Economic Relationships by Timescale Using Wavelets', *Macroeconomic Dynamics*, vol. 2, pp. 49–71.

Rasmussen, S., Moskelide, E. and Holst, J. (1989), 'Empirical Indication of Long Waves in Aggregate Production', *European Journal of Operational Research*, vol. 42, pp. 279–93.

Samuelson, P. A. (1955), *Economics*. New York: McGraw and Hill.

Schön, L. (2006), *Tankar om cykler*. Stockholm: SNS.

Schön, L. (2009), 'Technological Waves and Economic Growth – Sweden in an International Perspective 1850–2005', *CIRCLE paper* 2009/06.

Schön, L. (2011), 'Tillväxt och strukturell omvandling – svensk ekonomi under 150 år'. In Hultkrantz, L. and Söderström, H. Tson (eds) *Marknad och politik*. 9th Edition. Stockholm: SNS.

Schön, L. (2012), *An Economic History of Modern Sweden*. Oxon: Routledge.

Schön, L. and Krantz, O. (2012), 'Swedish Historical National Accounts 1560–2010'. *Lund Papers in Economic History* 123.

Slutsky E. (1938), 'The Summation of Random Causes as the Source of Cyclic Processes', *Econometrica*, vol. 5, pp. 105–46.

van Duijn, J. J. (1985), *The Long Wave in Economic Life*. 2nd Edition. London: George Allen and Unwin.

Wong, H., Ip, W.-C., Xie, Z. and Lui, X. (2003), 'Modelling and Forecasting by Wavelets and the Application to Exchange Rates', *Journal of Applied Statistics*, vol. 30(5), pp. 537–53.

Woodford, M. (2003), *Interest and Prices: Foundation of a Theory of Monetary Policy*. New Jersey: Princeton University Press.

Appendix
Data sources

Data sources for the data used in the empirical analysis are presented in Table A3.1. Total factor productivity (TFP) growth is estimated as the Solow residual from a Cobb-Douglas production function with constant rate of returns. Specifically, TFP growth is estimated as

$$TFP_{it} = GDP_{it} - a_{it}L_{it} - (1 - a_{it})K_{it},$$ (A3.1)

where L is employment measured as the total number of working hours, K is an estimate of the real capital stock and a_{it} is the wage share in the economy.

Table A3.1 Data sources

	United States	*Sweden*	*Australia*
Real GDP		Schön and Krantz (2012)	Haig (2001), Butlin (1962), Datastream
Real capital stock	Maddison (1994), EU KLEMS	Own estimations using Maddison (1994) method and Schön and data from Krantz (2012)	Own estimations using Maddison (1994) method and data from Butlin (1962), Datastream
Employment	Huberman (2005), The Conference Board Total Economy Database	Huberman (2005), The Conference Board Total Economy Database	Huberman (2005), The Conference Board Total Economy Database
Wage share	Statistical Abstract of the United States, and Datastream	Schön and Krantz (2012)	Datastream
CPI	Measuring Worth, Datastream	Statistics Sweden	Measuring Worth, Datastream

4 Development blocks and structural analysis

Josef Taalbi

Introduction

Major technological breakthroughs have during the past 250 years brought about unparalleled changes in the organization and structure of economies. These breakthroughs were not single events, but rather protracted processes of interdependent advances in technology. For example, the first industrial revolution was centred around the interrelated innovations of the steam engine (for example Newcomen's in 1712 and Watt's in 1769), the Arkwright mill (1767) and Trevithick's locomotive (1792), and the breakthrough of the factory system. The insight that such processes of structural and technological change are stories not only of isolated events but also of interdependencies has called for the development of adequate theoretical tools. Among such notions are general-purpose technologies (Bresnahan and Trajtenberg, 1995; Helpman, 1998), technological systems (Carlsson and Stankiewicz, 1991; Gille, 1978a; Hughes, 1987) and innovation systems (Freeman, 1995; Lundvall, 1992). *Development blocks* are sets of complementary economic and technological factors that evolve by way of the resolution of imbalances. This concept, proposed originally by Erik Dahmén (1991 [1942], 1950), has played a particularly important part in Swedish economic historical research, such as Lennart Schön's studies of structural cycles and Sweden's modern economic history (Schön, 1991, 1994, 2012). This essay discusses the concept of development blocks, with the intention to examine its merits and its place in structural analysis and in our understanding of how structural and technological change takes place. Two unique facets of the concept are highlighted: its role as a bridge between micro and macro explanations of structural change, and the rich underlying ontology of the notion that allows analysis of emergence, conflict and inertia in processes of structural change.

The essay concludes with a brief discussion of the development of empirical and methodological strategies to study development blocks. The last section takes issue with the empirical difficulties in establishing the boundaries of interdependent factors and the difficulties involved in studying complementarities systematically.

Structure and interdependence in economic thought

There is an almost irresistible inclination among (economic) historians to describe historical processes and phenomena in terms of distinct epochs in which certain states of affairs have engendered a set of stable relations, which may aid historical explanation. Such compulsions can be translated into schedules based on demarcations that may be significant from some points of view, but from other points of views quite arbitrary. The succession of monarchs may possibly be meaningful demarcations from a political point of view, but to the unfolding of the first industrial revolution, say, it has mattered little whether the monarch was George II or George III. With 'structural analysis', one may refer to a systematic scientific endeavour to understand the mechanisms behind stable economic relations and their changes, which includes the driving forces, events and mechanisms that tend to both reproduce structures and occasion them to transform. This certainly is the domain of economic history. In Swedish economist Johan Åkerman's view, a structure could be understood as a 'within given temporal boundaries, the structural boundaries, rather stable economic mechanism' (Åkerman, 1949, p. 1, translation by J. T.). Structural analysis, i.e. the analysis of structural stability and how structures emerge and evolve, involves analysis of the structural boundaries as well as the driving forces of structural change, the behaviour of economic agents and the impact of choices of economic agents on their environment.

One cannot overlook the fact that economic theory contains a wide array of tools which can be put to use to carry out such structural analysis. Analysis of economic structure and especially economic interdependence is rather a vital aspect of economics, and has been so at least since Quesnay's *tableau économique*. With Marx's (1992 [1885]) schemes of extended reproduction, Walras's (1954 [1874]) system of general equilibrium, von Neumann's (1945) seminal work on general equilibrium, Leontief's (1941) input-output analysis, Sraffa's (1960) production of commodities scheme and Pasinetti's (1973, 1983) models of structural change, there is no lack of analytical accounts that stress the interdependence of choices of economic agents or the interdependence across industries in the process of economic growth. These analytical tools are valuable for understanding the long-run stability of regimes of inter-industrial economic relations as well as analysing the static and dynamic production interdependencies between sectors. However, rather than explaining structural change, an overshadowing focal point of these particular analyses has been to show the existence of equilibrium positions, or in the work of Pasinetti, the existence of a set of multi-sectoral growth paths in which the demand and output of sectors are equalized in a growing economy.[1]

Other approaches bring a dynamic element to structural analysis, focusing on not only an understanding of structural stability but also *the driving forces* of structural change, some of which are endogenous to economic mechanisms. This latter view of structural analysis was certainly contended by Schumpeter, inspired by Marx:

> Capitalism, then, is by nature a form or method of economic change and not only never is but never can be stationary. And this evolutionary character of

the capitalist process is not merely due to the fact that economic life goes on in a social and natural environment which changes and by its change alters the data of economic action; this fact is important and these changes (wars, revolutions and so on) often condition industrial change, but they are not its prime movers. Nor is this evolutionary character due to a quasi-automatic increase in population and capital or to the vagaries of monetary systems of which exactly the same thing holds true. The fundamental impulse that sets and keeps the capitalist engine in motion comes from the new consumers' goods, the new methods of production or transportation, the new markets, the new forms of industrial organization that capitalist enterprise creates.

(Schumpeter, 1942, pp. 82–3)

Similarly, in Johan Åkerman's perspective: 'The concept of economic structure [...] can never denote anything else but a relativistic reality: the position of a certain structure in relation to previous and subsequent structures, by which the concept becomes an instrument in the search of the forces that govern structural changes' (Åkerman, 1939, p. 262, translation by J. T.). Understanding *innovation*, in one sense or another, as one of these driving forces and understanding the *interdependencies* that are created in the process of technological and structural change is then adequately put at the centre of analysis.

Development blocks and techno-economic interdependencies

We are thus urged to consider the fact that innovation not only creates interdependencies but also takes place as a result of pressures and opportunities that are created by previous technological advances. Besides Dahmén, there has been a broad consensus about the interdependent character of innovation activity and technological change (Bresnahan and Trajtenberg, 1995; Freeman and Louçã, 2001; Gille, 1978a; Hughes, 1987; Lipsey *et al.*, 2005; Nelson, 1994, 2001; Rosenberg, 1969). Broader technology shifts have been discussed in terms of general-purpose technologies (Bresnahan and Trajtenberg, 1995; Helpman, 1998; Lipsey *et al.*, 2005), technological styles (Perez, 1983; Tylecote, 1992, 1994) and techno-economic paradigms (Freeman and Louçã, 2001; Perez, 2002), 'macro' versus 'micro' inventions (Allen, 2009; Mokyr, 1990) and technological systems (Hughes, 1983, 1987) or '*systèmes techniques*' (Gille, 1978a). While, at least superficially, these approaches appear to convey similar content the differences are rather profound, owing to the methodological context(s) in which the concepts are employed and to a significant extent on the intellectual and philosophical milieus in which they have emerged. If the objective is to study the driving forces of structural change, there are two issues of immediate importance: how are interdependencies in technology shifts characterized, and how are notions of interdependencies put into contact with structural analysis? Focusing on these two issues, I will first expound what defines the development block approach conceptually and methodologically and then make a comparison with other notions that have gained currency.

The notion of development blocks and its genesis

Development blocks can be broadly understood as sets of interdependent economic activities, in the sense that the fruition of one economic activity requires the coming into place of investment, infrastructure and complementary innovations in other firms or industries. Development blocks are a 'series of events in entrepreneurial activity, technical development (including innovations) where the different linkages [...] in one or another manifestable way have causal connections with each other or condition each other' (Dahmén, 1980, p. 50, translated by J. T.). Or, in brief: 'a sequence of complementarities which by way of a series of structural tensions, i.e., disequilibria, may result in a balanced situation' (Dahmén, 1991a, p. 138).

The notion of development blocks grew out of Dahmén's study of von Hayek's notion of malinvestment (Carlsson *et al.*, 1991; Erixon, 2011), which he, encouraged by Johan Åkerman, studied as a part of his licentiate thesis. From a methodological point of view, the notion was certainly intended to be put to use in structural analysis, following in the footsteps of Åkerman. Dahmén first mentioned development blocks in a 1942 essay entitled 'Economic Structural Analysis. Reflections on the Problem of Economic Development and Business Cycle Fluctuations',[2] when he discussed the structural tensions that emerge in investment activity characterized by interdependencies:

> There are tensions in the production structure during depressions because certain enterprises and branches exhibit a lack of profitability due to the lack of other specific investments. This lack of balance in the structure of production serves as an expansionary force; a structural gap is filled in if certain specific new investments are made.
>
> (1991 [1942], pp. 29–30, original emphasis omitted)

The notion of 'development blocks' was meant to clarify 'the meaning of such structural tensions in the development process' (Dahmén, 1991 [1942], p. 30). Two things were made perfectly clear from this initial exposition.

First, the notion was developed as an integral part of structural analysis, the aim being to understand business cycle phenomena, as the title of Dahmén's 1942 paper reveals. Dahmén had noted that the weakest point of business cycle theory was explaining economic recovery from a crisis. He noted that an explanation not only of the depression but also of the recovery could be obtained 'by distinguishing between different causes of unprofitability' present during a slump (Dahmén, 1991 [1942], p. 29). *Some* of these causes of unprofitability were found in structural tensions. The fact that such tensions were also an expansionary force could explain the ensuing recovery: 'When a crisis has prevented the completion of the blocks, the subsequent depression has been marked by a structural imbalance. This lack of equilibrium has been a driving force during the transition from depression to expansion' (Dahmén, 1991 [1942], p. 30). Later work, in particular by Schön (1991, 1994, 1998, 2012), has drawn on the connection between structural crises, imbalances and expansionary driving forces that may emerge during crises towards expanding development blocks.

Second, it is clear that development blocks are disequilibrium phenomena, in which different economic activities and investments are linked through relations of complementarity and where system expansion occurs through 'gap filling'. Structural imbalances provide incentives, or pressure, to innovate. While not the first to note imbalances in technological change, this exposition is, to my knowledge, the earliest theoretical contribution in economics that puts this key dynamic at the core of an account of economic development.[3] In this process there are two types of innovations: Schumpeter-type disequilibrating innovations that create structural tensions, and gap filling innovations that aim to resolve the imbalances:

> Innovations in certain sectors and branches without any vision of a development block *ex ante* bring about 'structural tensions' which are observed *ex post* in the markets as an opportunity by actual and potential entrepreneurs. In such cases entrepreneurship consists of 'gap filling' within the framework of a development block *ex post*.
>
> (Dahmén, 1991b, p. 131)

In this way, development blocks may be said to be concentrated to a set of core innovations that bring about structural tensions, which in turn may be resolved by problem-solving innovations or investments.

The notion of development blocks was not intended to explain a particular aspect of economic development or to focus on a certain level of economic life. Rather, it was intended at the outset as a generic approach to understand interdependencies and to synthesize historical and geographical aspects of economic development. Returning to Dahmén's original article of 1942, he underscored the potential to use the concept as a way of studying a broad set of aspects of economic development:

> It is an important task to explore various development blocks. In that way a synthesis between economic history, economic geography and economic theory may be achieved. In this context, economic-historical research ought to provide material that can be fitted into the theory, while at the same time this research should also benefit from studying development blocks. Economic geography – particularly location theory – has its business cycle theoretical aspect; not only should one explain geographic location of various units of economic life but one must also explain the timing of location i.e. a time-spatial 'Standortstheorie' is required.
>
> (1991 [1942], pp. 30–1)

In this remark, Dahmén not only perceived the historical, economic and geographical aspects of innovational and industrial complementarities but also envisioned a synthesis of historical, economic and geographical theory. Apparently, he also alluded to the study of what has much later been called 'geographical innovation clusters'.

Moreover, in contrast to accounts of general-purpose technologies and techno-economic paradigms (see the next section), the notion is not fixed to a certain level of interaction. Rather, development blocks can refer to industrial connections from the individual firm, actor networks, and co-evolving industries to the development of large technological systems. Quite importantly, Dahmén envisioned development blocks as a bridge between micro- and macro-pictures of industrial and economic transformation: 'The microanalysis must thus aim for a macro-picture, i.e. it must comprise the influence of the microunits on their environment' (Dahmén, 1980, p. 38, translation by J.T.). In this view, the notion of development blocks can help understand how innovation activity affects the economic environment of firms.

The notion of development blocks can thus help understand the process of structural change and structural boundaries, as has been elaborated in the work of Schön (1991, 1998, 2012). The development block approach is also appropriately employed to understand how innovation activity is shaped by problems, imbalances and opportunities that arise in the process of economic development. The links between an analysis of development blocks and a structural analysis can be mediated by Dahmén's underlying ontology of industrial transformation as being 'Janus faced'. Dahmén operated with a notion of structural change as having its centre 'somewhere between two extreme situations': a positive situation characterized by opportunities, and a negative situation characterized by declining demand and a 'strongly felt necessity to adjust and adapt' (Dahmén, 1991a, p. 138). Thus, in industrial transformation there is a steadily ongoing conflict between new and old ways of doing things. In his doctoral dissertation, Dahmén (1950) coined the term 'transformation pressure' to describe the fundamental aspects of the industrial transformation process. Positive transformation pressure characterizes a situation dominated by opportunities, such as opportunities to increase production or advance or exploit new technologies. Conversely, a negative transformation pressure characterizes a situation dominated by declining profits or demand and a felt need for response (Dahmén, 1991a, 1993). Positive and negative transformation pressure may also be understood as sources of innovation as a creative response (Dahmén, 1993; Schumpeter, 1947; Taalbi, 2014), referring to response to new opportunities, or the 'cases where innovations are induced by a destructive threat and thus would not otherwise have been forthcoming' (Dahmén, 1993, p. 23).

Thus, as development blocks evolve, innovations may to a varying extent be induced by different pressures, problems and opportunities that arise in the process of transformation. Development blocks may be said to have a life cycle, which is intertwined with patterns of industrial crisis and growth. Schön (1991, 1994) in particular has described the evolution of development blocks as connected with two infrastructural long swings of roughly 15 to 25 years' duration. One has had a focus on transformation and renewal:

> After the creative destruction of a structural crisis, the road is opened in industrial countries for the expansion of new development blocks that have been formed during the preceding period. Innovations lead to increasing investments in both manufacturing industry and infrastructure. A rising share of investments is directed towards development power, i.e. long-term investments in new industrial plants and knowledge.
>
> (1991, p. 73)

A second phase has meant increasing focus on rationalization and efficiency:

> With reduced imbalances in the development blocks, expansionary forces are weakened. Structural stability and growing competition increasingly turn industrial investments towards lowering production costs through specialization with increasing emphasis on foreign trade: concentration on more productive units and new machinery. Emphasis is decidedly shifted from development power to competition power.
>
> (1991, p. 74)

The evolution of development blocks can also be described in terms of a sequence of widening imbalances (see Figure 4.1). In a first gestation phase, a core technology is known and possibly even in use, but technological obstacles remain to be solved before a technical breakthrough can be reached. For instance, the phenomenon of electricity was known long before its economic breakthrough, but it was in the 1890s that innovations of alternating current in a three-phase system solved the critical problem of transforming higher and lower voltage (Schön, 1990). Breakthroughs of new technologies are followed by a phase of innovations applying and improving on the core technology. Complementary innovations are necessary to enable the wider use and diffusion of the core technology. In particular, these followers enable a wider use of the core technology by lowering production costs and improving the performance of the technology. When a price fall takes place, the technology may be diffused on a broader basis.[4] When the development block expands it may enter what may be referred to as a 'network phase', in which the block encompasses interrelated components that require coordination in a system or network. Infrastructures such as railroads, the electricity grid, automotive transportation system or data and telecommunication networks come to mind.

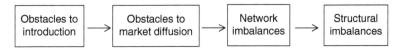

Figure 4.1 A sequence of widening imbalances.

Imbalances here appear as 'systemic', in the sense of requiring the alignment of components of a larger system. As imbalances are solved by innovation and investment activity, the development potential is exhausted. The focus of innovation may then be directed towards efficiency (as argued by Schön, 1991, 1994, 2012). As new technologies have been incorporated into the backbone of society, structural imbalances may emerge that add to structural crises. Such structural imbalances may give impetus for the development of new technologies, for example the oil crisis sparked development efforts to develop renewable energy technologies in the 1970s (Taalbi, 2014). The Dahménian view of a positive and negative side of industrial transformation also implies that development blocks can be situated on either side of the process of industrial transformation. Indeed, vested interests in mature development blocks (Glete, 1994) or locally increasing returns may provide obstacles to the diffusion of new technologies, something referred to as 'lock-in' (see Arthur, 1989; Unruh, 2000).

Major technology shifts and technological systems

What does the development block approach add to the current state of the art? I will return to this question towards the end of this section. Given the pervasive society-transforming impact of radical technologies such as the steam engine, the dynamo, the combustion engine and microelectronics, in the past 250 years or so, it is only natural that approaches to understanding the systemic character of innovation and technological change have been predominantly macro-focused. A set of different notions have emerged to describe and explain these shifts and their economic impact. One may distinguish very roughly between economic and historical theories of innovational interdependencies. Such a distinction may be crude since a notion of innovational interdependencies that covers only the economic or historical aspects is quite unthinkable. It is, however, not an unwarranted distinction, as the first notions have centred on relating the diffusion of technologies to economic growth (and crisis) and are promoted by economists or economic historians, and the second kinds are relatively more focused on describing and analysing the history of technological systems, often in minute detail, and are used by historians of technology. I will contend below that these approaches also differ in other methodological respects.

GPTs and TEPs

The notion of general-purpose technologies (GPTs) seems to account for important mechanisms in the process of diffusion and improvement on key innovations such as the steam engine, the electric motor and the microprocessor (Bresnahan and Trajtenberg, 1995; Helpman, 1998; Lipsey *et al.*, 2005). Lipsey *et al.* (2005, pp. 131–4) argue that throughout human history there have been 24 technologies that can be understood as GPTs, among which are found the domestication of plants and animals, printing, the steam engine, the factory system, electricity, the computer and the Internet. The requirements of a GPT are identified as follows: 'a single generic technology, recognizable as such over its whole lifetime that initially has much scope for improvement and eventually comes to be widely used, to have many uses and to have many spillover effects' (Lipsey *et al.* 2005, p. 98).

At the outset the notion drew from a discussion of the 'productivity paradox' in the diffusion of microelectronics, explained by Paul David (1990) to originate from the time involved in bringing forth complementary investments and solving technical problems in major technology shifts, as was evident as regards the development of the dynamo and the electric motor and what has been called the 'second industrial revolution'. The notion of GPTs therefore also builds on the notion of increasing returns in economic processes and network externalities (Arthur, 1989; Kaldor, 1981; Young, 1928). The core aspect of GPTs is the 'innovational complementarities' enhancing the marginal value of improving the technology of the application sector. In Bresnahan and Trajtenberg's formulation (1995), the application sector is assumed to maximize the private returns to technical advance with respect to its state of technology:

$$\prod^a(w, z, T^a) - C(T^a)$$

where w and z are the price and quality of the GPT, T^a is the technology in the application sector, $\prod^a$ is the value of enhancing the technology and C invention costs. The marginal value of enhancing the technology T^a in the application sector is positive in the quality of the GPT, z:

$$\frac{\partial^2 \prod^a}{\partial T \partial z} \geq 0.$$

Thus, increases in the quality of the GPT enhance the private returns and create incentives to innovate in the application sector.[5] Conversely, the GPT sector maximizes payoffs with respect to its state of technology (the quality of GPT, z):

$$\prod^g(z, T^a, c) - C^g(z)$$

where c is marginal costs of producing the goods embodying the GPT.[6] It follows that there is a mutual inducement mechanism in which the incentives for enhancing the GPT are also enhanced by the level of technology of the application sector. A Nash equilibrium is formulated in terms of reaction functions $z = R^g(T^a)$ and $T^a = R^a(z)$ when (if) $z^* = R^g(T^*)$ and $T^* = R^a(z^*)$, and thus it is in deviations from equilibrium that an impetus for technological change emerges. This formulation of the underlying complementarities that characterize broad technology shifts explains the increasing returns that give this process momentum and the strong linkages between the producer of the GPT and user industries.

The notion of techno-economic paradigms (TEPs) likewise has emphasized the interactions and complementarities between producers and users in networks and develops a typology of the relation between producers and users of new technologies. This approach, with an emphasis on historical analysis, has been developed in close connection with theories of long waves by several scholars (see Freeman and Louçã, 2001; Tylecote, 1992, 1994), recently in particular by Carlota Perez (1983, 2002, 2010). Carlota Perez (1983) suggested the concept of 'technological styles', later rephrased as 'techno-economic paradigms', to describe the successive technological revolutions brought about by sets of radical innovations (Freeman and Louçã, 2001; Perez, 2002). Technological styles were 'a kind of paradigm for the most efficient organization of production, i.e. the main form and direction along which productivity growth takes place within and across firms, industries and countries' (Perez, 1983, p. 360). The notion of paradigms (Kuhn, 2012 [1962]) stresses that key technologies open up opportunities and that there is a strong direction and sense of progress in technological change. In Dosi's seminal contribution, technological paradigms are 'a set of procedures, a definition of the "relevant" problems and of the specific knowledge related to their solution' while also defining 'its own concept of "progress" based on its specific technological and economic trade-offs' (Dosi, 1982, p. 148; see also Sahal, 1985). As in the notion of GPTs, the pulse of systemic evolution is mediated by feedback mechanisms or complementarities: 'major innovations tend to be inductors of further innovations; they demand complementary ones upstream and downstream and facilitate similar ones, including competing alternatives' (Perez, 2010, p. 188).[7] Perez (1983) makes a highly useful distinction between three types of industries in such major technology shifts. The motive branches produce the 'key inputs', such as micro-electronic components, and have 'the role of maintaining and deepening their relative cost advantage' (Perez, 1983), thereby being analogous to the producers of a GPT. Carrier industries implement the 'key input' and induce new investment opportunities: since the 1970s these have been computers, software and mobile phones (Perez, 2010). The 'induced industries' follow and innovation is a consequence of the introduction of key innovations in the motive branches. Moreover, the infrastructures, for example railroads, electricity, roads and the Internet, are pivotal in a mature TEP.

Historical approaches: technological systems and systèmes techniques

Two other approaches, one American and one French historical tradition, have to a larger extent stressed the role of problems and imbalances in the evolution of 'technological systems' (Gille, 1978a; Hughes, 1983, 1987; see also Rosenberg, 1969 on 'imbalances'). In contrast to the GPT and TEP approaches, these concepts have been developed mostly by historians (or historians of technology) working autonomously from economic issues such as the debate on long waves, rather employing the notion(s) of technological systems as frameworks to understand the often richly detailed and minute history of technologies. The French tradition of studying large technical systems has developed an understanding of the dynamics of 'systèmes techniques' (Aït-El-Hadj, 2002; Gille, 1978a; Simondon, 1969 [1958]). The notion of technical systems was launched in the seminal work *Histoire des techniques* of which Bertrand Gille was editor (however, he wrote 1,300 of the 1,500 pages). Gille's methodological approach departed from coherence between technical objects. A technical ensemble (*'ensemble technique'*) is an entity, such as a blast furnace, requiring the alignment of several parts indispensable to the overall performance. A technical path (*'filière technique'*) is a suite of technical ensembles aimed at arriving at a desired product. A technical system could be understood as an aggregate ensemble of such coherences at different levels in which the functioning of one part is dependent on the functioning of another part (Gille, 1978b, p. 19).

The history of such technical systems is characterized by constant adaptation and the becoming organic of technical objects, which Gilbert Simondon described as a 'concretization process' (*'procesus de concrétisation'*): 'the technical Being evolves through its convergence and adaptation; it unifies within according to a principle of internal resonance' (Simondon, 1969 [1958], p. 20, translation by J. T.).[8] The process of concretization departs from an 'abstract' primitive form of the technical object that evolves through the solution of compatibility problems between parts of the technical system.[9] In Gille's view, through this process of concretization technical systems tend towards a systemic equilibrium, in which the impulses towards further development vanish.

The American tradition gives a similar characterization of the evolution of technological systems but emphasizes the inventors, engineers and historical problems that emerge for such historical agents to solve. The seminal contribution is Thomas Parkes Hughes's (1983, 1987) analysis of 'technological systems', consisting of 'messy, complex, problem-solving components' (Hughes, 1987, p. 51) that evolve through the emergence of 'salient' and 'reverse salients'. In comparison with Dahmén and Gille, Hughes's interest lies more in understanding the social determinants of technological change, defining a technological system as consisting of not only technical components (technological artefacts) but also social components, including economic, scientific, and legislative or ideological components, such as organizations, scientific articles, research programs and regulatory laws. A system defined broadly in this sense consists of the interaction of the components, contributing to a 'system goal'.[10] Against technological determinism, this framework stresses the social shaping of technological systems, i.e. how social preferences interact with technical requirements to determine the evolution of technologies. Through his notions of critical problems and reverse salients, Hughes identified driving forces perfectly analogous to Dahmén's 'structural tensions'. Reverse salients are backwards, underperforming components of the sociotechnical system that hamper the development of the sociotechnical system as a whole. The system evolves as engineers and inventors identify and resolve 'critical problems', problems that hinder the technological expansion. In the view of Hughes, '[i]nnumerable (probably most) inventions and technological development result from efforts to correct reverse salients' (Hughes, 1983, p. 80).

Basing his argument on the history of the electricity system, Hughes also theorizes on phases of evolution of technological systems, in which the types of critical problems or reverse salients vary (compare the notion of widening imbalances in Figure 4.1). In a first phase, invention and development of the system take place, primarily through the inventor-entrepreneurs, who make the core inventions profitable and feasible in real-life situations. In a second phase, there is technology transfer from one location to another, i.e. technology diffusion. A third phase is characterized by system growth, acquiring 'momentum', i.e. *mass*, the involvement of machines, devices and capital, and *velocity*, a rate of growth (Hughes, 1983, pp. 14–17).[11] Reverse salients thus move from the area of invention and development to diffusion, to for example the problem of acquiring external finance.

Development blocks in comparative perspective

The reviewed notions embody, to a non-negligible extent, different analytical aims, methodologies and different views on the driving forces of innovation and economic change. In comparing the development block approach, two major differences should be clear. First, the Dahménian approach is, in principle, applicable to various levels of analysis: GPTs, large technological systems and networks of actors or technologies could all fit the description of development blocks. Thus, the notion of development blocks can be used to expound mechanisms in the history of the evolution of technological systems and GPTs. However, it is then important to distinguish clearly between development blocks, GPTs and broader technological systems. Working in the Dahménian approach, Carlsson and Stankiewicz (1991) and Carlsson (1995) reserve 'technological systems' for broader networks between actors linked by knowledge and competence networks:

> a network of agents interacting in a specific economic/industrial area under a particular institutional infrastructure or set of infrastructures and involved in the generation, diffusion, and utilization of technology. Technological systems are defined in terms of knowledge competence flows rather than flows of ordinary goods and services. They consist of dynamic knowledge and competence networks.
>
> (Carlsson and Stankiewicz, 1991, p. 111)

Arguably, such networks or systems of technologies can be *transformed* into development blocks, as defined by Dahmén, in the presence of entrepreneurial and innovation activity that solve problems and imbalances appearing in the process of industrial transformation.[12] The notion of development blocks thus specify a mechanism at the core of industrial transformation, which may (or may not) come to encompass technological systems, GPTs or TEPs.

In this context, one may also note that there are several benefits in combining the development block approach with the notion of GPTs. An advantage of the GPT approach is that there is a clear set of criteria for defining GPTs, though these criteria may be subject to debate (Lipsey *et al.*, 2005, p. 94–5). As regards the notion of GPTs, it is clearly set apart by answering a different set of questions about broad technology shifts than does the notion of development blocks, for example what technologies are widely used, have broad spillover effects and are improved by downstream innovation. Arguably, the Dahménian approach may illuminate key historical aspects of the diffusion of GPTs, for instance how GPTs have evolved historically, both by way of the resolution of imbalances and by the exploitation of innovational complementarities in different areas of industrial activity.

A second difference is that the discussed approaches tend to emphasize a single mechanism – either innovational complementarities or the resolution of critical problems and reverse salients. The Dahménian approach instead stresses both a 'negative' and a 'positive' side of industrial transformation. Both innovational complementarities and imbalances are understood as factors that enable and create incentives for innovation and investment activity. This enables an understanding of interdependent technologies as being intimately connected with the history of economic development and patterns of economic growth and crisis. Thus, the Dahménian approach should be understood as aiming for a structural analysis and account of alternation of periods of growth and crisis. Connecting the description of the evolution of development blocks with a chronology of crisis and growth, Schön (1991, 1994, 1998, 2012) in particular has developed this aspect of the Dahménian approach into an account of modern Swedish economic history. In the history of economic development, innovation is both shaped by and shaping the imbalances and opportunities that appear in the course of economic development. Structural crises break down barriers to innovation and pave the way for investment in new development blocks. Conversely, the investment in new development blocks, the resolution of imbalances and exploitation of new opportunities lie at the basis of economic growth processes.

This perspective enables a chronology of investment and growth related to the expansion and coming to maturity of various development blocks, some of which coincide with the diffusion of GPTs and can be described as broad TEPs, and some of which are of a less pervasive nature but equally important to economic growth. For instance, important development blocks in the Swedish post-war period were not only based on exploiting the alleged GPTs of electricity and combustion engines, but also could be found in the development of plastics, packaging systems and production and distribution systems for foodstuff, the advances in the pharmaceutical industry and medical equipment, and in the interdependencies in the shipbuilding and steel industries.

On the boundaries and composition of development blocks

> What are, in fact, the boundaries of technological systems, and how are they determined?
>
> (Carlsson and Stankiewicz, 1991, p. 112)

A major challenge to putting notions of technological interdependencies to work in empirical analysis is how to determine the boundaries of development blocks, GPTs and technological systems. In keeping with Dahmén's definition, one may suggest that, in principle, such boundaries are determined by innovational complementarities and imbalances that induce innovation. Development blocks become manifest when one can document the development of innovations or investment activity as connected to either new technological opportunities or the existence of a disequilibrium situation, an imbalance or tension pertaining to another innovation or other economic activities. If a development block is a 'series of events in entrepreneurial activity, technical development (including innovations) where the different linkages [...] in one or another manifestable way have causal connections with each other' (Dahmén, 1980, p. 50, translated by JT), determining its boundaries in time and space is tantamount to observing innovations that exploit technological opportunities, and observing imbalances and the attempts (successful or not) to overcome them and supply gap-filling innovations or carry out gap-filling investment.

I will shortly return to this suggestion, but I must first point out that this proposal certainly entails a minimalist definition, as it overlooks how innovations create new complementarities between functions and competences within production processes or between production activities, infrastructure and institutions on a number of different levels (for example firms or industries). Such broader complementarities created by development blocks must be studied using a greater number of historical approaches, including, for instance, historical case studies of industries and technologies (for example Carlsson, 1995; Schön, 1990), analysis of dynamic production relations between industries (Enflo *et al.*, 2008), input-output analysis of economic flows (Lind, 2014), industrial ownership structures (Glete, 1994), development pairs (Fridlund, 1993), the evolution of agglomeration externalities (Neffke *et al.*, 2011), collaboration networks of innovating firms or inventors (see, for example, Ahuja, 2000) and intra-firm or intra-industry knowledge spillovers (see, for example, Verspagen, 1997). Such broader complementarities can also be well understood in terms of GPTs and technological systems that are connected in terms of knowledge or competence complementarities.

Development blocks thus may encompass all of these types of interdependencies in their effects. However, it is useful to separate the wider effects of development blocks from the core mechanism specified by Dahmén, which relates to innovation or investment as responding to imbalances and exploiting (and creating) innovational complementarities. Such an analysis is possible in theory by qualitative analysis of the driving forces of innovation, and by quantitative study of the industries of origin and use of innovations (Taalbi, 2014). A new innovation output database for Sweden, 1970–2007 (Sjöö *et al.*, 2014; Sjöö, 2014; Taalbi, 2014), has enabled such empirical analysis, the results of which I will outline.

First, qualitative analysis of imbalances and opportunities that have incited innovation activity gives insights into the history of technological interdependencies. Examples of the major imbalances that spurred innovations in Sweden during the period 1970–2007 are described in Table 4.1. Notably, the main imbalances observed in a broader ICT development block were the many technological obstacles that appeared in the deployment of the Internet and telecommunication

Table 4.1 Imbalances that spurred innovation activity, 1970–2007

Industries	Imbalances
Pulp and paper	Replacement of chlorine
Foodstuff	Bacteria in thawing; temperature in distribution
ICT	Under-etching of micro-electronic components; secure payment and secure identification; capacity requirements in telecommunication networks
Automotive vehicles	Technical problems in catalytic converters
Electric and hybrid electric vehicles	Weight and density of batteries
Pharmaceuticals	Slow drug screening; incapacity to deal with vast amounts of data
Forestry	Obstacles to rational production methods
Solar power technologies	Limited exposure to sun; limited storing capacity of energy

Source: Based on Taalbi (2014).

networks during the 1990s and 2000s. Other imbalances that spurred innovation activity relate to the environmental problems that came to increased attention following the oil crisis of the 1970s. Some examples of energy technologies developed during this period were heating pumps and innovations for the use of biomass, bio power, solar power and wind power, each struggling with particular technical problems. The century-old critical problem of the weight and energy density of batteries for use in electric cars was also attacked by several innovation projects from the late 1960s and onwards.

While these imbalances and others indicate plausible development blocks, in complex systems a multitude of interrelations between firms and industries may in practice make delimiting the boundaries of development blocks an entangled affair. This empirical issue can be appeased by making use of *network analysis*. In principle, there is, as it were, an isomorphism between all studies of phenomena of interdependence, which can be represented by a graph, or a network. A graph $\Gamma(E,V)$ consists of a set of edges E (for instance, firms or industries) and a set of vertices between edges $V \in E \times E$ (for example innovations or economic flows between industries). Depending on what types of interdependencies we are concerned with, the vertices can be weighted or unweighted, directed or undirected. Social networks are often understood as unweighted undirected networks, i.e. a social connection between individuals is often mutual and binary (either-or). By contrast, economic networks are often weighted and directed, i.e. the direction and magnitude of economic flows matter. For a directed weighted network, each edge from vertex $i \in V$ to another vertex $j \in V$ has a weight W_{ij} that represents the network flows.

Networks can be sparse or highly connected. In highly connected complex systems (such as modern economies) the question arises of whether the network can be decomposed into subsystems or *communities*. Descriptive statistical techniques to isolate communities describe what industries (or firms) are most related in terms of the supply and use of innovations. Many approaches to find such subsystems in networks maximize a statistic called 'modularity', defined as[13]

Q = (share of edges within communities)
  − (expected share of edges within communities).

In other words, we find the sets of industries that have highest share of edges within communities as compared with the expected share. Using this method, Taalbi (2014) finds ten communities in the network of supply and use of innovations for Sweden 1970–2007. These communities describe innovations centred on 1) pulp and paper, 2) foodstuff, 3) ICT, 4) automotive vehicles, 5) medical equipment and health, 6) forestry, 7) construction, 8) military defence and shipbuilding, 9) electricity, and 10) textiles. The most encompassing of these communities is the one centred on ICT, illustrated in Figure 4.2. Industries marked with grey are industries that are primarily using innovations, while black indicates supplier industries. Clearly, within this community, there are strong linkages between electronic components, computers, software ('computer & related serv') and telecommunications, while these also find wide use in service and other industries.

One should also note that it is possible with this methodology to analyse broader technology shifts by examining what innovations have exploited general-purpose technologies. As an indication, Figure 4.3 shows the main types of product innovations that have exploited micro-electronic technologies in their core functions, what Carlota Perez has called 'carrier industries'. These industries by and large correspond to the supplier industries in Figure 4.2. These microelectronics-based innovations made up 1,379 out of 4,140 Swedish product innovations in the period 1970–2007 (Taalbi, 2014, pp. 93–8).

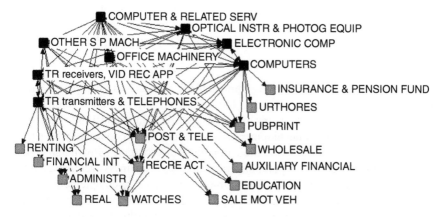

Figure 4.2 The community of innovations centered on ICT technologies: grey indicates industries that are primarily using innovations.[14]

Source: SWINNO database; see Taalbi (2015) for methods and calculation.

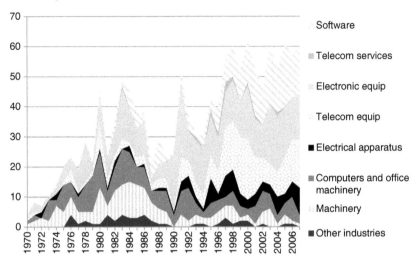

Figure 4.3 Carrier industries (count of innovations exploiting technologies based on micro-electronics) in Sweden, 1970–2007.

Source: SWINNO database and author's calculations.

Combining qualitative and quantitative accounts of the history of supply and use of innovations suggests that community detection analysis can be used to give a crude, yet useful, delimitation of closely related industries, while qualification from innovation biographies informs of imbalances and opportunities as the core mechanism in the evolution of development blocks. To assess the importance and broader dynamics of development blocks, however, requires a larger and more heterogeneous body of methodologies and approaches, such as analysis of inter-dependencies among industries, actor-networks, employing both quantitative and qualitative data.

Concluding discussion

This chapter has discussed the development block approach in a comparative perspective. The notion of development blocks was an original contribution to the economics of innovation dating from a paper by Erik Dahmén in 1942. The essay showed that evolution of development blocks is intimately connected with structural analysis of economies, and the chronology of economic growth and crisis, making it a most useful concept for historical analysis of business cycles and longer variations in economic activity. The notion can be argued to complement current wide-spread economic and historical approaches, such as the notions of general-purpose technologies and technological systems, by describing interdependencies from the factory level to broader systems and by specifying both 'positive' and 'negative' mechanisms that drive the evolution of development blocks. In particular, the chapter argues that the notion of development blocks should be clearly distinguished from other notions of technological interdependencies, according to Dahmén's definition, as sequences of innovations that respond to imbalances and opportunities. The notion of development blocks thus specify a mechanism at the core of industrial transformation, which may (or may not) evolve into technological systems, general-purpose technologies or techno-economic paradigms.

One major issue common to those approaches that analyse interdependencies in innovation activity has been how to delimit the boundaries of development blocks, technological systems or general-purpose technologies. The final section has discussed one viable path for further research that centres on innovations as responding to imbalances and opportunities created in other firms or industries. This method combines qualitative analysis from innovation biographies and quantitative analysis to suggest roughly the boundaries and components of development blocks. The exploration of historical innovation data is therefore an important path for further research into technological interdependencies.

Notes

1   John von Neumann's (1945) multi-sectoral model (inspired by Gustav Cassel) proved mathematically the existence of a general equilibrium growth rate across sectors. In a different vein, considering vertically integrated sectors, Pasinetti (1973) derived steady-state growth paths, along which the demand and output of sectors are equalized. In a multi-sectoral environment in which process innovation increases the input-output coefficients (output increases with respect to capital goods and labour), productivity increases, caused by process innovation, lead to disproportionate growth of investment and final demand – or 'technological unemployment' (Pasinetti, 1983). The counteracting tendency that contributes to instability is the creation of new sectors through product innovation, or increases in variety enabling growth of employment (and demand for capital goods).

2   Original title in Swedish: 'Ekonomisk strukturanalys: några synpunkter på den ekonomiska utvecklingens och konjunkturväxlingarnas problem.'.

3   While Dahmén was arguably the first to put these mechanisms at the centre of his analysis of economic development, clearly, the notion of development blocks may have had predecessors in embryonic forms, such as the Hicksian notions of complementary goods (as opposed to substitute goods) or empirical observations of imbalances or problems that have engendered complementary investment or innovation. As regards the former, see John R. Hicks' *Theory of Wages* (1932). As regards the latter, historians and other observers have for a long time observed sequences of problems and solutions in the eighteenth-century textile industry (for example Kay's flying shuttle) and the improvement of steam engines.

4   In Schön's (1994, 2012) account of structural cycles, this breakthrough of new machinery equipment is a central facet of the diffusion of new development blocks, occurring in the 1900s, 1940s and 1980s, roughly ten years after major structural crises.

5   This could of course take place by way of other innovational complementarities. The improvement of a GPT could, for instance, lower the costs of invention in the application sector.

6   The original formulation concerns a set of application sectors instead of one.

7   'The particular historical form of such a paradigm would evolve out of certain key technological developments, which result in a substantial change in the relative cost structure facing industry and which, at the same time, open a wide range of new opportunities for taking advantage of this particular evolution. In essence we assume a strong feedback interaction between the economic, social and institutional spheres which generates a dynamic complementarity centred around a technological style' (Perez, 1983, p. 370).

8 'L'être technique évolue par convergence et par adaptation à soi; il s'unifie intérieurement selon un principe de resonance interne' (Simondon, 1969 [1958], p. 20).
9 'L'intégration à l'ensemble offre dans ce cas une série de problems à résoudre qui sont dits techniques et qui, en fait, sont des problems de compatabilité entre des ensembles déjà donnés' (Simondon, 1969 [1958], p. 21).
10 'An artifact – either physical or nonphysical – functioning as a component in a system interacts with other artifacts, all of which contribute directly or through other components to the common system goal' (Hughes, 1987, p. 51).
11 Hughes's concept of momentum is an analogy to classical mechanics: 'A system with substantial momentum has mass, velocity, and direction' (Hughes, 1983, p. 17).
12 With this wording I wish to add emphasis to Dahmén's notion that development blocks are characterized by interdependencies that evolve by the resolution of imbalances. Carlsson and Stankiewicz (1991, p. 111) phrase the requirement a bit differently, suggesting that technological systems can be transformed into development blocks 'in the presence of an entrepreneur and sufficient critical mass'.
13 Formally, in a weighted directed network W_{ij}, modularity is defined as
$Q = \sum_{ij}(W_{ij}/k) - (k_i^{out}k_j^{in}/k^2)\delta_{c_ic_j}$. W_{ij}/k is the actual shares of flows between industry i and j, where k is the sum total of flows in the network. The expected share of flows from industry i to j is calculated as the product of the share of innovations supplied by i, k^{out}/k and the share of innovations used by jk_j^{in}/k. The Kronecker delta $\delta_{c_ic_j}$ is 1 if $c_i = c_j$, i.e. if i and j belong to the same community, otherwise 0.
14 Abbreviations: S P MACH = special-purpose machinery, TR = television and radio, VID REC = video recording, EQ = equipment, URTHORES = uranium and thorium mines, PUBPRINT = publishing and printing, REAL = real estate activities, MOT VEH = motor vehicles, RECRE ACT = recreational, sport and cultural activities, POST & TELE = post and telecommunications, ADMINISTR = public administration.

References

Ahuja, G. (2000), 'Collaboration networks, structural holes, and innovation: a longitudinal study', *Administrative Science Quarterly*, vol. 45(3), pp. 425–455.

Aït-El-Hadj, S. (2002), *Systèmes Technologiques et l'Innovation: Itinéraire Théorique*. Paris: Editions L'Harmattan.

Åkerman, J. (1939), *Ekonomisk teori. 1. De ekonomiska kalkylerna*. Lund: Gleerup.

Åkerman, J. (1949), 'Strukturgränser i svensk industrialism', *Ekonomisk tidskrift*, vol. 51(1), pp. 1–18.

Allen, R. C. (2009), *The British Industrial Revolution in Global Perspective*. Cambridge: Cambridge University Press.

Arthur, W.B. (1989), 'Competing technologies, increasing returns, and lock-in by historical events', *Economic Journal*, vol. 99(394), pp. 116–131.

Bresnahan, T. F. and Trajtenberg, M. (1995), 'General purpose technologies: "engines of growth"?' *Journal of Econometrics*, vol. 65(1), pp. 83–108.

Carlsson, B. (1995), *Technological Systems and Economic Performance: the Case of Factory Automation*. Dordrecht: Kluwer.

Carlsson, B. and Stankiewicz, R. (1991), 'On the nature, function and composition of technological systems', *Journal of Evolutionary Economics*, vol. 1(2), pp. 93–118.

Carlsson, B., Henriksson, R. G. and Dahmén, E. (1991), *Development Blocks and Industrial Transformation: the Dahménian Approach to Economic Development*. Stockholm: Industrial Institute for Economic and Social Research.

Dahmén, E. (1950), *Svensk industriell företagarverksamhet: kausalanalys av den industriella utvecklingen 1919–1939*, vol. 1. Stockholm: IUI.

Dahmen, E. (1980), 'Hur studera industriell utveckling?' In Eliasson, G. and Dahmén, E. (eds) *Industriell utveckling i Sverige: teori och verklighet under ett sekel*. Stockholm: Industriens Utredningsinstitut.

Dahmén, E. (1991a), 'Development blocks in industrial economics'. In Carlsson, B., Henriksson, R. G. H. and Dahmén, E. (eds) *Development Blocks and Industrial Transformation: the Dahménian Approach to Economic Development*. Stockholm: Industrial Institute for Economic and Social Research.

Dahmén, E. (1991b), 'Schumpeterian dynamics: Some methodological notes'. In Carlsson, B., Henriksson, R. G. H. and Dahmén, E. (eds.) *Development Blocks and Industrial Transformation: the Dahménian Approach to Economic Development*. Stockholm: Industrial Institute for Economic and Social Research.

Dahmén, E. (1991 [1942]), 'Economic-structural analysis. Reflections on the problem of economic development and business cycle fluctuation'. In Carlsson, B., Henriksson, R. G. H. and Dahmén, E. (eds) *Development Blocks and Industrial Transformation: the Dahménian Approach to Economic Development*. Stockholm: Industrial Institute for Economic and Social Research.

Dahmén, E. (1993), 'Research on railways in a historical perspective'. In Dahmén, E., Whitelegg, J., Hultén, S. and Flink, T. (eds) *High Speed Trains: Fast Tracks to the Future*. Hawes: Leading Edge, in association with Stockholm School of Economics.

David, P. A. (1990), 'The dynamo and the computer: an historical perspective on the modern productivity paradox', *American Economic Review*, vol. 80(2), pp. 355–61.

Dosi, G. (1982), 'Technological paradigms and technological trajectories: a suggested interpretation of the determinants and directions of technical change', *Research Policy*, vol. 11(3), pp. 147–62.

Enflo, K., Kander, A. and Schön, L. (2008), 'Identifying development blocks – a new methodology', *Journal of Evolutionary Economics*, vol. 18(1), pp. 57–76.

Erixon, L. (2011), 'Development blocks, malinvestment and structural tensions – the Åkerman–Dahmén theory of the business cycle', *Journal of Institutional Economics*, vol. 7(01), pp. 105–29.

Freeman, C. (1995), 'The "National System of Innovation" in historical perspective', *Cambridge Journal of Economics*, vol. 19(1), pp. 5–24.

Freeman, C. and Louçã, F. (2001), *As Time Goes By: the Information Revolution and the Industrial Revolutions in Historical Perspective*. New York: Oxford University Press.

Fridlund, M. (1993), 'The "development pair" as a link between systems growth and industrial innovation: cooperation between the Swedish state power board and the ASEA company', *Trita-HST, 1103–5277; 93/9*. Stockholm: Royal Institute of Technology.

Gille, B. (1978a), *Histoire des Techniques: Technique et Civilisations, Technique et Sciences*. Paris: Gallimard.

Gille, B. (1978b), 'Prolegomènes à une histoire des techniques'. In Gille, B. (ed) *Histoire des Techniques: Technique et Civilisations, Technique et Sciences*. Paris: Gallimard, pp. 1–118.

Glete, J. (1994), *Nätverk i näringslivet. ägande och industriell omvandling i det mogna industrisamhället 1920–1990*. Stockholm: SNS.

Helpman, E. (1998), *General Purpose Technologies and Economic Growth*. Cambridge, Mass.: MIT Press.

Hicks, J. R. (1932), *Theory of Wages*. London: Macmillan.

Hughes, T. P. (1983), *Networks of Power: Electrification in Western Society, 1880–1930*. Baltimore: The John Hopkins University Press.

Hughes, T. P. (1987), 'The evolution of large technological systems' In Bijker, W. E., Hughes, T. P. and Pinch, T. J. (eds) *The Social Construction of Technological Systems: New Directions in the Sociology and History of Technology*. Cambridge, Mass.: MIT Press, pp. 51–82.

Kaldor, N. (1981), 'The role of increasing returns, technical progress and cumulative causation in the theory of international trade and economic growth', *Economie Appliquée*, vol. 34(6), pp. 593–617.

Kuhn, T. S. (2012 [1962]), *The Structure of Scientific Revolutions*. Chicago: University of Chicago press.

Leontief, W. W. (1941), *Structure of American Economy, 1919–1929*. Cambridge, Mass.: Harvard University Press.

Lind, D. (2014), *Value Creation and Structural Change during the Third Industrial Revolution: the Swedish Economy from a Vertical Perspective*. Lund studies in economic history, 64 (diss.).

Lipsey, R. G., Carlaw, K. and Bekar, C. (2005), *Economic Transformations. General Purpose Technologies and Long Term Economic Growth*. New York: Oxford University Press.

Lundvall, B. A. (1992), *National Innovation System: towards a Theory of Innovation and Interactive Learning*. London: Pinter.

Marx, K. (1992 [1885]), *Capital: a Critique of Political Economy, Volume II*. London: Penguin Books.

Mokyr, J. (1990), *The Lever of Riches*. New York: Oxford University Press.

Neffke, F., Henning, M., Boschma, R., Lundquist, K.-J. and Olander, L.-O. (2011), 'The dynamics of agglomeration externalities along the life cycle of industries', *Regional Studies*, vol. 45(1), pp. 49–65.

Nelson, R. R. (1994), 'The co-evolution of technology, industrial structure, and supporting institutions', *Industrial and Corporate Change*, vol. 3(1), pp. 47–63.

Nelson, R. R. (2001), 'The coevolution of technology and institutions as the driver of economic growth'. In Foster, J. and Metcalfe, J. S. (eds) *Frontiers of Evolutionary Economics: Competition, Self-organization and Innovation Policy*. Cheltenham: Edward Elgar.

Pasinetti, L. L. (1973), 'The notion of vertical integration in economic analysis', *Metroeconomica*, vol. 25(1), pp. 1–29.

Pasinetti, L. L. (1983), *Structural Change and Economic Growth: a Theoretical Essay on the Dynamics of the Wealth of Nations*. Cambridge: Cambridge University Press.

Perez, C. (1983), 'Structural change and assimilation of new technologies in the economic and social systems', *Futures*, 15(5), pp. 357–375.

Perez, C. (2002), *Technological Revolutions and Financial Capital: the Dynamics of Bubbles and Golden Ages*. Cheltenham: Edward Elgar.

Perez, C. (2010), 'Technological revolutions and techno-economic paradigms', *Cambridge Journal of Economics*, vol. 34(1), pp. 185–202.

Rosenberg, N. (1969), 'The direction of technological change: inducement mechanisms and focusing devices', *Economic Development and Cultural Change*, vol. 18(1), pp. 1–24.

Sahal, D. (1985), 'Technological guideposts and innovation avenues', *Research Policy*, vol. 14(2), pp. 61–82.

Schön, L. (1990), *Elektricitetens betydelse för svensk industriell utveckling*. Vällingby: Vattenfall.

Schön, L. (1991), 'Development blocks and transformation pressure in a macroeconomic perspective – a model of long-term cyclical change', *Skandinaviska Enskilda Banken Quarterly Review*, vol. 20(3–4), pp. 67–76.

Schön, L. (1994), *Omvandling och obalans: mönster i svensk ekonomisk utveckling. Bilaga 3 till Långtidsutredningen.* Stockholm: Finansdepartementet.
Schön, L. (1998), 'Industrial crises in a model of long cycles: Sweden in an international perspective'. In Myllyntaus, T. (ed.) *Economic Crises and Restructuring in History. Experiences of Small Countries.* Katharinen: Scripta Mercaturae.
Schön, L. (2012), *An Economic History of Modern Sweden.* Oxon: Routledge.
Schumpeter, J. A. (1942), *Capitalism, Socialism, Democracy.* New York: Harper Perennial.
Schumpeter, J. A. (1947), 'The creative response in economic history', *Journal of Economic History*, vol. 7(2), pp. 149–59.
Simondon, G. (1969 [1958]), *Du mode d'existence des Objets Techniques.* Paris: Aubier.
Sjöö, K. (2014), *Innovation and Transformation in the Swedish Manufacturing Sector, 1970–2007.* Lund studies in economic history, 65 (diss.).
Sjöö, K., Taalbi, J., Kander, A. and Ljungberg, J. (2014), 'SWINNO – A Database of Swedish Innovations, 1970–2007', *Lund Papers in Economic History*, 133.
Sraffa, P. (1960), *Production of Commodities by Means of Commodities: Prelude to a Critique of Economic Theory.* Cambridge: Cambridge University Press.
Taalbi, J. (2014), *Innovation as Creative Response: Determinants of Innovation in the Swedish Manufacturing Industry, 1970–2007.* Lund studies in economic history, 67 (diss.).
Taalbi, J. (2015), 'Development blocks in innovation networks. The Swedish manufacturing industry, 1970–2007', unpublished manuscript.
Tylecote, A. (1992), *The Long Wave in the World Economy: the Current Crisis in Historical Perspective.* London: Routledge.
Tylecote, A. (1994), 'Long waves, long cycles, and long swings', *Journal of Economic Issues*, vol. 28(2), pp. 477–88.
Unruh, G.C. (2000), 'Understanding carbon lock-in', *Energy Policy*, vol. 28(12), pp. 817–30.
Verspagen, B. (1997), 'Measuring intersectoral technology spillovers: estimates from the European and US patent office databases', *Economic Systems Research*, vol. 9(1), pp. 47–65.
von Neumann, J. (1945), 'A model of general economic equilibrium', *Review of Economic Studies*, vol. 13(1), pp. 1–9.
Walras, L. (1954 [1874]), *Elements of Pure Economics or the Theory of Social Wealth.* Homewood, Ill.: Irwin.
Young, A. A. (1928), 'Increasing returns and economic progress', *Economic Journal*, vol. 38, pp. 527–42.

5 The Gerschenkron effect, creative destruction and structural analysis

Jonas Ljungberg

It is well known that electronic equipment such as personal computers or LCD television-sets have become much cheaper with time. The phenomenon of falling prices is, however, not particular to ICT goods. In general new products that are the outcome of innovation display falling prices, at least in relative terms but often absolutely also. Had, for example, the price of an ordinary bicycle followed the general price level as indicated by the CPI since the beginning of the twentieth century, it would cost more than 1,200 euro today. The current price of a single-geared bicycle is about a third or even less. However, the whole of this fall in the relative price of a bicycle took place in the first three to four decades after its appearance. Broadly speaking, relative prices fell in the period when the bike was a new commodity, some basic innovations or improvements such as the free-wheel were introduced, new manufacturers appeared and the industry was in its formative years.

In economic theory prices are usually connected with sellers' and buyers' behaviour in the market place. Buyers' demand drives a price up or down, and sellers supply a certain quantity in response to the prices. Mostly they act according to a given demand or supply function, and important changes, described as outward or inward shifts in any or both of these functions, are perceived as exogenous and causal factors. Basically, this is a static approach and little interest has been devoted to integrate the shift factors into the behaviour of prices. In other words, little interest has been devoted to the price effects of innovation, a notable exception, though, being Bresnahan and Gordon (1997).

The aim of this chapter is to present evidence of how relative prices of manufactures changed over an 'antedated twentieth century' (1888–1992), and how the changes were related to the transformation and growth in manufacturing. The contribution is, thus, to extend the analysis in Ljungberg (1990), which ended with 1969, through the 1970s and 1980s. More specifically, the aim is to examine the role of positive and negative transformation in Swedish manufacturing from 1888 to 1992 through the lens of relative prices and volumes. Are there any periodical patterns across industries and, if so, could these be related to Schön's structural cycles in the Swedish economy?

Points of departure

The economic historian Alexander Gerschenkron (1962) found that prices could be an indicator of dynamic macroeconomic change. Moreover, Gerschenkron developed an analytical method for exploring economic transformation in a study of whether industrialization took place in early twentieth-century Bulgaria. His argument was that an aggregate index for the volume of production may give quite different results if the weights are taken from the end of the period compared with weights from its beginning:

> Those discrepancies in measurements are known as the index-number problem and are gall and wormwood to the statistician and theoretical economist. By contrast, their existence, magnitude, and change over time are a subject of very positive interest to the economic historian who regards them as an integral part of the processes of economic change.
>
> (Gerschenkron, 1962, p. 204)

Gerschenkron discussed an industrial production index but exactly the same could be said about price indices, and it is the change in relative prices that play havoc with differently weighted volume indices. Furthermore, instead of just shifting the weights between the beginning and end of the period, one could extract more information by comparing different index types. For example, a Paasche price index with annual quantity weights could be compared with a Laspeyres price index with constant quantity weights obtained from the beginning of the period.[1] If economic transformation takes place and new goods with falling relative prices are providing an increasing share of the aggregate output, then the Paasche price index will show lower values than the Laspeyres price index. Goods that are becoming relatively cheap get increasing weight in the Paasche index whereas the weights do not change in the Laspeyres index. Thus, to be precise, they are showing different things. While the Laspeyres price index shows how much the base year's basket changes in price over a period, the Paasche price index shows how much the price of today's basket has changed from what it would have cost in the base year. The different outcomes of the two calculations yield, as Gerschenkron noted, the annoying index problem but if we take the ratio between the Paasche and Laspeyres indices, we can pretend to have another index indicating economic transformation. The more the Paasche/Laspeyres ratio declines, which has been labelled the *Gerschenkron effect*, the more the economy has transformed. In a historical study of prices for commodity production in Sweden over the period 1885–1969, it was shown that such transformation was concentrated to the two decades around the turn of the twentieth century and again during the 1940s (Ljungberg, 1990, 1991). This can also be seen in Figure 5.1, which shows the Paasche/Laspeyres ratio for manufacturing prices over the years 1888 to 1992. Thus, the previously existing price indices for 1888 through to 1969 have been extended with 23 years to 1992. To take account of the changing composition of production, the long series have been linked together from indices of about twenty-year-long periods, overlapping

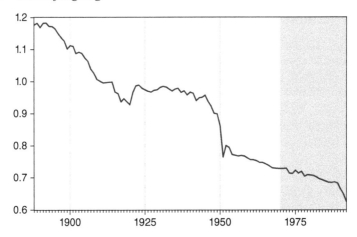

Figure 5.1 Ratio between Paasche and Laspeyres price indices for manufacturing, 1888–1992.

Source: Author's calculations based on Ljungberg (1990, 1999) and SOS *Industri*; reference year (1910/12=100).

in 1911, 1930, 1953, and 1969. The shaded area from 1970, in the graph, highlights a change in estimation method, which may have implications for the comparability as discussed on p. 83. The most striking decline in the ratio occurs between 1945 and 1951 as well as in the final years 1988–1992. In comparison with the downward sloping ratio from the 1950s through the 1980s, the decline before World War I is also noticeable. The annual percentage rate of change of the trend 1895–1910 was –0.93, and just –0.37 for the period 1953–1987.

Considering the interpretation of the Paasche/Laspeyres ratio, it should be noticed that the transformation can be of two sorts, positive or negative, to use the wording of Erik Dahmén (1970 [1950]). This idea of the two sides of transformation corresponds to Schumpeter's (1942) *creative destruction*: new industries expand at the expense of the old, which fall behind. Dahmén, in his seminal study of entrepreneurship and innovation in the manufacturing industry in interwar Sweden, classified branches of manufacturing at a low level of aggregation according to their economic performance in interaction with the market. In a later paper (Dahmén, 1980), he considered four different categories: advancing industries characterized by either *supply-push* or *demand-pull*, and stagnating industries by either *supply-contraction* or *demand-reduction*. In two of the categories, the entrepreneurial capability of the industry itself is a key or major causal factor behind the performance. A major factor behind the supply-push was thus innovation in the industry, whereas conservative or defensive entrepreneurship caused supply-contraction, often as a reaction to innovations elsewhere which had made the products in question obsolete. In the two other categories, demand-pull and demand-reduction, the major forces were identified as external to the firms and these only passively responded to developments in the market.[2]

Dahmén did not comprehensively include prices in his analysis, which was subsequently incorporated by Ljungberg (1990) who classified more than 35 sectors of the manufacturing industry according to Dahmén's scheme on the basis of changes in relative prices and relative sales volumes. Generally, there was a negative correlation between relative prices and volumes as already indicated by the *Gerschenkron effect* and the decreasing Paasche/Laspeyres price index ratio. The question could be raised whether this was mainly the result of a supply-push, with falling prices and expanding sales, or of supply-contraction, with increasing prices and declining sales. The secular trend was more on the positive side of transformation, that is, supply-push, than on the negative side with supply-contraction. Also, in the periods of the more pronounced Gerschenkron effects, around the turn of the twentieth century and in the 1940s, there was more of a positive supply-push than a negative supply-contraction. Furthermore, when it comes to the role of innovation, new commodities or product innovations seem to have been more connected with significant cases of supply-push, whereas process innovation typically was connected with a more moderate development (Dahmén, 1950, p. 124; Ljungberg, 1990, p. 74). At first this difference between the impact of product and process innovation might seem counterintuitive, since economies of scale, largely driven by process innovation, could be assumed to be the primary cause of falling relative prices. On the other hand, it is reasonable to assume that product innovation is followed by imitation which successively erodes the technological monopoly of the innovator. As a result relative prices of new commodities typically decline due to downward pressure from both economies of scale and growing competition.

Whilst the normal case was a negative correlation between relative prices and volumes, there were also cases of a positive correlation classified as demand-pull, with increasing prices and volumes, and demand-reduction, with decline in both. However, these were more rare cases. Demand-reduction signified obsolete products, for which over-capacity and competition were pressing prices. Falling prices of raw materials could also counteract the loss of economies of scale and result in a relative decline of product prices. The other atypical case is demand-pull. Although conforming with the textbook case of demand driving up the prices, cases of demand-pull were in fact often connected with particular conditions in the market. This applied time and again to sales in export markets where the producer had the advantage of technological leadership, as in ball bearings, produced by SKF, or stainless steel, produced primarily by Avesta Jernverk, in the interwar period. It could also apply to new consumption goods which were in high demand when personal earnings rose, as during much of the twentieth century. However, the background could also be more institutional, such as the building materials industry, which in the post-war period benefited from government policy that aimed to stimulate residential construction (Ljungberg, 1990, pp. 154, 215).

Before we move ahead and have a look at some relative prices over 'the antedated twentieth century' and examine the positive and negative transformation within manufacturing, the data deserve a presentation.

Data, prices and quality change

So far nothing has been said about the construction of the price series for individual commodities that make up the price indices. It is not obvious, however, that price series are available for commodities which undergo frequent technical change, let alone for historical periods. The construction of price indices should start from the commodity level and be weighted by subsectors, sectors and the aggregate economy. A particular problem that can only be handled at the commodity level is quality change. In principle, quality change could be accounted for under the assumption that the same price at the same point in time (and market) implies the same quality. Then continuous price series can be spliced or matched together from various price quotations, as illustrated in Table 5.1.

If there is a large amount of data with price quotations for well-specified products for each time period, but with frequent changes of model or type between the periods, then a hedonic index might be a solution. For every period (usually a year) the price is treated as a function of the technical specifications. With a regression for each single year, the technical parameters are given coefficients which can be used for deriving the 'typical' price for any model of a given specification. For example, assume we have access to catalogues for electrical motors with prices and specifications for 1930 through to 1969 but do not know which should be taken as 'representative' or we find it difficult to match changing models. Say that there is a consecutive series of a slip-ringed, closed motor 'type R' with specifications 'CC, 12 kW, 2000 rpm, and 220 V' for the years 1935–51 but before and after there are slip-ringed, closed motors with other specifications. If we estimate coefficients for the specified parameters in each single year 1930–1969, it is possible to simulate a price of a 'type R' for the whole period.[3] It might be used as a representative or 'typical' price series, or used for extrapolation of the actual 'type R' quotations backwards and forwards. However, the splicing or matching method shown in Table 5.1 achieves the same result in principle, under the assumption that the price quotations are representative.

Representativity is another problem that might not depend on the amount of data but more on the source. For example, catalogue prices may offer a sufficient

Table 5.1 Construction of a commodity price index from scattered observations: an example

	Type R	Type Q	Type P	'Type R' extrapolated
1929			195	96.9
1930			190	94.4
1931			180	89.5
1932		170	190	94.4
1933		175		97.2
1934		180		100
1935	200	180		100
1936	210			105

Note: The relations of the underlined observations determine the link to one series.

amount of data for statistical analysis but may not truly reflect prices in the market. Therefore, actual transaction prices found in, for example, sales or acquisition records of a firm could arguably be more representative even if they do not provide sufficient data for a hedonic index.

The price indices for 35 to 38 sub-branches of manufacturing in the period 1888–1969, used in this chapter, are built up from price series for individual commodities, with one or a few together taken as representative for product groups. For the product groups, Sweden's Official Statistics reported annual sales values, which (recalculated to volumes) were used as weights in the Paasche indices. Sales values are 'gross', reflecting to some extent also the price changes of intermediate products, and ideally series of value added should be used for weights. Another reason to prefer value added is that the share of intermediate products in the final price differs between industries and the relative weight of an industry might deviate from its share in total value added. However, for practical purposes value added entails other difficulties, such as not being available before 1959 for the sub-branches of manufacturing, and only from 1968 for the product groups used for the construction of the indices. Another shortcoming is that historic shares of value added are interpolated between benchmark estimates (Schön, 1988).

Not only do the quantities of the weights change over time but also the composition of commodities in production and consumption. To take account of this both the Laspeyres and the Paasche price indices have been constructed with different 'baskets', and base years, for different, slightly overlapping, periods and then linked together with the same reference year (1910/12=100) for the whole period. These periods are 1888–1912, 1910–1931, 1929–1954 and 1952–1969. The theoretical considerations for the choice of periods are essentially discussed in Chapter 2 (and in the extract from Krantz and Nilsson, 1978). It should be added that even if the secular slope is different in a Paasche/Laspeyres ratio with just one base year, the periodical patterns of twists and turns are very similar. The indices for the remaining years 1970–1992 differ, however, somewhat in the construction, as discussed later in this section. After 1992 the primary material in the official price statistics changed, which motivates the end of the period under study.

The individual commodity prices from 1935 onwards, and to some extent from 1920, are based on the primary material of the official wholesale price index, provided to the author by Statistics Sweden. For the preceding years price quotations are taken from printed price lists and catalogues, various business acquisition and sales records, and less so from other printed statistics or literature. All the commodity price series for the years 1885–1969 are available in Ljungberg (1990).

For the years 1970–1979 (overlapping backwards to 1968 and 1969 and forwards to 1980), Statistics Sweden has provided indices with 80 product groups. These are of Laspeyres type, where 1968 is the base year. The indices for the product groups have been weighted with sales volumes (from Sweden's Official Statistics, *Industri*) to 42 sub-branch indices. For the preceding period 1953–1969, 40 sub-branches were weighted together from 187 product groups and a higher number of commodity price series. Earlier data are scarcer, and for the period 1888–1910 the 35 sub-branch indices are constructed from weights for 85 product groups, most of which were matched with several commodity price series. Hence, there is an obvious problem with the consistency of the indices in the 1970s with those both before and after. While the Paasche price indices for the preceding years could be based on individual commodity prices and weights down to roughly five-digit level, for the 1970s only a hybrid Paasche could be constructed. Hence, Statistics Sweden has provided Laspeyres price indices (1968=100) at about the four-digit level, and these have been weighted with corresponding annual sales volume weights and grouped to 42 sub-branches at broadly the four-digit level. As a consequence, the Paasche/Laspeyres ratio for the 1970s is strictly speaking a 'hybrid Paasche'/Laspeyres ratio and it can be expected to underestimate any Gerschenkron effects, compared with the 'true' ratio for the preceding years.

For the following years 1980–1992, the validity of the Paasche indices is higher but there are other data problems that limit the comparability with the years 1888–1969. Prices and weights at about the six-digit level have been provided by Statistics Sweden and are also used in the official domestic market producer price index (HMPI). The indices used here, however, are not the official HMPI, for reasons dealt with in Ljungberg (1999).[4] The original price quotations, said to be about 1,800 commodities in the early 1990s (SCB, 1991b, p. 6), were unfortunately not available so indexed monthly prices had to be matched with corresponding weights in the reconstruction of Paasche price indices. The indexed prices were usually short series, sometime less than a year. Only those providing annual links were used. The number of useful links increased from about 440 in the early 1980s to 650 by end of the period. As a result 42 sub-branch indices could be constructed. The sub-branch sales data, used for the aggregation of the Paasche price index for total manufacturing as well as for the analysis of volumes, have been collected from SOS *Industri*.

The matching together of the short price series implies some consideration of quality change. Unfortunately, treatment of quality change in the individual series is a bit unclear. Statistics Sweden explained that quality change is considered proportionate to change in the cost of production (SCB, 1991a, p. 20; SCB, 1991b, p. 10). However, this implies that price decrease due to competition, which is typical for new and innovative products, will be ignored and hence the index biased upwards. Other methods were described by Dalén (1992) according to whom splicing or matching (as shown in Table 5.1) should apply to 35 per cent of the links in a series, while no comparison between old and new products was deemed possible for 50 per cent which are 'linked in', that is, its index value is set at the level of the larger product group to which it belongs. Dalén (1992, p. 8) thought this involved 'a rather great potential for error since large price changes could be "linked off" this way'. However, the problem would actually be *when* new products are introduced. A problem in the official statistics has been that they are introduced too late, when relative price reductions have stabilized. Thus, uncertainty remains around the treatment of quality change for the period 1980–1992, although it could be assumed as better than 1970–1979. For the preceding years there is at least a higher transparency, since all the links are documented together with the individual price series.

Another problem is that the representativity of the price data, that is, product groups with at least one price series as a share of total manufacturing output, decreased from about 70 per cent over the first four decades, to about 50 per cent in the 1960s (Ljungberg, 1990, p. 49). This decrease in representativity occurred despite an increase in the number of price series, due to the growth and diversification of output. More problematic than the representativity as such is that new products were probably included later in the official wholesale price material from the interwar period than in the data collected from other sources in the earlier period. It could therefore not be ruled out that some part of the retardation in the Gerschenkron effect in the interwar period, as can be seen in Figure 5.1, reflects ignorance of new products in the data. From 1935 the amount of price data increased and the marked Gerschenkron effect in the late 1940s corroborates the validity of the data until 1969. The trend of the Paasche/Laspeyres ratio (Figure 5.1) is unbroken from the early 1950s to the late 1980s. One can speculate whether more consistently constructed indices in the 1970s would have accelerated the fall.

Nevertheless, the steep fall visible in the late 1980s might support Schön's contention that the new development blocks show up in declining relative prices of new products a decade after the structural crisis, labelled supply-push in the typology used here. It could also be an outcome of the reverse, a supply-contraction with increasing relative prices and diminishing sales volumes. We will have a closer look at these patterns but first the broader picture is useful in order to have a more concrete perception of the long-term movement of relative prices.

Relative prices of significant products[5]

It is well known that over the long term the cost of services has increased much more than commodity prices. This is due to the fact that while most services have remained labour intensive, commodity production has become increasingly mechanized and automatized. This divide is also manifest among commodity prices. Product prices in industries with faster productivity growth have fallen relative to those with slower productivity growth, even though there are notable exceptions, as will be shown.

Figure 5.2 shows relative prices in some major product groups of industrial society. One is machinery, encompassing a wide range from ploughs and other agricultural machinery, to machine tools, sewing machines and office machinery. There are also significant price differences among these products but a weighted average (Paasche index) is displayed. It is notable that there are distinct trends, not over the whole 'antedated century' but for some decades, and then changes in direction. The fall in the decades down to World War I came with the introduction of a modern, specialized, engineering industry that superseded the older workshops with diversified production. Besides improvements in the methods of production, the 'new American style' in contrast to the 'old English way', an important factor was the emergence of imitating firms that challenged the technological monopoly of the original innovator, which contributed to lower prices.

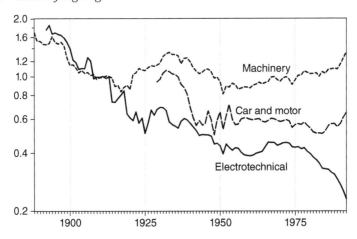

Figure 5.2 Prices of machinery, electrical equipment and cars, relative to prices of all manufactures, 1888–1992.

Source: Reference year (1910/12=100), semilog scale; Ljungberg (1990, 1999).

Note: The index for cars has been 'linked in' to the level of all metal and engineering products in 1930.

The relative prices of machinery stabilized well before World War I but fell again during the war, when production peaked in 1917. Subsequently, relative prices rose significantly until the early 1930s.

The rise in the relative price of machinery came along with a stagnation of output once the industry had reached a level of maturity. A success story before the war had been the milk separator for use at the farmstead, but major export markets disappeared with the Russian revolution and domestically the growth of industrial dairies, despite their need for larger machinery, did not replace the previous demand. A would-be success that failed were combustion engines, which had seemed promising in the early century. However, even if useful, for example for boats, these engines could not challenge electrical motors for use in manufacturing. Over the period 1912–1929 the horsepower from combustion engines in manufacturing only increased by 54 per cent, to 22,000 hp, while that of electrical motors increased more than fivefold, to almost 1.5 million hp. Another innovation that failed was the milking machine, which after a long process of development reached a technological breakthrough around 1910 but had to await two world wars before becoming a success in the market. Yet, there was a success story in the ball bearings produced by Sven Wingquist and SKF, a company that was in the early stage of international expansion when major patents expired in 1923. SKF could retain its advantage, however, and charge increasing prices which in 1930 were 20 per cent above the index (1910/12=100) for all manufactures, and just about the same for the overall machinery index.

By the end of the depression, in 1934, machinery prices turned down and continued to fall relatively until 1951, when they were roughly 20 per cent below the index for all manufactures. This fall was driven by new products such as office machinery and domestically produced cars, notably Volvo but also montage production of Ford and GM, and after the war SAAB as well. The fall in the relative price of machinery was, however, also driven by stiff competition in ball bearings, where notwithstanding continued high output growth, SKF saw its share of the world market decline from an impressive 18 per cent in 1934 to a slightly less impressive 15 per cent in 1950. Office machinery became a new success story with mechanical calculating machines and typewriters, which had annual output growth of nearly 20 per cent over the 1930s and 1940s. Calculating machines fell absolutely in price while all office machinery fell relatively. This industry is a rare case in which Swedish twentieth-century engineering had its origin in the old, even early modern, iron works industry. The iron works in Åtvidaberg, a bit peripheral as it was situated about 250 kilometres south of the old iron district *Bergslagen* in central Sweden, thus transformed into a leading high-tech industry.[6] The success ended in the 1980s, however, with the failure to change from mechanical to electronic technology. The output of cars, together with trucks and tractors, also grew very fast at an annual rate of about 10 per cent during the two decades after the depression. This was slower than office machinery, and the relative price of cars displayed a somewhat less steep fall. Nevertheless, as displayed in Figure 5.2, relative car prices fell very sharply in the 10 years after the depression. They moved broadly similarly to machinery prices from the early 1950s to the early 1970s. Despite that output was now at a higher level, the growth of the car industry accelerated in the post-war period. Given this and the competition among several producers in a global market, the relative price was remarkably stable. Unless the price estimations underestimate quality change in the production of cars, it can only be explained by a high income elasticity of demand. After a dip in the structural crisis of the late 1970s, relative car prices displayed a distinct increase from the mid-1980s. Actually, this development in relative prices largely matched output growth, a relation which makes cars stand out in comparison with the typical case where relative prices and output are negatively correlated.

Figure 5.2 also shows the relative price of electrical equipment, encompassing electrical motors, cables, bulb lamps, later extended to refrigerators, vacuum cleaners and radio apparatuses. This is an industry with a backlog of many new products. The relative prices show a persistent and secular decline, only interrupted in the late 1920s and by a stabilization from 1960 to the late 1970s. There then began a new decline that by the early 1990s had cut the relative prices of these products to a half of what they were in 1978. Remarkable as this decline was, one historical and one methodological remark should put it into perspective. From the mid-1930s to the early 1950s an even steeper decline of relative prices was displayed by bulb lamps (filled with gas instead of vacuum, an innovation of the 1920s), office machinery and refrigerators (another innovation). The decline in the relative price of electrical equipment since 1980 is hence not historically unique. The methodological remark is, however, a reminder that the price indices from 1970 cannot be decomposed into single commodities, while the label of 'electrical equipment' arguably hides a distribution of products with diverging relative prices, of which some might have fallen steeper than the precursors in the earlier period.[7]

It is noticeable in Figure 5.2 that there are three periods of 10 to 20 years in length with a pronounced fall in relative prices: around the turn of the twentieth century, from the early or mid-1930s, and from the late 1970s. While the first two periods saw a unison fall (though cars were not represented before 1929), in the latest period only electrical equipment became relatively cheaper. The development of car prices has already been commented on but what could explain the slow but persistent rise of machinery prices since the mid-1950s? Broadly speaking, it had reached a stage of maturity demonstrated by the marginally higher volume growth, in comparison with total manufacturing, over the 1950s and 1960s, and stagnation of output that was clearly behind total manufacturing from the 1970s. As almost an exception, office machinery was still growing fast until about 1970, but relative prices were rather stable. In ball bearings a large, unchanging share was exported but the technological advantage had gone and SKF competed by cutting relative prices. This could not stop foreign competitors from even seizing a large share of the domestic market. The fall of the relative price of ball bearings was neither due to innovation nor to output growth with economies of scale but simply to stiffening competition. Agricultural machinery saw some innovations, the reaping-machine (half a century after its introduction in the USA), for example, but output growth was modest and probably the dominance of two big producers marked up the prices. The efficiency of machine tools had been drastically improved in the 1940s by the innovation of ceramic edges but it seems that the links in the price series have accounted for quality changes (Ljungberg, 1990, p. 313n). Thus, their steeply rising relative prices are presumably not due to deficiencies in the data, that is, ignorance of quality change but explained by high demand. A conjecture is further that makers were highly specialized and competed more on technology than on prices. This conjecture is suggested by the circumstance that Swedish machine tools lost out to imports in the domestic market while exports grew faster than the rate of total manufacturing output.

It is worth going into some detail on the machinery industry, since this was the mainstay of the engineering industry, the flagship of Sweden's post-war manufacturing. In the last decade of the nineteenth century, the share of the machinery, electrotechnical, and shipbuilding industries in total manufacturing sales (in current prices) was some 5 per cent. In the 1950s and 1960s their share, now with cars and trucks included, was above 20 per cent. However, machinery had already reached its share in the 1940s and the continued expansion of the engineering industry was due to the other branches, in particular the car industry which in the 1980s had more than 7 per cent of total sales. How different the composition of manufacturing had been in the last decade of the nineteenth century, with almost 20 per cent of sales made up of sawn and planed wood, while the second biggest product group was flour, followed by textiles, and liquor and sugar, each with bigger sales than machinery!

The relative price of an industry that was among the biggest a century ago, textiles, is shown in Figure 5.3. Also shown is the relative price of butchery, fresh

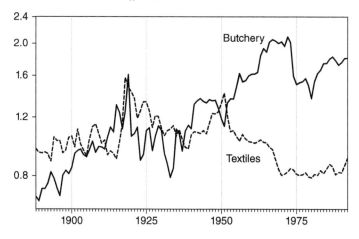

Figure 5.3 Prices of butchery and textiles, relative to prices of all manufactures, 1888–1992.

Source: Author's calculations based on Ljungberg (1990, 1999); reference year (1910/12=100), semilog scale.

meat and pork as well as more processed products, which was rather small having less than 1 per cent of manufacturing output around the turn of the twentieth century, yet grew and by the post-war years matched the electrotechnical industry with close to 5 per cent of total sales. Textiles and butchery followed similar though not identical trajectories until about 1950, after which point in time they diverge and broadly mirror each other. Before World War I the relative price of textiles was stable while that of butchery rose. This reflected a slow growth in sales output of the latter and a rather fast growth of textiles. Like other consumption goods they rose with inflation during the war, which hit consumables more than other manufactures. In about 1920 a relative decline in textiles began, which from 1970 was followed also by an absolute decline of sales volumes. The fall in relative prices down to the late 1930s was a consequence of stiff competition. However, in contrast to the traditional textiles, the new product rayon, made of synthetic fibre, displayed the typical pattern of an innovation: fast growing volumes and steeply falling relative prices. When war limited the imports of cotton and wool, rayon could expand even more without increasing prices. Overall, however, the relative price of textiles rose and continued to do so until 1951. Then, the fall through the 1950s and 1960s reflected increased competition even if the volume of sales continued to grow in absolute terms. However, over the 1970s and 1980s output diminished by about a third, and the remaining products were, as can be seen in Figure 5.3, those which could be sold at stable relative prices.

The relative price of butchery displays a secular rise except for the period 1911–1930 and between 1972 and 1980. It is noticeable that the rate of output growth was the highest in the 1920s and 1930s, clearly above the average of manufacturing, at the same time as prices lagged behind. In other periods output has been slightly above the manufacturing average or, from 1950, clearly below.

Productivity change in the industry was below that of total manufacturing. In particular, this seems to have been the case in the interwar period (Ljungberg, 2004; 1990, p. 541), which is consistent with the secular rise in relative prices although not with the interwar trend. However, the pattern in prices, at least up to 1970, broadly followed those of livestock and pigs. The connection, and disconnection, with an international market seems ultimately to explain the variation of butchery prices. In the interwar period international prices for beef and pork fell, and the Crisis Policy of 1932 (the so-called *Cow Deal*) seems, from a comparison with Danish prices (assumed to be representative of an international market), mostly to have had an impact on milk and butter. Only at the end of the interwar period, with the introduction of war regulations, and retained from 1956 by increasing foodstuff tariffs, were Swedish consumers of beef and sausages disconnected from international trends. The steep fall in relative prices of butchery in the 1970s was, paradoxically, most likely a result of the insulation. It was more a result of the price hike of other manufacturers and it preceded the international fall in meat and pork prices, and also recovered when the latter still kept falling. In summary the secular trend follows the prediction by Adam Smith that smaller possibilities for division of labour in agriculture than in manufacturing would lead to rising relative prices of foodstuffs. The international market changed these preconditions, but when the regulation of agriculture and tariff policy implemented a closed economy in agriculture, the development returned to Adam Smith.

Finally we look at 'mineral goods', which were mostly building materials such as bricks, cement and concrete. Relative prices for these goods, shown in Figure 5.4, do not follow any typical pattern. Productivity change seems generally to have been above average, in particular in the early decades although

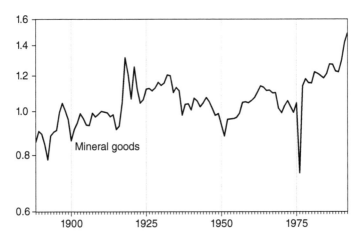

Figure 5.4 Prices of mineral goods (building materials), relative to prices of all manufactures, 1888–1992.

Source: Author's calculations based on Ljungberg (1990, 1999); reference year (1910/12=100), semilog scale.

with the exception of the interwar period. Hence, relative prices rose with fast productivity growth and fell with slow productivity growth. Output also grew rapidly in the early decades but stagnated in the interwar period and through the 1940s. An inference is that prices were demand-driven, at least until 1950. This interpretation also finds support in an inspection of the series in Figure 5.4, which irrespective of the longer trends show fluctuations very similar to the timing and length of building cycles. Such is the pattern after 1950 also, when the trend is rising, despite a productivity change about average. In the 1950s and 1960s, when we can trace prices of different goods in this industry, price developments differed, however. Cement and concrete goods were stable or even falling, while bricks and tubes of concrete had rising relative prices. Overall building materials seemed a bit inflationary, even to contemporaries, and were the object of several public investigations between the 1940s and 1960s. Cartelization was suspected but evidence pointed to a competitive industry. A conjecture is that the policy in support of an improved housing standard, which had been quite poor in international comparison before 1950, created a market where producers could very much determine prices. This might explain the rising trend from 1950 onwards.

This section has explored relative prices over the 'antedated twentieth century' for a selection of products or industries. Even though they have, through the whole century, made up nearly a third of all manufacturing output, they are in no sense representative of all manufactures. However, they represent some typical developments. One typical pattern shows falling relative prices with growing volumes of output, particularly pronounced when radical innovations and new products are involved. Also the opposite pattern has not been unusual, for mature products that are becoming obsolete. Technological advantage or particularly strong demand has in different ways violated or modified these patterns. Typically, I would argue, relative prices have not fluctuated around a stable trend but annual fluctuations have drifted in one direction over several decades before changing direction.

In economic modelling a usual assumption is 'international prices' for tradables, whereas only goods and services that are not involved in foreign trade are priced domestically. However, in the present discussion the international market has been considered only in the cases of textiles and butchery. Arguably, 'international prices' are a creation of the mind, a logical construct that may be necessary in a model of the economy. In the real world friction, information asymmetries, and industrial dynamics create enough deviations from the fictitious equilibrium of international prices to necessitate purchasing power parity adjustments of exchange rates in international comparisons.[8] Hence, there is reason to go further from the somewhat *ad hoc* discussion in this section to a more systematic analysis of relative prices and transformation in Swedish manufacturing.

Positive and negative transformation pressure

Schumpeter (1942) coined the concept *creative destruction* which has often received an intuitive or narrative meaning for the perennial transformation of a capitalist economy. Dahmén (1970 [1950]) gave the concept a more instrumental interpretation with the *positive side* and *negative side* of industrial transformation to which a typology of development patterns is subsumed. Schön, in several works, has also examined the positive and negative sides in the development of structural cycles in the Swedish economy, notably during structural crises. Hence, from being more on the positive side in the crises of the 1890s and 1930s, Sweden in the 1970s moved more towards the negative side (Schön, 2012, pp. 320ff.). This conception of transformation pressure is further developed by Taalbi (2014), who in an examination of innovations in Swedish manufacturing develops an endogenous model that explains the origin for about two-thirds of innovations between 1970 and 2007. From positive transformation pressure originates two kinds of innovation: those responding to 'new opportunities' and those 'solving technological bottle-necks'. From negative transformation pressure, on the other hand, originates innovations that aim to solve problems of rising cost, or problems of negative externalities (mostly environmental), or problems that relate to the organization (often working conditions). The highest number of innovations came in a surge around 1980, in the midst of the structural crisis, with a large share responding to negative transformation pressure. Another surge of innovations, particularly in ICT and software, came in the 1990s as a response to positive transformation pressure. These elaborations of *transformation pressure* are reiterated here because they have a great deal in common with the present analysis of relative prices.

To begin with, Table 5.2 gives an overview of the average annual percentage rate of change in relative prices for sub-branches of manufacturing. The century-long period 1888–1992 has been divided into five approximate 20-year-long sub-periods. Only two industries had either a positive or negative trend over the whole period: tobacco with rising relative prices and chemicals with falling relative prices. Fourteen industries have had two or three periods with either positive or negative trends, while 16 had positive trends in four periods and 7 negative trends. Despite the persistent rise or fall, neither chemicals nor tobacco had the greatest change over the century. The biggest rise was assigned to sawn and planed wood, with an almost eightfold increase in relative prices. Printed matter came close behind with a more than a sixfold increase. On the other hand, rubber products fell to a sixth, while electrical equipment and ores to a fifth. This again emphasises that changes have been both sizeable and discontinuous over longer periods.

When did the trend breaks occur? Assessed from machinery (Figure 5.2), it could be argued that trend breaks came before World War I, in the early 1930s, early 1950s, and, if we include electrical equipment, in the mid-1970s. These junctures also appear as discontinuities in textiles, butchery and mineral goods, even if mixed up with other instances of change. It is not the aim here to test when these discontinuities actually appeared (it would be the topic for a separate paper). Instead, the task is to examine how these discontinuities in relative prices affected the transformation of manufacturing. This is done by investigating how relative prices and output volumes have changed over periods of transformation and rationalization in structural cycles. An exact dating of the periods seems elusive since

Table 5.2 Average annual percentage rate of change in product prices relative to all manufactures, 1888–1992

	Iron and steel	Metals	Iron and metal goods	Machinery	Electrical equipment	Ships
1888–1910	0.88	1.63	0.95	−2.63	−3.65*	−0.97
1911–1930	−1.90	−4.83	−0.14	1.52	−1.89	−0.95
1931–1952	1.85	1.84	−0.45	−2.00	−2.00	2.85
1953–1973	−0.43	0.94	2.32	0.64	0.62	0.01
1974–1992	−1.11	0.97	0.54	1.46	−3.13	0.33
1888–1992	0.42	−0.62	0.66	−0.24	−1.55	0.79

	Bicycles	Car and motor	Instruments	Ores	Glass	Mineral goods
1888–1910	−3.67	—		2.16	0.93	0.62
1911–1930	−2.14	—		−0.35	0.38	0.88
1931–1952	−1.46	−3.63		−0.93	−1.51	−1.00
1953–1973	−0.10**	−0.23		−6.03	0.91	0.32
1974–1992	—	0.56	0.11	−4.27	1.01	2.15
1888–1992	−1.49	−0.75†		−1.57	0.27	0.23

	Sawn and planed wood	Joinery	Pulp and paper	Packaging products	Printing	Butchery
1888–1910	1.77	—	−1.87	—	1.42	1.76
1911–1930	1.10	—	−0.80	—	5.38	−0.78
1931–1952	3.38	—	2.74	—	−0.42	2.06
1953–1973	2.10	1.42	−1.01	0.99	1.61	2.16
1974–1992	−0.28	1.80	−0.29	0.08	4.15	1.33
1888–1992	2.00	1.27‡	0.23	0.88‡	1.79	0.90

	Dairy	Fats and margarine	Flour	Bakery	Sugar	Confectionery
1888–1910	1.00	2.17	0.49	1.58	−1.60	0.19
1911–1930	−0.20	−2.53	−0.06	1.88	−2.66	0.59
1931–1952	−0.06	1.66	−0.48	−0.81	0.57	3.74
1953–1973	1.39	−1.43	1.80	3.51	−0.25	−0.72
1974–1992	1.28	0.36	1.19	2.90	−1.63	2.14
1888–1992	0.25	0.21	0.41	1.40	−0.66	1.25

	Other food	Liquor	Beer etc.	Tobacco	Canned and frozen food	Fodder
1888–1910	−2.12	1.27	0.67	0.13	—	
1911–1930	1.45	0.75	2.31	2.55	—	
1931–1952	1.22	−1.20	−2.16	0.45	—	

(continued)

Table 5.2 (Continued)

	Other food	Liquor	Beer etc.	Tobacco	Canned and frozen food	Fodder
1953–1973	−3.10	0.03	0.87	0.77	—	
1974–1992	−1.91	−0.79	1.32	2.69	0.94	−0.92
1888–1992	0.31	−0.12	0.34	0.78	—	—

	Textiles	Clothing	Shoes	Tannery and leather	Rubber products	Fertilisers
1888–1910	0.57	0.30	0.37	1.72	1.30	−2.40
1911–1930	0.80	1.05	0.12	−2.25	−1.12	−2.52
1931–1952	1.01	1.22	−0.52	−0.10	−4.53	−0.48
1953–1973	−1.46	−0.11	0.39	−0.42	−2.64	−2.26
1974–1992	0.50	1.36	2.17	−0.12	2.40	1.24
1888–1992	−0.22	0.40	0.16	0.11	−1.74	−0.96

	Dyes	Soap and detergents	Chemicals	Techno-chemical products	Petrol etc.	Pharma-ceuticals
1888–1910	0.11	0.74	−0.89	0.35	1.54	—
1911–1930	−2.09	−0.93	−0.88	0.29	−2.80	—
1931–1952	1.37	−1.28	−0.90	0.67	1.21	—
1953–1973	0.23	−0.83	−2.74	−0.32	−0.18	—
1974–1992	1.38	0.52	−2.63	0.91	0.52	−0.67
1888–1992	−0.08	−1.06	−1.40	0.19	0.47	—

Notes
* start year 1892;
** end year 1969;
† start year 1931;
‡ start year 1953.

they are defined by different characteristics, which change with some leads and lags (for a discussion of the structural cycle see Chapter 1 and references there). From 1888 to 1992 there are roughly five such periods of transformation and rationalization. The first period 1888–1910 actually begins before the structural crisis of the early 1890s, yet covers the following transformative period that turned into rationalization about 1910. The second period 1911–1930 corresponds to the rationalization of the 1910s and 1920s, ending with the structural crisis of the early 1930s. Most of this crisis and the following transformation are covered by the third period, 1931–1952. A change to rationalization occurred in the 1950s and continued until the structural crisis of the 1970s. Rationalization thus broadly characterized the fourth period 1953–1973. The fifth period covers the structural crisis and the early transformation, 1974–1992. The intense transformation created a bubble that burst in the financial crisis of the early 1990s. As mentioned on p. 83, data

Table 5.3 Classification of industries according to change in relative prices, with sales volumes during five periods, 1888–1992

1888–1910

Steeply falling	*Falling*	*Stable*	*Rising*	*Steeply rising*
<–1%	*–1 to –0.34*	*–0.33 to 0.33*	*0.34 to 1%*	*>1%*
Machinery, Electrotechnical, Bicycles, Pulp and paper, Sugar, Other food, Fertilisers, Petrol products	Ships, Chemicals	Confectionery, Tobacco, Clothing, Dyes	Iron and steel, Iron and metal goods, Glass, Mineral goods, Flour, Beer etc., Textiles, Shoes, Soap and detergents, Techno-chemical products	Metals, Ores, Sawn and planed wood, Printing, Butchery, Dairy, Fat and margarine, Bakery, Liquor, Tannery and leather, Rubber products

Annual percentage rate of change of sales volumes, total manufacturing 4.36 (value added 5.19)

10.41	8.74	2.28	3.87	2.28

1911–1930

Steeply falling	*Falling*	*Stable*	*Rising*	*Steeply rising*
Iron and steel, Metals, Electrotechnical, Ships, Bicycles, Ores, Fat and margarine, Sugar, Tannery and leather, Fertilisers, Dyes, Chemicals, Petrol products	Pulp and paper, Butchery, Rubber products, Soap and detergents	Iron and metal goods, Dairy, Flour, Shoes	Glass, Mineral products, Confectionery, Liquor, Clothing, Techno-chemical products	Machinery, Sawn and planed wood, Printing, Bakery, Other food, Beer etc., Tobacco, Textiles

Annual percentage rate of change of sales volumes, total manufacturing 2.50 (value added 2.66)

3.47	5.24	1.23	2.20	1.34

(continued)

Table 5.3 (Continued)

1931–1952

Machinery, Electrotechnical, Car and motor, Bicycles, Glass, Liquor, Beer etc., Rubber products, Soap and detergents	Iron and metal goods, Ores, Mineral products, Printing, Flour, Bakery, Shoes, Fertilisers, Chemicals	Dairy, Tannery and leather	Sugar, Tobacco, Techno-chemical products	Iron and steel, Metals, Ships, Sawn and planed wood, Pulp and paper, Butchery, Fat and margarine, Confectionery, Other food, Textiles, Clothing, Dyes, Petrol products
8.25	4.32	5.02	1.72	3.97

Annual percentage rate of change of sales volumes, total manufacturing 5.00 (value added 4.64)

1953–1973

Ores, Pulp and paper, Fat and margarine, Other food, Textiles, Rubber products, Fertilisers, Chemicals	Iron and steel, Confectionery, Tannery and leather, Soap and detergents	Ships, Car and motor, Bicycles, Mineral products, Sugar, Liquor, Clothing, Dyes, Techno-chemical products, Petrol products	Metals, Machinery, Electrotechnical, Glass, Packaging, Beer etc., Tobacco, Shoes	Iron and metal products, Sawn and planed wood, Joinery, Printing, Butchery, Dairy, Flour, Bakery
5.78	6.28	6.58	5.70	3.78

Annual percentage rate of change of sales volumes, total manufacturing 5.57 (value added 4.81)

1974–1992

Iron and steel, Electrotechnical, Ores, Sugar, Other food, Chemicals	Liquor, Fodder, Soap and detergents, Pharmaceuticals	Ships, Instruments, Sawn and planed wood, Pulp and paper, Packaging, Tannery and leather, Plastic products	Metals, Iron and metal products, Car and motor, Fat and margarine, Canned and frozen food, Textiles, Techno-chemical products, Petrol products	Machinery, Glass, Mineral products, Joinery, Printing, Butchery, Dairy, Flour, Bakery, Confectionery, Beer etc., Tobacco, Clothing, Shoes, Rubber products, Fertilisers, Dyes
4.83	2.59	1.42	2.49	0.13

Annual percentage rate of change of sales volumes, total manufacturing 2.62 (value added 1.07) constraints motivated a stop with 1992; otherwise the continued transformation until the end of the century could have been included in the fifth period.

Table 5.3 classifies industries according to their rate of change in prices relative to the average of manufactures over the different periods. Five categories are used: steeply falling, falling, stable, rising and steeply rising. Stable indicates prices that have moved 0.33 per cent at most annually, up or down, relative to the aggregate price index. Rising (falling) have increased (decreased) between 0.33 and 1 per cent, while steeply rising (or steeply falling) have moved at least at an annual rate of 1 per cent. These limits are of course arbitrary, as with any classification. One might consider using a more relative standard such as the coefficient of variation. This would smooth the differences, however, between periods and therefore the fixed percentages are preferred.

Besides classifying the industries according to changes in relative prices, Table 5.3 also shows the rate of change in the sales output of the industries in each category and each period. It is notable that in the three periods of transformation the industries with steeply falling relative prices have the fastest growth in output. In the periods of rationalization industries with either falling (1911–1930) or stable (1953–1973) relative prices grow the fastest. Overall, the negative correlation between relative prices and output growth is clearer during periods of transformation. On the other hand, the variations of aggregate growth of manufacturing and mining are not related to the pattern of transformation and rationalization. This holds independent of whether growth is measured as total sales values of the represented industries or as value added of manufacturing in national accounts (Schön and Krantz, 2012), as can be seen in Figure 5.3. For example, the two periods with lowest growth were in the rationalization of 1911–1930 and in the transformation of 1973–1992. Even if the whole period of transformation had been included, down to 2000, this would not change.[9]

Another similarity between periods, observed just by a glance at the number of industries in different classes, is the broad spread of change in relative prices. What changes in this respect, though, is while only a few industries had stable relative prices in the first three periods, in the fourth period the distribution is more even, and in the last period the distribution is towards more industries with rising or steeply rising relative prices. However, so far only the change in relative prices but not the relation to output growth for the individual industries has been considered. It is in this relation we might find clues about the transformation pressure and whether it is of a positive or negative nature. To this issue we now turn.

In the discussion on p. 80 about the Gerschenkron effect, a typology with four different combinations of relative prices and output was introduced. Two of these types have a negative correlation between relative prices and output: *supply-push* with falling prices and growing volumes, and *supply-contraction* with rising prices and decreasing volumes. Both of these result in a negative slope of the Paasche/Laspeyres price index ratio. In line with Dahmén's argument, the causal factor here is largely the entrepreneur or the strategy of the firm. With *demand-pull* and *demand-reduction*, on the other hand, the driving forces are outside of the firm and determined by broader market conditions. The latter two types of forces counteract the

Gerschenkron effect and if dominant would show up in a rising Paasche/Laspeyres ratio, or 'negative Gerschenkron effect'. To operationalise the typology, only those industries deviating more than 1 percentage point from the aggregate change in prices or sales volumes qualify for any of the four categories. The relations between correlations and transformation pressure is not straightforward, though, since the supply-push implies a positive transformation pressure and supply-contraction a negative transformation pressure; similarly, demand-reduction means a negative transformation pressure and demand-pull a positive.

In Table 5.4 only industries from the two extreme categories in Table 5.3 reappear, those with steeply falling and steeply rising relative prices, and only those also having steep changes in the sales volumes. The table broadly outlines which industries were facing positive transformation pressure and which were facing negative transformation pressure. The electrotechnical industry responded to positive transformation pressure with supply-push in four out of the five periods. In the period 1953–1973 electrical equipment had rising relative prices and the growth of sales volume was, compared with before and after, only modestly above that of total manufacturing. This signified that the electrotechnical industry was coming to maturity but it managed, by exploiting new electronic technology, to achieve supply-push in the following period. Chemicals is another successful industry that achieved supply-push during the three periods, 1911–1930, 1953–1973 and 1974–1992. No other industry could achieve supply-push in more than two periods. It is notable that a positive transformation pressure coming from the demand side, as demand-pull, only occurred in the three periods before 1953. An interpretation is that competition increased and it became more difficult to retain a technological advantage over longer periods.

Sawn and planed wood responded to negative transformation pressure with supply-contraction over four consecutive periods down to 1973. Also in the period 1974–1992 the sales volumes developed far below that of total manufacturing, but relative prices could not be sustained steeply rising and were in the range defined as stable. Despite the fact that industries in supply-contraction had the largest share of sales output over all periods, no single industry except the saw mills appeared in this category more than twice. This might be seen as a feature of creative destruction, a phase that industries have to go through before adapting to new circumstances.

A closer look at the changes behind the distinct Gerschenkron effects, shown in Figure 5.1, reveals a great turbulence in both 1945–1951 and 1988–1992. In the 1940s it was mostly due to more industries coming into supply-push or supply-contraction. There were also some changes on the demand side where more industries faced demand-reduction while all those facing demand-pull fell out of this category. The turbulence in the late 1980s was even more complex and several industries faced demand-pull, for example shipbuilding, instruments, liquor and detergents. However, these were industries with a low weight in the aggregate index and a more important factor was that the paper and pulp industry moved to supply-push, and also that metal products, the car industry, the glass industry and joineries turned to supply-contraction. As a conclusion these distinct Gerschenkron effects in price indices should not be taken as breakthroughs of innovations and development

Table 5.4 Typology of market forces for industries during different periods, 1888–1992

	Supply-push	Supply-contraction	Demand-reduction	Demand-pull
1888–1910	Machinery, Electrotechnical, Bicycles, Sugar, Other food, Fertilisers, Petroleum products	Metals, Sawn and planed wood, Liquor		Ores, Fats and margarine, Bakery, Tannery and leather, Rubber products
Percentage shares of total sales value of manufacturing, 1888–1910				
	13.0	21.0	0.0	4.1
1911–1930	Metals, Electrotechnical, Ships, Bicycles, Fats and margarine, Dyes, Chemicals	Sawn and planed wood, Printing, Textiles	Iron and steel, Ores	Bakery, Other food, Tobacco, Dyes
Percentage shares of total sales value of manufacturing, 1911–1930				
	8.3	18.0	7.4	5.6
1931–1952	Machinery, Electrotechnical, Car and motor, Rubber products	Sawn and planed wood, Pulp and paper, Confectionery, Other food, Textiles	Liquor, Beer etc.,	Metals, Fats and margarine, Petroleum products
Percentage shares of total sales value of manufacturing, 1931–1952				
	16.5	22.1	2.2	5.1
1953–1973	Ores, Rubber products, Chemicals	Iron and metal goods, Sawn and planed wood, Butchery, Dairy, Flour, Bakery	Fats and margarine, Other food, Textiles, Fertilisers	
Percentage shares of total sales value of manufacturing, 1953–1973				
	2.8	18.1	4.1	0
1974–1992	Electrotechnical, Chemicals	Machinery, Mineral goods, Printing, Butchery, Dairy, Flour, Bakery, Confectionery, Beer etc., Tobacco, Clothing, Shoes, Rubber products, Fertilisers, Dyes	Iron and steel, Sugar	
Percentage shares of total sales value of manufacturing, 1974–1992 (36.8 which supply 32.0)				
	7.1	24.9	4.8	0

blocks from the preceding structural crisis. The more disaggregated price data also indicate that big falls in the relative prices of new products came earlier in the cycle, as was the case with several engineering products in the years before 1900, again in the 1930s, and electrical equipment from the late 1970s. The distinct Gerschenkron effects in the 1940s and 1980s were more mixed, creative destruction as it were. These developments were arguably anticipations of the crises of transformation which occurred in the early 1950s and early 1990s. The latter is well known and was reinforced by 'the banking crisis' and an international currency crisis. In the 1950s regulations of the capital market constrained a bubble but the crisis is clearly seen in the sales volumes of some industries. For example, the car industry had reduced sales of more than 10 per cent in 1951, and in 1952 the electrotechnical industry had reduced sales of almost 6 per cent and shipbuilding was down by nearly 25 per cent. In the perspective of the structural cycle these crises in the early 1950s and early 1990s preceded a somewhat later turn from transformation to rationalization (Schön, 2012, pp. 16–17; see also Chapter 1 in this volume about the structural cyce).

Concluding remarks

Relative prices of different products change profoundly over the long term and often with a trend that lasts several decades. Such discontinuities are reflected in the Gerschenkron effect but the underlying character of the development might be of a different kind. However, an examination of relative prices and the concomitant development of output volumes provides insights about phases of development that are hidden if just the variations in growth are studied. In general there is a negative correlation between relative prices and output. New products typically have falling relative prices and grow fast in output. Since the origin of such cases is an innovation, they are defined as supply-push and as implying a positive transformation pressure. A negative transformation pressure, on the other hand, is implied by supply-contraction with rising relative prices and diminishing output. Positive transformation pressure is an important element in the period of transformation that together with the period of rationalization and the structural crisis composes the structural cycle. Increasing negative transformation pressure prepares for the end of the transformation period and the beginning of rationalization. The Swedish price history over the examined period 1888–1992 provides further support for this interpretation.

Notes

1 Denoting the price series p, and volume series q, with subscripts o for initial year or base year and t for any following year, or year of comparison, the Paasche index is calculated as $P = \Sigma p_t q_t / \Sigma p_o q_t$ whereas the Laspeyres is $L = \Sigma p_t q_o / \Sigma p_o q_o$.

2 Dahmén was, at least originally, very critical of conventional supply-demand curves since they 'eliminate important instruments for the causal analysis which are useful for the tracking of the driving forces in a process' (1950, p. 50n., translation by J. L.). In Leijonhufvud's translation of Dahmén (1970) this note is omitted. Furthermore, the supply-push, supply-contraction, demand-reduction, and demand-pull, have no exact match in the Swedish original (Dahmén, 1950). Dahmén did not use 'supply', neither

'demand' in this context but different 'market' processes. Dahmén (1980) can be seen as loyal to Dahmén (1950), but I have kept supply and demand in a typology of market processes since, contrary to Dahmén, I think they clearly indicate the origin of change. What Dahmén was probably after was to avoid the idea that supply and demand necessarily meet in equilibrium, and with that intention I fully comply.

3 The example is hypothetical. In the present data price lists and firm acquisition records are used up to 1935 and thereafter the primary quotations of the official wholesale index. The hedonic method, however, is used for a comparison of prices for electrical motors in Germany, Britain, and Sweden in Ljungberg (1998; 2015).

4 The official HMPI (1980=100) was part of a 'family' of the official producer price indices (PPI), also including exports (EXPI), imports (IMPI) and domestic supply (ITPI), which differed in the composition of weights. PPI was declared as a Laspeyres price chain index with annual links. That is, the weights should be composed by the preceding year's basket. However, since the statistical record of manufacturing was released with a lag of several years, accurate weights for the preceding year were not available for those calculating the contemporary PPI. Their solution was to use weights that were three years old and adjust these with the corresponding price changes ('inflation'). In retrospect it was possible to recalculate the index with the correct weights, and as I showed in my paper, official HMPI performed a kind of double-counting and overestimated the price increases from 1983 to 1993 by at least 30 per cent, or at an average annual rate of change of 5.5 instead of 4.4 per cent.

5 This section draws on Ljungberg (1990), in particular Chapters 6 to 10.

6 From a bird's perspective it is near at hand to infer that the engineering industry of the second industrial revolution in Sweden originated from the age-old industry of iron works. It was typically not so and Åtvidaberg stands out in this respect.

7 Hedonic price indices were introduced by Statistics Sweden (for radio, television and communication equipment) for the first time in 1992. Reconstruction of the price links in HMPI for the 1980s implies, as discussed on p. 84, that the present indices take better account of quality change than the official price index.

8 Cross-country differences in 'international prices' are treated more in detail by Kravis and Lipsey (1971), and Ljungberg (1998, 2015).

9 It is notable, however, that the differences between growth of sales volumes and value added are conspicuously large only for the period 1973–1992, with 2.6 per cent for the former and 1.1 per cent for the latter. It is not a question of representativity because in this period the sum of the industries' sales values makes up more than 95 per cent of the total for manufacturing and mining. For this period Schön and Krantz (2012) use the official national accounts, which might suffer a problem with deflation (compare note 4).

References

Bresnahan, T. F. and Gordon, R. J. (1997), *The Economics of New Goods*. Studies in Income and Wealth, vol. 58. Chicago: University of Chicago Press.

Dalén, J. (1992), 'Operationalising a hedonic index in an official price index program. Personal computers in the Swedish import price index', *SCB R&D Report*, 1992:15.

Dahmén, E. (1950), *Svensk industriell företagarverksamhet. Kausalanalys av den industriella utvecklingen 1919–1939*. Stockholm: IUI.

Dahmén, E. (1970), *Entrepreneurial Activity and the Development of Swedish Industry, 1919–1939*. Published for the American Economic Association, Homewood, Ill.: Richard D. Irwin.

Dahmén, E. (1980), 'Hur studera industriell utveckling.' In Dahmén E. and Eliasson G. (eds) *Industriell utveckling i Sverige. Teori och verklighet under ett sekel. Uppsatser till ett IUI-symposium i anledning av Marcus Wallenbergs 80-årsdag*. Stockholm: IUI.

Gerschenkron, A. (1962), 'Some aspects of industrialization in Bulgaria, 1878–1939.' In *Economic Backwardness in Historical Perspective*. Cambridge, Mass.: Harvard University Press.

Kravis, I. B. and Lipsey, R. E. (1971), *Price Competitiveness in World Trade*. New York: NBER.

Ljungberg, J. (1990), *Priser och marknadskrafter i Sverige 1885–1969. En prishistorisk studie*, Lund: Skrifter utgivna av Ekonomisk-historiska föreningen, vol. 64 (diss.).

Ljungberg, J. (1991), 'Prices and industrial transformation', *Scandinavian Economic History Review*, vol. 39, pp. 49–63.

Ljungberg, J. (1998), 'Prices and growth accounting. On the use of deflators in international benchmark comparisons'. In van Ark, B., Buyst, E. and van Zanden, J. L. (eds) *Historical Benchmark Comparisons of Output and Productivity*. *Proceedings Twelfth International Economic History Congress, Madrid*, Seville: Fundación Fomento de la Historia Económica.

Ljungberg, J. (1999), 'A revision of the Swedish producer price index, 1968-1993.' *Lund Papers in Economic History*, vol. 68.

Ljungberg, J. (2004), 'Earnings differentials and productivity in Sweden, 1870–1980'. In Heikkinen, S. and van Zanden, J. L. (eds) *Explorations in Economic Growth*. Amsterdam: Aksant.

Ljungberg, J. (2015), 'International price competition and catch-up in high-tech sectors, 1850–1940', paper presented at the Economic History Society Annual Conference, University of Wolverhampton, 27–29 March 2015.

SCB (1991a), 'Prisindex i producent- och importled. Produkthandbok version 1', januari, Statistiska centralbyrån, Stockholm.

SCB (1991b), 'Prisindex i producent- och importled. Innehålls- och metodbeskrivning', augusti, Statistiska centralbyrån, Stockholm.

Schön, L. (1988), *Industri och hantverk 1800–1980*. Lund: Ekonomisk-historiska föreningen.

Schön, L. (2012), *An Economic History of Modern Sweden*. Oxon: Routledge.

Schön, L. and Krantz, O. (2012), 'Swedish Historical National Accounts, 1560–2010', *Lund Papers in Economic History, 123*.

Schumpeter, J. A. (1942), *Capitalism, Socialism and Democracy*. New York: Harper & Brothers.

Taalbi, J. (2014), *Innovation as Creative Response: Determinants of Innovation in the Swedish Manufacturing Industry, 1970-2007*. Lund studies in economic history, 67 (diss.).

6   The gold standard and industrial breakthrough in Sweden

Håkan Lobell

Research in the 1980s by Lennart Schön on the role of Swedish capital imports in the process of industrialization during the second half of the nineteenth century underpinned a rethinking of the predominant view that Sweden's industrial breakthrough could be characterized as a case of export-led industrialization. Schön claimed that at least equal emphasis on foreign investments could better explain the shift of investments towards urban infrastructure and housing, as well as modern industries, from the 1880s. Thus, the combination of export earnings and capital imports appears to have reduced the problem of capital scarcity and investment costs. It enabled Sweden to rapidly increase investments in infrastructure as well as growing industries without increasing domestic savings and taxes to the same extent that would otherwise have been required. Simultaneously, massive emigration, primarily to North America, was important in terms of reducing labour supply and raising wages. The resulting relatively higher domestic consumption demand resulted in much wider, deeper and more rapid Swedish industrialization, and indeed modernization in a wider sense (Ljungberg and Schön, 2013; Schön, 1989, 1997, 2007, 2012, pp. 125–6). Capital imports not only enhanced a transition from a predominantly agricultural economy into an industrial one, but also facilitated a transformation from rural to more advanced, urban-based industries between the 1890s and 1914. In fact, on the eve of the First World War in 1914, Sweden was well on the way to completing the transformation into an industrial society, but was at the same time probably one of the most indebted nations in the world (Schön, 1989, p. 227). This chapter explores the development of monetary and credit market conditions of the gold standard related to the emerging capital imports in a long-term perspective.

The extent of Swedish capital imports

The extensive foreign borrowing did not pass unnoticed, of course, by contemporary decision-makers and observers. A number of public and academic inquiries were initiated between the 1870s and 1910 to estimate the size of the foreign debt, i.e. the country's financial position, and to review its possible consequences for the country and future generations. The size of the foreign debt was largely estimated by employing a direct method of adding different items reported by borrowing institutions, such as commercial banks and the government borrowing agency, the National Debt Office (*Riksgäldskontoret*) and the state association coordinating mortgage funding (*Sveriges Allmänna Hypoteksbank*). In the early 1910s, it was concluded that the total foreign borrowing amounted to about a total of SEK 1.1 billion in 1908 (Flodström, 1912). In the 1930s, new estimates were made by the pioneering National Income project by employing new, indirect methods based on estimates of current accounts and other items (Lindahl *et al.*, 1937). The results revealed that the foreign debt had been twice as large as the contemporary inquiries based on what direct methods had shown. Research by Lennart Schön, in connection with the National Debt Office's 200th anniversary in 1989, along with the aid of new results from the research programme Historical National Accounts for Sweden 1800–1980 (see an overview in Krantz and Schön, 2007), led to yet another upward revision of the pre-First World War foreign borrowing. The discrepancy arose because Schön accurately took into account parts of the amount of interest and dividends paid on the foreign debt, which the National Income project of the 1930s had failed to include. Total foreign borrowing was estimated by Schön to have amounted to approximately SEK 3.4 billion between 1850 and 1914 and the foreign debt to about three-quarters of GDP in 1914 (Schön, 1989, p. 234). Schön's estimate of Swedish capital imports between 1850 and 1913 is displayed in Figure 6.1.

Swedish nineteenth-century foreign borrowing, except commercial credit, started in the 1830s with agrarian so-called mortgage associations in connection with the enclosure movement. Government borrowing had been almost negligible since the post-war crisis in the 1810s and the 'termination' of the entire government foreign debt (Ahlström, 1989). Government borrowing was resumed in the 1850s and was mainly aimed at financing railroad construction. In the 1860s, municipalities also started to issue debt abroad to finance investments in public

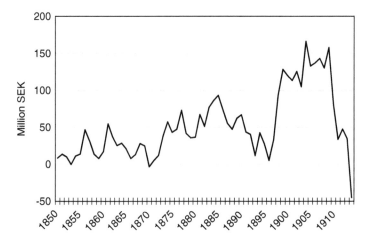

Figure 6.1 Sweden's capital imports, 1850–1913.

Source: Schön, 1989, p. 236.

utilities. Private railroad and industrial companies began to turn to the international market at the same time. Foreign borrowing increased in the 1870s and 1880s and virtually exploded after the Baring crisis in a wave that lasted until about 1910. The gap between the estimates by Schön relative to earlier studies, however, suggests that foreign borrowing must have been carried out by a wider range of actors and institutions and its uses must have been much wider than limited to infrastructure, public utilities, agricultural investments and urban housing construction.

The gold standard and capital imports

An indebtedness of this magnitude has proven difficult to sustain for many developing economies in the post-Bretton Woods world. There are, of course, many reasons why conditions for developing countries differ between the first and the present era of economic globalization. One important institution in international finance and trade is, of course, the International Monetary System. The stability provided by the international gold standard between the 1870s and the First World War is seen as one of the advantageous conditions for international capital movements and development. The symmetry and absence of currency risks, provided by the international gold standard, created an integrated and elastic international capital market that allowed funds to flow from developed to developing economies, without 'sudden stops' in the supply of funds, provided that investments led to growth and development and an increase in the receiving nation's ability to service its foreign debts (Schön, 2012, pp. 75–6). Recent studies have demonstrated that relatively larger shares of international capital flows went from developed to developing economies during the 'first' than during the present 'second era of globalization' from about 1990 until the 2010s (Schularick, 2006; Schularick and Steiger, 2010). Financial crises were not rare, but they did not deteriorate into currency or twin crises – at least not in core countries or the North-Western European or North American peripheries (Eichengreen, 1996, p. 39). On the other hand, it has been shown that when developing countries did suffer financial crises during the gold standard, it took longer for these countries to reach the pre-crisis growth rates, compared with the developing countries' resilience during the current era of globalization. However, Canada, Australia and the Scandinavian countries were exceptions and the reason given is that these countries had well-developed financial systems and credit markets (Bordo and Meissner, 2007a). This makes re-examining the Swedish case worthwhile.

Sweden transitioned from a silver standard into a gold standard and a Scandinavian Monetary Union with Denmark and Norway in the 1870s. In practice, a gold standard implies that a government makes gold coin legal tender and orders its central bank or other note-issuing institutions to redeem banknotes in gold (either coin or bullion). By maintaining convertibility, the value of money (metal and paper) is attached to the value of the minted metal. If other countries also tie their currencies to gold, an international gold standard such as the one that prevailed between the 1870s and 1914 is established. Since participating countries in practice use the same currency unit, expressed in weight of gold – and if gold is allowed to flow freely between nations – the exchange rates between different currencies in practice become fixed. Normally, however, transactions between countries were carried out with bills of exchange that were traded on foreign exchange markets. Under the gold standard the variations in foreign exchange rates were limited by 'gold points', which were determined by the transaction costs for using gold instead of normal payment or credit instruments since these could be substituted by gold if the exchange rates deviated more than could be absorbed by the transaction costs. By 1880, most countries in Europe and North America were on gold and in 1900 most of the world had gone to gold, creating a large international standard that would prove to last longer than any other international currency arrangement in modern times. The development of foreign exchange rates in Sweden between 1803 and 1914 is displayed in Figure 6.2. There is a clear difference in exchange rate movements between the gold standard (1873–1914) and the suspension period (fiat standard, 1809–1834) and the silver standard (1834–1872).

The fixed exchange rates and transmission of international prices during the gold standard may also have had implications for the particular pattern of transformation of the Swedish economy in the 1880s and 1890s. Although linkage to gold gave exchange rates and price levels a degree of stability, there was a deflationary trend during what has been called the 'Long' or 'Great' Depression between the mid-1870s and the mid-1890s. The deflation was a result of the integration of the world economy, but also a result of the broad transition to the gold standard, which created a demand for monetary gold, driving up the price of gold and thus putting a downward pressure on the price level. In the 1890s, gold production increased dramatically so that the gold supply could keep up with or even supersede demand. This gave prices a weakly rising trend which turned to war inflation after 1914. The deflationary period was difficult for large parts of the Swedish economy. Falling prices and crisis tendencies affected established industries, such as sawmills, iron producers and agriculture. Exchange rates were fixed and thus offered no relief for the declining industries, which instead managed to persuade the government to increase custom duties. However, there were other aspects of this development, according to Schön (2012, pp. 80, 101–11, 123–6). Deflation allowed real wages to rise thereby creating an increasing demand for consumer goods. Massive capital imports in this period were channelled into the creation of new industries and investments in new technologies, such as paper and pulp, steel production, and electrical production, distribution and equipment, thereby laying the foundation for a transformation and industrial breakthrough in the decades before the First World War.

Sources of gold standard stability

Besides its obvious symmetry and the fact that the pre-war gold standard was a relatively peaceful period, the automatic adjustment mechanisms are often seen as the source of the exceptional and long period of international monetary stability. It was – and often still is – thought that international flows in gold bullion or

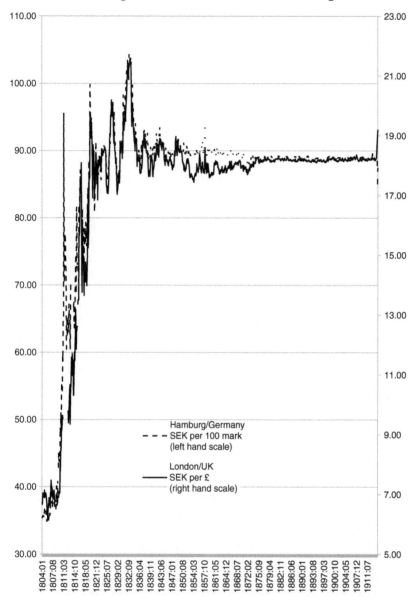

Figure 6.2 Stockholm exchange rates of bills payable in Hamburg and London, monthly 1804–1914.

Source: Lobell, 2010.

money automatically levelled out imbalances in money supply, and implicitly price levels, resembling Hume's *price specie flow mechanism* if central banks played according to what Keynes characterized as the *rules of the gold standard game* (Eichengreen, 1996, pp. 28–32).[1] In reality, however, the gold standard did not work in the previously perceived manner. It has been shown that international gold flows had little to do with adjustment and that central banks did not follow 'rules' as they had been outlined in retrospect by Keynes and others. Modern interpretations from a rational expectation viewpoint instead claim that confidence and capital flows were the keys to stability. A credible commitment to gold convertibility signalled 'A good housekeeping seal of approval' (Bordo and Rockoff, 1996), which gave access to foreign funds, but also at considerably lower costs than if a country/currency was off gold. It even resulted in stabilizing international currency speculation and capital flows, according to another influential interpretation (Bordo and Kydland, 1995). These conditions also resulted in at least some leeway for monetary policy, which explains subsequent observations of frequent and more or less systematic violations of the rules of the gold standard game that have been acknowledged by a large number of studies ranging from Bloomfield (1959) to Ögren (2010, 2011). However, it is argued by Lobell (2000) that this type of monetary dynamics cannot be the most obvious characterization of how the system and its adjustment mechanism worked during much of the nineteenth century. Prior to the 1860s – Sweden entered the gold standard in 1873 – adjustment and responses to international shocks on goods and credit markets appear to have been accommodated by pro-cyclical flows of specie money, bullion and thereby associated domestic monetary expansions and contractions. In the Swedish case, regularly recurring external specie and bullion flows accompanied international business cycles and crises until the late 1850s. Thereafter, the switches between inflows and outflows of precious metals appear to have ceased, implying that either the shocks to the external balance were milder or that different external adjustment mechanisms were at work (see Figure 6.3). The outflows detected in the 1870s can largely be attributed to silver payments in exchange for gold during the transition from a silver to a gold standard. There appears to have been only some comparatively moderate gold exports in connection with the Baring crisis in the early 1890s. Apart from that, the national bank, the *Riksbank*, was able to accumulate gold reserves despite large and persistent current account deficits. The monetary system and credit markets were thus able to maintain and create liquidity due to access to foreign funds, channelled by a more sophisticated and integrated financial system.

A key feature of specie standards concerns the connection between the central bank's reserves of specie and bullion and money supply. As displayed by Figure 6.3 and Figure 6.4a–c, the relation between these reserves and money supply also appears to have changed with the implementation of gold. This detachment between silver and gold holdings and the money supply coincided with the growth, integration and expansion of the Swedish banking and financial system, which Ögren and Sylla (2010) have characterized as nothing less than a financial revolution. Thereby, both prerequisites for a specie standard, as modelled by Bordo and Rockoff (1996) and Bordo and Kydland (1995), a credible commitment to gold convertibility and the existence of a liquid, integrated and elastic financial system, appear to have become fulfilled.

A related problem facing many capital importing, developing countries today, which has been highlighted in recent years, is the fact that they cannot borrow

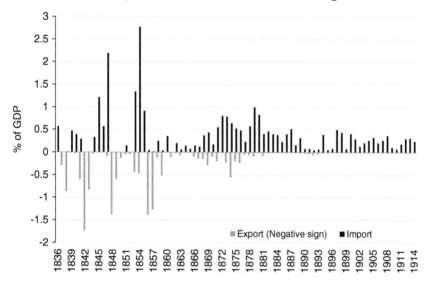

Figure 6.3 Sweden's import and export of specie and bullion as per cent of GDP, 1836–1914.

Source: Calculations based on Commerse-kollegii Underdåniga Berättelser on Sveriges utrikeshandel och sjöfart. BiSOS Litt. F. Utrikeshandel och sjöfart, Swedish Historical National Accounts 1560–2010. Schön and Krantz, 2012, available on Economic History Data website, Lund University, and Lobell, 2000, p. 205.

internationally in their own currency. The subsequent currency mismatch, sometimes referred to as the 'Original Sin' problem, has repeatedly been a source of volatility, crisis and interruptions in economic development. Original Sin limits the effectiveness of monetary policy since exchange rate changes have wealth effects for net borrowing developing countries, as foreign currency denominated debt will change in terms of domestic currency if the exchange rate changes. Wealth effects, thus, may offset any positive effects of the developing country's competitiveness. Moreover, since international financial market participants are aware of this problem, they will add a premium and also be more inclined to withdraw funds in cases of shocks to the external balance, or other sources of loss of confidence in the government's or central bank's capability to maintain currency stability, since it increases the risk of fiscal insolvency and default. Of course, a risk of capital flight will in itself increase the risk of a currency depreciation and default. Original Sin thus increases the incentive of central banks to introduce hard pegs and pursue tight monetary and fiscal policies (Bordo *et al.*, 2010; Bordo and Meissner, 2007b; Eichengreen and Hausmann, 2005).

The problem of Original Sin does not appear to lie in conditions in the borrowing, usually developing, country, but rather in the structure of the international capital market. Not even extremely 'well-behaved' developing countries, whose currency should enjoy confidence in the international market, such as Korea as a notable example, are able to borrow in their own currency. In a survey of capital markets in the nineteenth century, Flandreau and Sussman (2005)

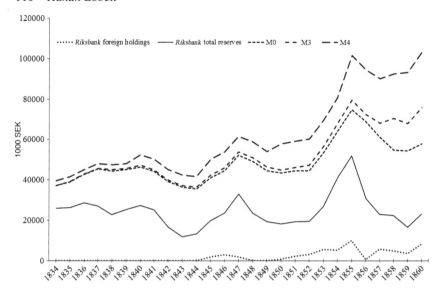

Figure 6.4a Composition of money and specie reserves, 1834–1860.

Source: Appendix, Ögren, 2003.

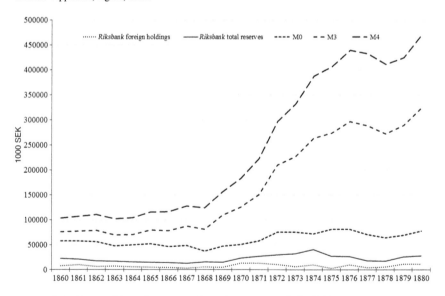

Figure 6.4b Composition of money and specie reserves, 1860–1880.

Source: Appendix, Ögren, 2003.

found that approximately the same conditions applied then as now. They found little correlation between countries with 'good institutions' and a stable, convertible currency, and countries that in fact could borrow in international financial centres in their own currency. However, Flandreau and Sussman found a perfect

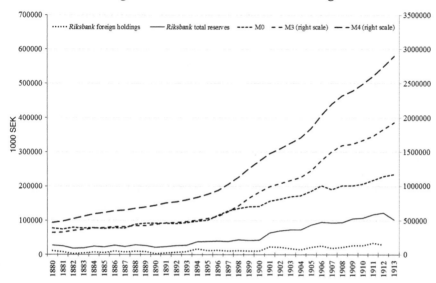

Figure 6.4c Composition of money and specie reserves, 1880–1913.

Source: Appendix, Ögren, 2003.

correlation between those countries whose currencies were viable internationally and that could borrow long term in their own currency, notwithstanding, of course, the countries with international key or vehicle currencies, Britain, France and Germany.

One can, of course, consider whether borrowing in a foreign currency was an equally dangerous problem for developing economies on gold, since countries, in practice, applied the same currency as the underlying basis for each country's currency. Nevertheless, the part of Swedish bond loans raised abroad was exclusively denominated in one or several international gold-based key currencies depending on which market they were marketed in (Franzén, 1998). From a Swedish perspective, however, this may have been of less significance because domestic crises of confidence, suspended specie payments and currency devaluations themselves would have been regarded as catastrophic events long before international borrowing became of significance. Overall, the incidence of capital flight and 'hot money' was much less significant under the gold standard than in the later era of globalization (see, for example, Eichengreen, 1996).

The remainder of this chapter examines the Swedish monetary authorities' commitment to maintaining currency stability, by describing the development of monetary and exchange policies from the resumption of the silver standard in 1834 until and including the gold standard. It assesses how Sweden, and in particular the *Riksbank*, managed currency convertibility, especially during international crises and recessions. The policy developments are related to capital imports along with the development and integration of the financial system.

Development of currency policies between the 'realization' in 1834 and the crisis of 1857

Sweden entered the nineteenth century with a paper standard after silver convertibility had been cancelled in 1789 in connection with the war against Russia. In 1803, specie payments were resumed, but were again suspended in 1809 during the Napoleonic wars, the war with Russia and the deposition of the king. After the wars followed a long period of preparation and political and theoretical battles about a return to the silver standard, which ended in the resumption of silver payments through the so-called 'realization' in September 1834. The *Riksdag* adopted laws to force the *Riksbank* to maintain convertibility as the primary objective. It was explained in the first paragraphs that convertibility of banknotes in silver at a certain rate was the foundation of the monetary system and the principal target for the *Riksbank*.[2]

It is of course only natural that a hard peg between currencies, in this case the domestic bank notes and domestically, but internationally, viable silver coins, is declared in an equally strict manner since the value of paper money is dependent on public confidence. During the period with paper currency that preceded the realization, the advantages and disadvantages of the silver standard and proposals for alternative solutions with a paper currency were discussed. The debate in Sweden resembled in many ways the somewhat earlier so-called 'bullionist controversy' in England. One difference, however, was that in Sweden a 'fund theory' approach was more prominent. According to the fund theory, the value of paper and bank-created money was dependent on public confidence that the notes could be redeemed in 'genuine coin', i.e. in metallic currency, which was thought to have, if not an inherent, at least an international value. In this context, the *Riksbank*'s reserves of precious metal became a key variable in the monetary system. It prompted widespread debate on whether the silver reserve was large enough to justify the resumption of silver payments without risking a run on the bank. Together with a power struggle between the king and the *Riksdag* for power over the *Riksbank*, this debate most likely delayed the implementation until 1834.

Once the silver standard was in place in 1834, it managed to survive until the transition to the gold standard and the Scandinavian Monetary Union with Denmark in 1873, joined by Norway in 1875. Overall, the specie standard lasted a full 80 years until it was suspended in connection with the outbreak of the First World War in 1914. The period up to the gold standard's implementation would prove, however, to be lined by international crises that tested the monetary system and the *Riksbank*'s ability to maintain the specie standard.

Already, after three years, economic conditions had deteriorated in Europe and a deep crisis had developed in the United States, which affected the Swedish export of staple goods, including fairly extensive iron exports to North America. Declining export earnings led to rising prices of foreign currencies on the foreign exchange market, which at that time carried on mainly at the Stockholm stock exchange. Foreign trade payments were made almost exclusively with bills of exchange payable in foreign financial centres and in their currencies, but predominantly in Hamburg and with the currency Hamburg banco. As trade deficits propagated to the foreign exchange market, the price of foreign currency rose and eventually reached the specie export point, where it became profitable instead to redeem bank notes for silver at the *Riksbank* and carry out payments abroad in silver instead of foreign currency. Thus arose outflows of silver at current account deficits and high exchange rates, as was the case to quite a large extent in the years 1837 and 1838 (Figures 6.2 and 6.3).[3]

An interesting feature in this context is that silver rarely flowed spontaneously into the country during favourable economic conditions and external balances accompanied by low foreign exchange rates. Instead the *Riksbank* itself imported silver as soon as the exchange rate had fallen down to parity.[4] Silver coins exported to international financial and trading centres were ordinarily melted down. The *Riksbank* therefore imported silver bullion, which then had to be coined into domestic currency, with all the costs it entailed. The bank regarded this as 'buy-backs' aimed at 'restoring' its reserves of specie and bullion (Lobell, 2000, pp. 219–20).

In the early 1840s, Sweden suffered further shocks to the external balance, which this time seems to have had more difficult consequences. A continental recession was coupled with an extraordinary event: the entire stock of Swedish riksdaler paper currency in the former Swedish province of Finland was transferred to the *Riksbank* for redemption in silver with the aim of creating a new currency system in the then Russian, but relatively autonomous, province. Furthermore, extensive arbitrage with the *Riksbank*'s stock of Spanish piastres took place due to high rates in East Asia. This gave rise to a substantial monetary tightening, although one can assume that the outflows of silver to Finland and Asia should not have had any domestic effects other than the *Riksbank*'s reserves falling to a minimum. Since certain branches of *Riksbank* lending continued despite the export of silver, however, the stock of banknotes finally exceeded the legal ratio between reserves and notes in circulation, which caused concern among policymakers and commentators. As a result of the currency crisis, but also influenced by the contemporary debate in England, the *Riksbank*'s policy was tightened considerably. The new regime reflected orthodoxy in many ways similar to that in England with the Bank Charter Act of 1844 (Lobell, 2006a).

As paper money was redeemed in silver, intended to be primarily used in payments abroad or, what seems to have been rarer, arbitrage, domestic money supply contracted to almost the same degree (cf. Figure 6.4a). Although the *Riksbank* had a certain margin, i.e. unused note issue rights, which could be used to cushion the impact on money supply, outflows are likely to have brought considerable tightening in credit markets. It is important to note in this context that the *Riksbank* at this time was not a central bank in the modern sense. The *Riksbank* also pursued commercial activities and did not see it as their responsibility to safeguard the banking system's liquidity. The bank, however, did its best to not unnecessarily tighten the domestic money market. On the other hand, the few at this time existing note-issuing unlimited liability bank companies based their note issuing and credit on reserves of *Riksbank* currency, which served as an additional liquidity buffer, according to Ögren (2006). Nonetheless, the *Riksbank* managed to achieve the main goal for the entire period, in contrast to the Bank of England, which was forced to temporarily suspend specie payments on several occasions.

Additional external disturbances in connection with political unrest and a widespread financial crisis across Europe affected Sweden in the late 1840s, resulting in a drastic reduction of exports, while at the same time the credit market conditions in international financial centres deteriorated or completely ceased. Nor at this point did the *Riksbank* suspend silver payments despite widespread export of silver and draining of its reserves until conditions improved in the summer of 1849. The drain resulted in a drastic monetary tightening and again voices were raised for reform. Contrary to a growing body of opinion, however, the *Riksdag* chose to constitutionally protect convertibility. Instead, focus was on improving the efficiency of the credit and banking system as a means to avoid the recurring liquidity crises. It was attempted in the Swedish case, among other things, and as in England at this time, to strike a blow against the private note-issuing banking companies by introducing non-note-issuing so-called 'branch banks' (*Filialbanker*), as well as attempting to create conditions for a functioning domestic bill market.

Developments after the crisis in 1857

The crisis in 1857 was in many ways a turning point. The international crisis broke out after the Crimean War and was one of the most intense in history. After the economic boom and monetary expansion during the war there followed a correspondingly sharp monetary contraction as the international economy slipped into recession. The recession and the international liquidity crisis led to a full-blown financial crisis in Sweden during the winter of 1857/1858. The *Riksbank* tried for some time, against regulations and despite fears of convertibility suspension, to support credit market liquidity (Ögren, 2010, pp. 80–1). As soon as international conditions improved, the National Debt Office precipitated a railway loan abroad, known as the 'emergency loan' in 1858, which was used to relieve the distressed domestic credit markets. Moreover, the *Riksbank* tried on this occasion, for the first time, to accommodate liquidity support with interest rate increases. Interest rates had hitherto been fixed, regardless of the situation regarding external trade and credit market conditions.

After the crisis in 1857, however, a somewhat paradoxical development followed when the *Riksbank*'s policies developed in an almost opposite direction to the established orthodox thinking. In the debate preceding the realization, relatively sophisticated ideas about a pure paper standard were expressed and an anti-bullionist opposition saw the obsession with precious metal convertibility as a remnant of medieval conceptions. During the 1840s, a more orthodox approach came to dominate monetary thinking, and its application through the so-called 'currency principle'[5] had an impact on legislation in Sweden, as it had in England at about the same time (Lobell, 2006a). Alternative ideas successively disappeared in public and parliamentary debates and finally seemed to have died out during the 1850s. By that time, silver convertibility and the *Riksbank*'s reserve had reached an uncontested status as the foundation for the monetary system. That approach lasted at least until Knut Wicksell presented alternative monetary theories in 1898. His ideas were far too premature and it would be a long time before they were implemented in practice. Even Wicksell himself believed that gold was the safest foundation for a currency system (Wicksell, 1966).

However, the *Riksbank* left, or was forced to leave, the strict application of the currency principle. The bank began to thin out the silver and later the gold reserves with bills of exchange in international key currencies that were considered as good as silver/gold, i.e. pounds, francs and thalers/marks. For a period during the 1870s and 1880s, the bank, moreover, counted bonds issued in key international currencies in the metallic reserve. The bank also began using currency operations in an effort to counter redemption of notes into metal currency and subsequent export. Selling foreign currencies was regarded as more cost-efficient than allowing precious metal to be exported, since the bank subsequently would have to import again and mint in order to maintain its reserves within the legal limits. The *Riksbank*'s illegitimate interest rate increase during the crisis in 1857 was also the start of a trend towards a more systematic interest rate policy, as illustrated in Figure 6.5. In short, international flows of precious metal were replaced by money market operations and interest rate changes, thereby resembling more and more a 'gold exchange standard' (see, for example, Lobell, 2000; Ögren, 2010).

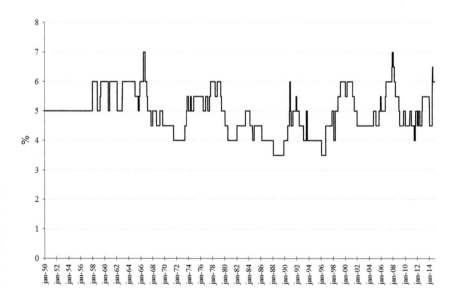

Figure 6.5 Riksbank official discount rate, 1850–1914.

Source: Sveriges Riksbank, 1931, Del V. *Statistiska tabeller.*

Before the crisis in 1857, there is little evidence that the *Riksbank* would have prevented the redemption of paper currency in silver despite the bank and the parliament repeatedly being concerned that the *Riksbank*'s reserves were running dry. This was the case during the crises in 1843/1844 and 1848/1849. The question is whether the *Riksbank* declined the redemption of banknotes for silver during the crisis in 1857. There is little direct evidence that it did. A circumstance indicating some kind of obstruction against redemption of bank notes, however, is that the exchange rate of foreign currencies rose far above what must have been the location of the silver export point (Lobell, 2006b). This could indicate that the silver export point had been made ineffective and a likely explanation would then be that the bank prevented redemption. On the other hand, the prices of foreign exchange were peaking during winter when transaction costs of silver exports may have been particularly high due to icy conditions, possibly preventing or hampering shipping between Stockholm and the continental financial centres.

A single concrete example of the *Riksbank* openly obstructing the redemption of banknotes and export of silver is when *Stockholms Enskilda Bank* requested to withdraw silver intended for a payment in Hamburg in the 1860s. However, the *Riksbank* solely paid out silver in worn and clipped coins at par value, which according to their weight did not correspond to the value of silver. The incident is known since it led to a rather fierce exchange in the newspapers (Lobell, 2000). However, the *Riksbank* had increased their efforts, as stated on p. 115, to try to replace the precious metal transactions with foreign bills and securities, which were considered as good as silver or gold if the bills were denominated in a key currency and issued by first-class banks. There is, to our knowledge, no further evidence that the *Riksbank* would later have actively thwarted redemption and export, but the example, even if it was caused by special circumstances, fits at first glance into the pattern of how the *Riksbank*'s currency operations developed during this stage.

In this context, of course, institutions and the symmetry with the outside world were important from the viewpoint of credibility. Developments in, at this time, peripheral Sweden were not entirely different from those of other comparable countries. Credit and financial institutions in Sweden were not even very far behind those in the more advanced economies in the developed core. The gap that still existed was picked up at a relatively fast pace in the period up to 1914. The new domestic and international monetary conditions are probably an important reason why Sweden relatively quickly switched to a gold standard and the Scandinavian Monetary Union in 1873. From a Swedish perspective, in the late 1860s there existed network externalities indicating that Sweden had much to gain from joining the international movement towards the gold standard. It was believed that silver would be destined to depreciate and become unstable if many countries transitioned to the gold standard, which would, of course, have resulted in less monetary stability had Sweden remained on the silver standard.

The development and integration of the payment and banking system, foreign borrowing and the *Riksbank*

The emergence of banking companies and savings banks occurred comparatively early in Sweden. The first savings banks were founded already in the 1820s and in the 1830s commercial banking companies were formed. These were unlimited liability companies that based their activities on equity capital and the issuance of banknotes. Lending was offered mostly against guarantees and mortgages. Deposits were a less important part and the domestic bill market was rather undeveloped, at least until the 1850s. The banking system's growth was moderate before the 1860s when modern deposit banks and joint stock limited liability credit companies started to emerge. Prior to the 1860s, the growth of the banking system was inhibited, for example, by the previously mentioned conflict between the king and the *Riksdag* about the influence over the *Riksbank* and the monetary system. Moreover, there was a reluctance against private banknote issuing among decision-makers, which was considered to potentially jeopardize currency convertibility (Lilja, 2010 and Table 6.1).

After the crisis in 1857, a reformation, expansion and transformation of the banking system began, which, as mentioned earlier, was considered to almost resemble a revolution. There was a wave of credit market re-regulation and liberalization in the 1860s which was particularly important for the major cities of Stockholm and Gothenburg. New corporate legislation allowed joint stock limited liability credit companies, usury laws were relaxed, and geographical restrictions of bank company establishment were eased. New credit instruments and banking practices attracted both banks and their customers to use bank deposits. A more formal and deepened clearing cooperation between banks created conditions that allowed a domestic market for bills of exchange to start to grow and expand. The expanding and integrating deposit banking system also produced conditions for the public and companies to use bills of exchange for payments and as credit instruments to a much larger extent. Taken together, this was an acceleration in the development of a modern banking system in Sweden, alongside an equally strong growth of the savings and postal savings banks which can be traced in Table 6.1. This development is also reflected in the broad money indicators in Figure 6.4b with M3, including commercial bank deposits and M4 savings bank deposits.

Simultaneously, there was also an international credit market integration. It has long been recognized that this development accelerated during the economic boom of the 1850s that also involved Sweden's credit markets. During the 1850s, however, it was not primarily banks that spearheaded the integration of international financial centres, but businessmen and merchant bankers. These actors made transactions on their own account, but also acted as agents for the Swedish banks on the international money market. Many of these actors were hit hard by the crisis in 1857. The newspaper *The Economist* once even claimed that the intensity of the crisis in 1857 had been caused by extensive so-called 'bill jobbing' in the Stockholm–Hamburg–London triangle.[6] An example is the so-called

Table 6.1 The number of banks and savings banks in Sweden, 1830–1910

	Savings banks	Savings banks offices	Post-savings bank offices	Commercial banks	Commercial banks offices
1830	25	25	—	—	—
1840	60	60	—	6	14
1850	86	90	—	8	25
1860	151	151	—	30	50
1870	234	234	—	36	136
1880	341	921	1575	44	205
1890	378	909	1942	43	190
1900	388	748	2652	67	269
1910	436	854	3245	80	625

Source: Lilja, 2010, p. 46.

'Holm disaster', a bankruptcy named after one of these actors, which drew several other older esteemed firms with it in the aftermath of the crisis in 1857. For existing and reorganized banks, as well as newly founded banks, in the 1860s it became important to establish international connections. In these years banks developed foreign exchange trading and brokering of international loans to the Swedish market. Thereby, the foreign exchange market developed from being dominated by stock exchanges to more of an interbank market, also supported by the *Riksbank*'s activities in the area (Lobell, 2010a, pp. 120–4).

The breakthrough of modern commercial banking during the 1860s and up until the First World War resulted in the money supply being decoupled from the *Riksbank*'s metallic reserves to an increasing extent during the period up to the First World War, as mentioned earlier and shown in Figure 6.4b,c on pp. 113–14. On top of the reserve currency and bullion piled more and more bank deposits and other financial instruments, bills, bonds and eventually company shares, which changed the whole dynamics of the credit market and the monetary system, and resulted in new conditions that the *Riksbank* had to accommodate.

International integration and the increasing long-term foreign borrowing were most likely crucial in this development. The National Debt Office's loan in 1858 became a prelude to the extensive capital imports that characterized the period up to the first decade of the twentieth century. It has been shown that the government institutions, the National Debt Office and the Swedish General Mortgage Bank, which accounted for a large part of public foreign borrowing, assisted a stable development of credit markets and the banking system in two important respects (Nygren, 1989; Schön, 1989). First, foreign borrowing certainly increased liquidity in the Swedish economy on a macro level. As banks that primarily had based their operations on note issuing increasingly evolved towards modern deposit banks, the expanding banking system could simultaneously expand liquidity and thereby deposits and lending via multiplier effects. Second, the National Debt Office and the Swedish General Mortgage Bank also more directly affected the stability of credit markets and the banking system due to their practice of investing the imported but not yet used funds in interest-bearing deposits. These operations were particularly important during times of crisis. Thus, these institutions functioned as a liquidity reserve, or lender of last resort, for the Swedish credit market on several occasions during the first part of the 1860s, between 1874 and 1878, in the mid-1880s and during the Baring crisis in the 1890s. These practices very likely eased crises and enabled a relatively steady expansion of the Swedish banking system until the *Riksbank* became a more reliable lender of last resort and pronounced central bank in the modern sense around the turn of the 1900s. Moreover, the National Debt Office obtained foreign loans with the sole purpose of mitigating the acute distress of the foreign exchange market in both 1878 and 1899, and again for the relief of the *Riksbank* when it was in a difficult position during the crisis in 1907 (Lindahl *et al.*, 1937, p. 273).

Currency mismatches

During this time of increasing foreign borrowing, the state or local government's long-term bond issues abroad were, as far as is known, exclusively carried out in foreign currencies, despite Sweden's long-standing adherence to a silver and later gold standard. Flandreau and Sussman (2005) reveal that Swedish bonds quoted in London and Paris were issued in key international currency, in several different currencies and with gold clauses until at least 1883. What distinguished countries that did get their bonds quoted in their domestic currency in international centres is that these countries had a working domestic bond market and an international market for bills of exchange in the domestic currency. A good institutional framework and macroeconomic stability seem to have been of lesser importance (Flandreau and Sussman, 2005, pp. 154–84). One such example is Russia, which quite early was able to borrow in its own currency.

In Sweden, however, a domestic market at the Stockholm Stock Exchange for both stocks and bonds became increasingly important as secondary markets in the 1870s and 1880s, and had its breakthrough in the decades before the First World War (Lindgren, 2010). With the emergence of a secondary market – though not in one of the leading financial centres – there is of course the possibility that Swedish bonds denominated in Swedish currency may have become attractive to foreign investors. Since there is a relatively large discrepancy between direct measures of external debt and the indirect measures by Lindahl *et al.* and Schön, it is likely that financial instruments other than those that were directly marketed abroad in key international currencies were attractive for foreign investors – including bonds intended for the domestic market and denominated in local currency. However, so far there is only some sporadic evidence suggesting this would have been the case. Thus, Schön quotes a contemporary source claiming that on one occasion 80 per cent of locally emitted bonds in domestic currency were found abroad when a conversion of an 1872 government bond loan was made in the 1880s (Schön, 1989, p. 232).

Similarly to bonds, Swedish payment and credit instruments, i.e. bills of exchange denominated in Swedish currency, were not viable either in international financial centres until the early 1880s. Up until then, international transactions had been conducted almost exclusively in foreign currency, i.e. bills of exchange drawn on banks or bankers in the financial centres. In 1882, bills of exchange, denominated in kronor and issued by Swedish banks, started to be quoted on the London, Paris and Hamburg stock exchanges. A functioning Swedish bill market had emerged only during the 1860s, in close liaison with the growth, diffusion and transformation of the banking system. Efforts for the establishment of a functioning domestic bill market had been made since at least the early 1840s. These efforts were partially linked to the silver standard and its rigid monetary supply, while it was believed that a functioning bill market would make the payment and credit system more efficient and thereby relieve credit markets of the often-perceived 'money shortages'. Bill legislation after the German pattern was adopted in 1852, but the domestic bill market did not take off until the Swedish banking system had been widened and integrated to make bills of exchange comfortable enough to use as credit instruments and means of payment (Lobell, 2010b). The domestic currency began to be quoted regularly in financial centres in the early 1880s, which can thus be seen as a sign that the Swedish credit market had reached a certain degree of maturity, integration and sophistication.

Figure 6.6 compares the call rates of Swedish, Danish and Norwegian bills denominated in the Scandinavian Monetary Union common currency kronor at the Hamburg Stock Exchange with the corresponding prices in Stockholm on bills drawn on Hamburg/Berlin and denominated in marks. The figure shows that the Scandinavian bills appear to have been charged with a not insignificant premium. This premium seems to have decreased over a considerable period of time. Not until the turn of the century does the trend of the price differential appear to have decayed and ceased. The premium might be explained by a relative insecurity in Hamburg concerning the Scandinavian credit market conditions. However, contrasting with the explanation that the premium was due to country-specific credit markets and other conditions is the fact that prices for Danish, Norwegian and Swedish currencies were highly correlated. This could indicate a common factor and it is, of course, easy to suspect that the common currency, the *krona*, did not enjoy the full confidence of the international market until around the turn of the 1900s.

Summary and conclusions

Sweden had its industrial breakthrough in the last decades before the First World War. In this process, extensive capital imports played an important role since the Swedish economy was able to utilize savings in the leading economies for investment while still maintaining domestic consumption, which influenced the pace, breadth and depth of industrialization. In this context, the international gold standard is of great significance since it facilitated and created stability both domestically and in international financial relations. Such conditions have often been lacking in the recent era of globalization, implying a constraint on

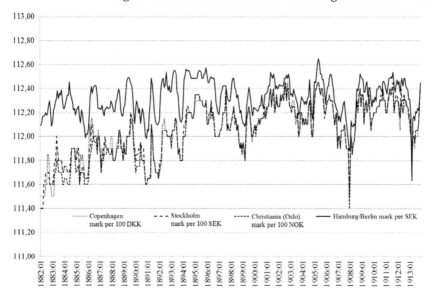

Figure 6.6 Exchange rates for Scandinavian bill of exchange in Hamburg compared with rates for Hamburg/Berlin bills in Stockholm, monthly 1882–1913.

Source: Lobell, 2010, p. 313.

the industrialization in developing countries. This chapter describes the long-term development of monetary and credit conditions up to and including the gold standard in a context of increasing foreign borrowing and from an international capital market perspective.

It is shown that the way in which the specie standard worked was changing in a very profound way during the transition to the gold standard. Throughout the preceding silver standard, regularly recurring external specie flows indicate that international financial flows played a subordinate role in external adjustment. By the 1860s, financial flows had begun playing an increasingly important role as a result of an increasing international integration and development of the domestic credit markets. The dynamics of Sweden's external monetary and financial relations changed accordingly, thereby gradually resembling the dynamics described in time consistency models of the gold standard. Metal money, gold, was at the same time gaining a more symbolic, but nevertheless important, role as the foundation of the system and signalling device.

Up to the 1850s, monetary and exchange rate policies were relatively passive, largely reflecting a belief that flows of metal currency induced automatic adjustment. The changing conditions more or less forced the *Riksbank* to adapt its policies to introduce a larger element of active monetary and credit market management, but without losing sight of its primary objective of the convertibility of paper money into specie at fixed rates. Swedish policymakers and the *Riksbank* were able to adapt to changing conditions; however, institutional and policy changes often ensued in the wake of monetary and financial crises, particularly in the aftermath of the crisis of 1857.

Besides market forces, however, there were more tangible elements of capital movements stabilizing the Swedish currency, the banking system and even the *Riksbank* on several occasions. The National Debt Office specifically took up foreign loans to support the Swedish foreign exchange market in some cases and to rescue the *Riksbank* in at least one instance. A price differential that existed between Swedish and German foreign exchanges for instruments in the respective currency also raises questions about how solid the Swedish gold standard currency really was. On the other hand, emergency loans, for instance during the severe international crisis in 1907, would scarcely have been possible without a credible commitment to reducing the exchange rate and country risks involved. The last hundred years since the gold standard show that not even the largest central banks are powerful enough to withstand capital flight if confidence in its currency is lost for one reason or another.

The process of development and integration of credit and capital markets further facilitated the international viability of Swedish financial instruments denominated in domestic currency. First, Swedish currency began to be traded in international financial centres in the early 1880s. Second, a liquid domestic capital market started to emerge, which probably made domestic bonds and shares in domestic currency more attractive internationally. There are also indications and evidence that domestically issued bonds found their way into the hands of international investors. Even though loans intended for foreign markets were exclusively issued in international key currencies, and Swedish bills of exchange quoted in international financial centres appear to have carried a premium until the turn of the century, these findings to some degree qualify the findings of Flandreau and Sussman (2005) that Sweden was among the 'well-behaved' developing countries on gold in the nineteenth century that could not borrow abroad in their own currency.

In this process, capital imports contributed to changing conditions by facilitating the development and integration of modern credit and financial markets, thereby changing the dynamics of Sweden's monetary system as well as external financial relationships to which monetary policy and the *Riksbank*'s management practices had to be adapted. A growing foreign debt increased the incentive to maintain the hard peg between the domestic currency and gold in order to maintain confidence, since rapidly growing domestic credit markets and the foreign debt diminished the actual stock of gold in relative terms. Thus, capital imports contributed to a dynamic economic development and at the same time to a complex interaction and dynamic development of the financial system and monetary policies during the gold standard.

Notes

1 See McKinnon (1993).
2 'Lag angående Myntbestämningen' and 'Lag för Rikets Ständers Bank' in 1830.
3 See a comprehensive theoretical and empirical analysis of commodity points and flows of specie and bullion in Officer (1996).

4 Mint parity under a specie standard represents the number of foreign currency units in terms of domestic currency corresponding to the same weight in terms of monetary metal.
5 The 'currency principle' asserts that a mixed monetary system with specie, paper money and banks should be designed to operate as if it consisted solely of specie.
6 'A Lesson for the Future,' *The Economist*, 2 January 1858.

References

Ahlström, G. (1989), 'Riksgäldskontoret och Sveriges statsskuld före 1850-talet'. In Dahmén (ed.) *Upplåning och utveckling. Riksgäldskontoret 1789–1989*. Stockholm: Allmänna förlaget.
Bloomfield, A. J. (1959), *Monetary Policy under the International Gold Standard: 1880–1914*. New York: Federal Reserve Bank of New York.
Bordo, M. and Kydland, F. E. (1995), 'The Gold Standard as a Rule: An Essay in Exploration', *Explorations in Economic History*, vol. 32, pp. 423–64.
Bordo, M. and Rockoff, H. (1996), 'The Gold Standard as a "Good Housekeeping Seal of Approval"', *Journal of Economic History*, vol. 56, pp. 389–428.
Bordo, M. D. and Meissner, C. (2007a), 'Foreign Capital and Economic Growth in the First Era of Globalization', *NBER Working Paper 13577*.
Bordo, M. D. and Meissner, C. (2007b), 'Financial Crises, 1880–1913: The Role of Foreign Currency Debt'. In Edwards, S., Esquivel, G. and Marquéz, G. (eds) *The Decline of Latin American Economies: Growth, Institutions, and Crises*. NBER: University of Chicago Press.
Bordo, M. D., Meissner, C. and Stuckler, D. (2010), 'Foreign Currency Debt, Financial Crises and Economic Growth: A Long-run View', *Journal of International Money and Finance*, vol. 29, pp. 642–65.
Eichengreen, B. (1996), *Globalizing Capital. A History of the International Monetary System*. Princeton: Princeton University Press.
Eichengreen, B. and Hausmann, R. (eds) (2005), *Other People's Money. Debt Denomination and Financial Instability in Emerging Market Economies*. Chicago: University of Chicago Press.
Flandreau M. and Sussman N. (2005), 'Old Sins'. In Eichengreen, B. and Hausmann, R. (eds) *Other People's Money. Debt Denomination and Financial Instability in Emerging Market Economies*. Chicago: University of Chicago Press.
Flodström, I. (1912), *Sveriges nationalförmögenhet omkring år 1908 och dess utveckling sedan midten av 1880-talet*. Finansstatistiska utredningar V. Stockholm.
Franzén, C. (1998), *Skuld och tanke. Svensk statsskuldsproblematik i ett internationellt perspektiv före 1930-talet*. Stockholm: Almqvist & Wiksell International (diss.).
Krantz, O. and Schön, L. (2007), *Swedish Historical National Accounts 1800–2000*. Lund Studies in Economic History, 41.
Lilja, K. (2010), 'The Deposit Market Revolution in Sweden'. In Ögren, A. (ed.) *The Swedish Financial Revolution*. Basingstoke: Palgrave MacMillan.
Lindahl, E., Dahlgren, E. and Kock, K. (1937), *National Income of Sweden, 1861–1930*. 2 vols. London: P. S. King.
Lindgren, H. (2010), 'The Evolution of Secondary Markets, 1820–1920'. In Ögren, A. (ed.) *The Swedish Financial Revolution*. Basingstoke: Palgrave MacMillan.
Ljungberg, J. and Schön, L. (2013), 'Domestic Markets and International Integration: Paths to Industrialisation in the Nordic Countries', *Scandinavian Economic History Review*, vol. 61, pp. 101–21.

124   *Håkan Lobell*

Lobell, H. (2000), *Växelkurspolitik och Marknadsintegration. De utländska växelkurserna i Sverige*. Lund Studies in Economic History, 14. (diss.).

Lobell, H. (2006a), 'Institutions, Events and Theory. A Comparison of the Monetary Policy Shifts of 1844/45 in England and Sweden.' *Lund Papers in Economic History, 102.*

Lobell, H. (2006b), 'The Range of Stockholm-Hamburg and Stockholm-London Specie Points 1834–1880,' *Vierteljahrschrift für Sozial- und Wirtschaftsgeschichte*, vol. 93, pp. 304–21.

Lobell, H. (2010a), 'Financial Market Integration, 1830–1890'. In Ögren, A. (ed.) *The Swedish Financial Revolution*. Basingstoke: Palgrave MacMillan.

Lobell, H. (2010b), 'Foreign Exchange Rates 1804–1914'. In Edvinsson, R., Jacobson, T. and Waldenström, D. (eds) *Historical Monetary and Financial Statistics for Sweden. Exchange Rates, Prices and Wages, 1277–2008*. Stockholm: Ekerlids.

McKinnon, R. I. (1993), 'The Rules of the Game: International Money in Historical Perspective', *Journal of Economic Literature*, vol. 31, pp. 1–44.

Nygren, I. (1989), 'När lång upplåning blev korta krediter 1840-1905'. In Dahmén, E. (ed.) *Upplåning och utveckling. Riksgäldskontoret 1789-1989*. Stockholm.

Officer, L. H. (1996), *Between the Dollar-Sterling Gold Points*. Cambridge: Cambridge University Press.

Ögren, A. (2003), *Empirical Studies in Money, Banking and Credit. The Swedish Credit Market in Transition under the Silver and Gold Standards, 1834–1913*. Stockholm School of Economics (diss.).

Ögren, A. (2006), 'Free or Central Banking? Liquidity and Financial Deepening in Sweden, 1834–1913', *Explorations in Economic History*, vol. 43, pp. 64–93.

Ögren, A. (ed.) (2010), *The Swedish Financial Revolution*. Basingstoke: Palgrave MacMillan.

Ögren, A. (2011), 'Central Banking and Monetary Policy in Sweden during the Long Nineteenth Century'. In Ögren, A. and Øksendal, L. F. (eds) *The Gold Standard Peripheries. Monetary Policy, Adjustment and Flexibility in a Global Setting*. Basingstoke: Palgrave Macmillan.

Ögren, A. and Sylla, R. (2010), 'What can we Learn from the Swedish Financial Revolution: An International Comparison'. In Ögren, A. (ed.) *The Swedish Financial Revolution*. Basingstoke: Palgrave MacMillan.

Schön, L. (1989), 'Kapitalimport, kreditmarknad och industrialisering 1840–1905'. In Dahmén, E. (ed) (1989), *Upplåning och utveckling. Riksgäldskontoret 1789-1989*. Stockholm: Riksgäldskontoret.

Schön, L. (1997), 'Internal and External Factors in Swedish Industrialization', *Scandinavian Economic History Review*, vol. 45, pp. 209–23.

Schön, L. (2007), 'Capital Movements, Exchange Rates and Market Integration: The Baltic Area 1870–1913'. In Cottrell, P. L., Lange, E. and Olsson, U. (eds) *Centres and Peripheries in Banking. The Historical Development of Financial Markets*. Ashgate, Hampshire.

Schön, L. (2012), *An Economic History of Modern Sweden*. Oxon: Routledge.

Schön, L. and Krantz, O. (2012), 'Swedish Historical National Accounts 1560–2010', *Lund Papers in Economic History, 123*.

Schularick, M. (2006), 'A Tale of Two "Globalizations": Capital Flows from Rich to Poor in Two Eras of Global Finance', *International Journal of Finance & Economics*, vol. 11, pp. 339–54.

Schularick, M. and Steiger, T. M. (2010), 'Financial Integration, Investment, and Economic Growth: Evidence from Two Eras of Financial Globalization', *Review of Economics and Statistics*, vol. 92, pp. 756–68.

Sveriges Riksbank (1931), *Statistiska tabeller. Sveriges Riksbank 1668–1924. Bankens tillkomst och verksamhet*, Del V. Stockholm: Nordstedts.

Wicksell, K. (1966), In Sommarin E. (ed.) *Föreläsningar i Nationalekonomi*. 5th ed. Lund: Gleerups.

7 The development of economic growth and inequality among the Swedish regions 1860–2010

Evidence from regional national accounts

Kerstin Enflo and Martin Henning

History is a core aspect in the analysis of spatial patterns of economic growth. Long-term perspectives lend themselves well to understanding the nature of the regional economic growth process. A core question is whether economic growth follows a linear process, or whether criticalities in the form of economic crises and the introduction of new generic technologies can be interpreted as meaningful events of technological and institutional transformation which are endogenous to the capitalist system. The latter view has received recent attention from advocates of evolutionary economic geography who champion a 'view of evolution in which episodes of relative stability or gradualism alternate with major shocks or "criticalities" that shift the system to a new configuration and phase of relative stability or gradualism' (Boschma and Martin, 2007, p. 543). While gradual change was indeed also central to Schumpeter's (for example 1939) understanding of the economy, so were episodes of more dramatic transformation and creative destruction (Boschma and Martin, 2007; Svensson Henning, 2009). Some scholars have even argued that the growth process is not only marked by alternating periods of stability and crisis, but also is cyclical in nature. For example, the structural analysis of Lennart Schön (2006, 2012) follows in the footsteps of Schumpeter by emphasizing that periods of creative destruction are followed by periods of stability and the formation of development blocks. The pattern is a cyclical process of crisis, transformation, rationalization and crisis. The structural crisis marks the demarcation of the industrial cycles, as they occur once a cycle has come to maturity. At the same time, structural crises start new cycles by opening opportunities for innovation, and pave the way for new growth paradigms or even entire industrial revolutions (see Schön, 2012).

Previous contributions have investigated the geographical patterns of the most recent industrial cycle, from the 1970s and onwards, through detailed industry and regional decompositions of national growth patterns (Lundquist and Olander, 2001; Lundquist *et al.*, 2008; Henning *et al.*, this volume). This chapter takes a longer-time perspective and analyses the long-run evolution of regional disparities in Sweden over more than 140 years. For the analysis, we use a data set, the Swedish Regional National Accounts, which we have developed as a regional equivalent to the Swedish Historical National Accounts (SHNA) (Schön, 1988, 1995; Krantz and Schön, 2007; Schön and Krantz, 2012a). The construction of the data set draws on a method that has gained wide acceptance in the economic history literature (Geary and Stark, 2002) and has proven to yield precise results for a variety of countries, such as England (Crafts, 2005), Spain (Rosés *et al.*, 2010), Italy (Felice, 2011) and Belgium (Buyst, 2010). The Swedish regional data set has been published and discussed elsewhere (Enflo *et al.*, 2014a; Henning *et al.*, 2011).

We will be primarily concerned with three variables for analysing the stability and change of economic activities in the Swedish regions: regional GDP, regional GDP per capita, and population. The use of regional GDPs will show how concentration versus dispersion of economic production evolves over time, while regional GDPs per capita are analysed to measure production per inhabitant in the regions. This will be compared with the regional distribution of population in Sweden, as migration and population changes are important historical mirrors of spatial redistribution of economic activities.

Sweden is an interesting case study for historical analyses on changes in geographical patterns of production. It has a characteristic geography of scarcely populated but resource-rich regions in the north, whereas the major population centres, such as the largest cities of Stockholm, Göteborg (Gothenburg) and Malmö, are all located in the southern half of the country. In addition, the Swedish production capacity has been relatively insulated from wars and major natural disasters during the period investigated. Also, during the period analysed in our study, no major changes in the definitions of the 'regions' have taken place.

An account of the related literature and the Swedish empirical context will be followed by a discussion of the construction of our data set and the measurement techniques we use. Thereafter we account for and discuss the empirical findings. After discussing the caveats of our study and specificities connected to the Swedish case, we conclude by making a few suggestions for an enlarged historical research agenda around the dimensions of structural analysis and economic geography.

The Swedish growth experience from a regional perspective

Over the last 150 years, the Swedish economy has undergone dramatic changes in terms of economic growth and improvements in standards of living. Whether such growth has taken place in a linear fashion or in a stepwise fashion with certain periods involving great leaps in terms of technology and societal transformation is a question that has lured economic historians for decades. There is a long tradition of emphasizing the discontinuous nature of the growth process, by introducing terms like 'the great spurt' (Gerschenkron, 1962) or 'take-off' (Rostow, 1960). What is less discussed is if and how the transformation periods also translate to discontinuous patterns in geographical space in the long run. Yet, some previous studies have touched upon the subject, for example Freeman and Perez's (1988) study of changes in technological systems that have a major influence on the behaviour of the entire economy. In their words, this new techno-economic paradigm brings a 'new pattern in the location of investment both nationally and internationally as the change in relative cost structure transforms comparative advantages […]' (p. 59).

Williamson (1965) discussed the development of regional disparities over time using quantitative indicators for several countries and suggested that the long-term evolution of regional disparities followed an inverted U-shape curve, with rising regional inequality during industrialization and decreasing inequality there-after. However, Williamson's study only covered about 40 years (the data set stretches between 1920 and 1960) and therefore could not investigate whether there are reoccurring patterns of convergence/divergence over successive waves of industrial transformation.

Recently there has again been a burgeoning interest in the issue of long-run regional inequality. This movement has mainly turned to New Economic Geography (NEG) (Krugman, 1991) for theoretical inspiration and has provided new estimates of regional GDPs for several European countries (Tirado *et al.*, 2002; Martinez-Galaragga, 2010).

There are few empirical descriptions of the regional character of Sweden's industrialization in the longer term, but some previous studies cover certain periods of regional economic conditions. For example, Andersson (1978) studied the distribution of income shares and population in Sweden between 1920 and 1975, and identified a high degree of stability during the period. The selected time period precluded the study of the major structural shifts in the Swedish economy during the late 1800s and after 1975, sometimes referred to as the Second and Third Industrial Revolutions (see Schön, 2012 and Lundquist *et al.*, 2008). However, Andersson (1978) assumed the period before 1920 to have been more region-ally turbulent due to higher capital mobility. In a study from the early 1980s, Söderberg and Lundgren (1982) noted the rural character of early industrialization in Sweden compared with other nations.

The above-mentioned studies about Sweden cover too short a period to provide answers to the research issues presented in this chapter. Moreover, they pay little attention to the spatial distribution of production or production per capita over time, but rather rely on related variables such as population or taxable income. In fact, little is known about the overall geographical distribution of production over time in Sweden (as in most other countries). In order to contribute to the emerging literature in historical economic geography, this chapter sets out to analyse the Swedish growth experience from a regional perspective from 1860 to 2010.

The technology shift model presented in Schön (2006, 2012) suggests that economic changes occur abruptly and give rise to cycles in the patterns of investment and growth. The first industrial cycle (1850–1890) was characterized by the early breakthrough of modern industrialization and the beginning of the expansion of the railway in Sweden. International integration and expanding trade promoted the export-led growth of oats, iron and wood products, but also the growth of some specific industries directed towards a domestic market, such as textiles and products of simple mechanical workshops. This early period started the process of market integration between the regions, with increasing potential to move people and goods over longer distances. Enflo *et al.* (2014b) show that internal and external migration resulted in fast regional wage convergence during this period. The Baring crisis at the beginning of the 1890s marks the end of this structural cycle of burgeoning industrialization and integration into the world economy.

During the second industrial cycle (1890–1930), the real breakthrough of the industries closely associated with the Second Industrial Revolution (such as advanced mechanical engineering and paper industries as well as the urban service industries) occurred. The nature of this growth paradigm was closely related to new technologies, such as electrification and the electric motor. Important innovations were especially connected to the early expansion of the electrical power grid and decreased relative cost of electricity transmission. In the latter part of this period, new industries, such as specialized shipbuilding and the car industry, expanded together with the paper industry in particular. This period ended with the crisis of 1931, which, however, turned out to be less dramatic in Sweden than in many other countries. During the 1930s and 1940s, average growth in Sweden was among the highest in the world. Steps towards an integrated electrical power grid were taken, but further integration of the electrical power system (the connection of geographically separated networks in different parts of the country) and decreasing relative transmission costs would continue all the way into the 1960s. Taken together, the first two industrial cycles moved Sweden from a relatively poor, peripheral country to one of the richer industrial nations in the world.

The structural cycle from 1930 to 1975 involved booming mechanical and engineering-based manufacturing industries and chemical industries. The period is often described as the heyday of the industrial society. The public sector expanded, and the 'Swedish model' of economic organization was implemented, with its greater public responsibility in terms of social security and human capital improvement. An additional part of the model was the regulation of labour and capital markets, constructed to sustain growth and increase economic equality. On the labour market, 'solidaristic wage policy' was a main element. It served to create income equality, simultaneously with high pressure for structural change as inefficient firms could no longer compete by lowering wages. High pressure for structural change created unemployment in certain regions, and the government responded with active labour market policies to stimulate workers to re-educate or move to more prosperous areas (Enflo and Rosés, 2015). Structural change in this period meant that the important sectors from the first waves of industrialization (food, sawmilling and textile industries) stagnated or decreased. The period reached an end in the structural crises of the 1970s, associated with booming oil prices, stagflation and increasing unemployment levels.

The last cycle runs between 1975 and 2010, often called the post-industrial era. After the international crises of the late 1970s, which seriously affected many of the traditional manufacturing industries in Sweden, the 1980s and the 1990s saw institutional reforms including liberalization of the capital and labour markets, and rapid diffusion of new innovations in electronics and their applications, called by some observers the Third Industrial Revolution.

With these four markedly different structural cycles in mind, we will now move to the regional analysis to investigate how these national and sectoral patterns have impacted on the spatial allocation of resources and patterns of regional convergence and divergence in the Swedish economy.

Data and measurement

For the empirical investigations, we venture to estimate the size of regional production through regional GDPs (we follow the convention from economic history literature of using 'regional GDPs' instead of 'GRPs'). One of the major obstacles to the estimation of historical regional GDPs is the lack of historical data. In fact, official GDP regional calculations are a relatively recent phenomenon in most countries. Geary and Stark (2002), however, presented a method that enables the estimation of regional historical GDPs using a minimum of input data. The simplest version of the method uses only productivity for an industry on the national level, numbers of workers per sector and region, and wages per sector and region, all for a specific year. In most countries, this is also the best available data, since first-hand historical regional productivity data is very rare. However, even this kind of information could be difficult to obtain for some historical time periods, especially for the service sectors. Therefore, Geary and Stark also suggested different theoretically grounded solutions to such data problems. The regional GDP estimation method, outlined by Geary and Stark, has recently been applied to estimate historical regional GDPs for some of the countries in Europe, for example (apart from the original estimations of Geary and Stark for the UK) Italy (Felice, 2011), Spain (Rosés *et al.*, 2010) and Belgium (Buyst, 2010). Comparisons with estimates from other sources indicate that the estimations made using the Geary-Stark method generally yield highly accurate results.

For the estimation of the Swedish regional GDPs, therefore, we have also used the method suggested by Geary and Stark (2002). The exact specification of the estimation, calculations and definitions of the variables for the Swedish case can be found in Enflo *et al.* (2014a), but the main characteristics of the estimations could be described intuitively. In essence, the national productivity (value added per worker) in an industry on the national level is taken as the point of departure (in our estimations we work with the four industries of agriculture, manufacturing, and public and private services). If we also know in each region how many workers are employed in this specific industry, a very rough estimate of the production value of an industry in a region is given by multiplying the value added per worker for the industry by the number of workers in the industry in a region. However, as the productivity for the industry is the national average, such calculations would completely disregard regional variations in productivity. This is an unfortunate compromise. Therefore, given the reasonable assumption that regional wage differentials also reflect productivity differentials, productivity is weighted by regional wage differentials for the industry. Then, regional estimates made for all the different industries in a region are added to produce the total regional GDPs for a specific year.

Even with these simplifying assumptions underlying the method, different empirical problems arise when dealing with historical data. We discuss these in detail in relation to the Swedish case in Enflo *et al.* (2014a), where the complete matrix of estimated regional GDPs can also be found. For the estimations, we used regional employment data from the Swedish Census and wage data from a wide variety of sources, such as published collections of wage series and the wage statistical yearbooks of Statistics Sweden. For the regional wage differentials, we sometimes had to rely on proxies. To adjust our calculations to the known total national GDP, we used the national estimates from the Swedish National Historical Accounts (Krantz and Schön, 2007; Schön and Krantz, 2012a), and total populations in the regions were given by Statistics Sweden.

In all, we were able to estimate regional GDPs for ten-year benchmarks since 1860 for the 24 Swedish counties (Swedish: län). Admittedly, these provinces are not functional regions but larger administrative units, and contain within them some degree of heterogeneity in terms of population density and production. However, the counties are sufficient to create an overall impression of the development of regional economic patterns in Sweden. For example, they give more detailed information about regional disparities than do the regional aggregations normally used by the European Union (NUTS 2). Moreover, to our knowledge, the counties are the lowest possible unit of spatial aggregation for estimation of production values covering a broader set of activities than only the manufacturing sector. However, this does not exclude the fact that our results should be treated as indications of broad trends in the Swedish regional system.

Operationalization and measurement techniques

We will consistently deal with three variables: regional GDPs (production value per region), regional GDP per capita and population per county. We use different techniques to measure changes in the regional distributions.

We use the coefficient of variation (CV) and a measure of population concentration. The coefficient of variation is one of the techniques normally employed to measure processes of regional sigma convergence (Monfort, 2008). We follow convention and calculate this as

$$CV_t = \frac{s_t}{\bar{x}_t},$$

where CV_t is the coefficient of variation at year t, s_t is the standard deviation of the variable among the regions at year t, and $\bar{x}_t$ is the (unweighted) average of the variable at time t. In our case, the CV is a measure of the regional dispersion in the Swedish regional system, and the higher the CV, the more unequal the regions in terms of the variable investigated.

To measure the geographic concentration of our variables, we use the adjusted EG index proposed by Spiezia (2003). The index is a development of the regional concentration index (EG) proposed by Ellison and Glaeser (1997):

$$EG = \sum_{i=1}^{N} (y_i - a_i)^2,$$

Where y_i denotes population or production in region i as a percentage for Sweden and a_i is the area of region i as a percentage of the country area. If the production share of each region equals its relative area, then there is no concentration and EG equals 0. Therefore, the bigger the value of EG, the higher the geographic concentration.

A major drawback of the EG index is that it is not suitable for international comparisons because it is very sensitive to the level of aggregation of regional data. This is because the differences between the production share and relative area of each region are squared. To correct this bias due to aggregation, the EG index can be reformulated as the adjusted geographic concentration index (AGC) (see Spiezia, 2003).

The CV and the AGC only measure changes in the dispersion of the distribution and do not necessarily take into account individual regional changes within the distribution. To study regional mobility more closely, we use two different descriptive techniques: one based on correlations and one based on a simple transformation matrix where regions move between regional groupings of GDP or GDP per capita.

The long-term development of regional inequality

Results

Figure 7.1 shows the names of the different regions and the location of the major cities in Sweden. We will refer to these names in the discussion of the results. Figures 7.2 and 7.3 display the distribution of regional GDP and the population in the regions in 1860 (first year of our data) and 2007 (last year). Figure 7.2 clearly shows the highly unequal distribution of regional GDP, with the main shares of production located in the Stockholm, Göteborg and Bohus, and Malmöhus regions. In 1860, 27 per cent of the nation's GDP was located in these regions, but in 2007 the share had increased to 47 per cent. This means that almost half of Sweden's GDP was located in the three regions of the metropolitan cities, a dramatic increase compared with the 1800s. As for the more peripheral regions, the situation is reversed, and the north/south gap in the allocation of GDP widened between 1860 and 2007. While the five most northern provinces hosted 13 per cent of the national GDP in 1860, the corresponding figure in 2007 was 11 per cent. Figure 7.3 shows that the regional shares of population display much the same tendencies, but mark an even more pronounced concentration pattern. While about 7 per cent of all Swedes lived in the capital in 1860, the share had risen threefold to one-fifth (21 per cent) in 2007.

Figure 7.4 displays the AGC index of population concentration from 1860 to 2010. A striking feature of the graph is that the Swedish counties actually became less geographically concentrated during the first two industrial cycles (1860 to 1930). The pattern is a clear U-shape, indicating that the first two industrial cycles of transformation in Swedish growth involved a strong decentralization of productive forces and people, while, in contrast, the last two industrial cycles created higher levels of agglomeration and centralization in the core regions.

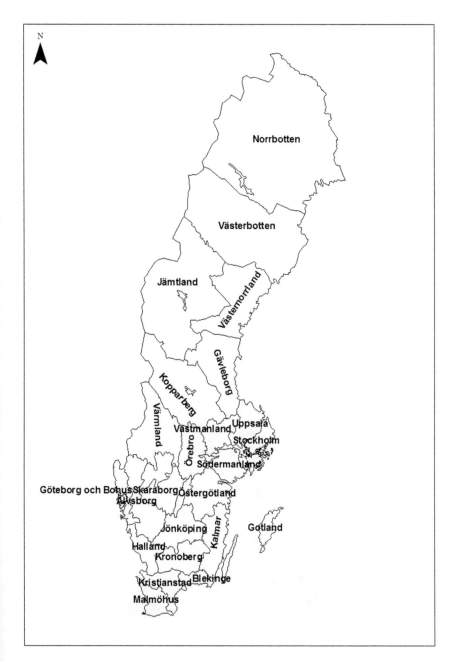

Figure 7.1 Location and names of the Swedish regions.

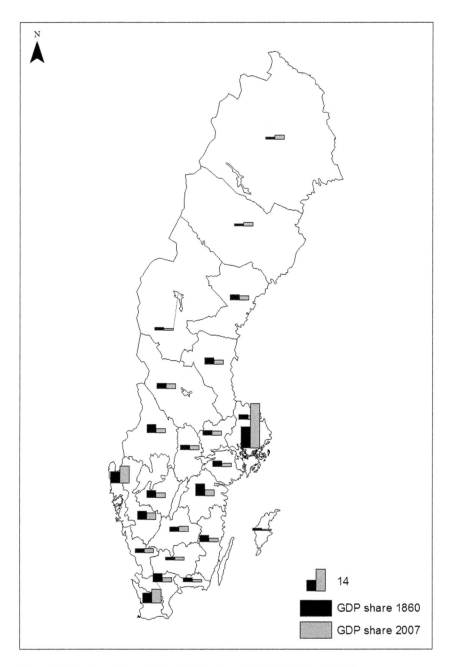

Figure 7.2 Regional shares (%) of total national GDP in 1860 and 2007.

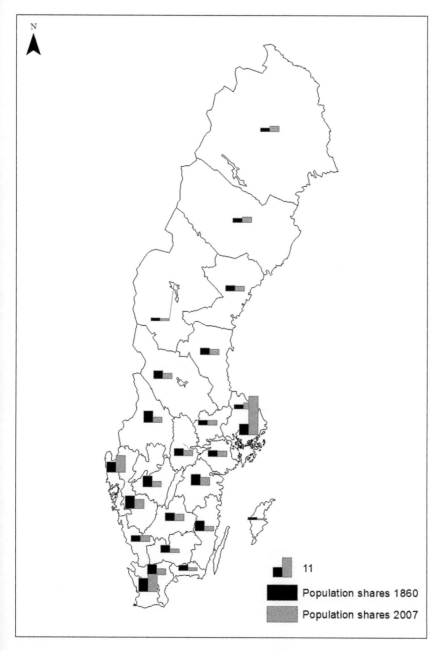

Figure 7.3 Regional shares (%) of total national population in 1860 and 2007.

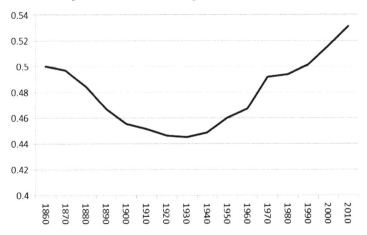

Figure 7.4 Long-run Adjusted Geographic Concentration (AGC) index of population in Sweden, 1860–2010.

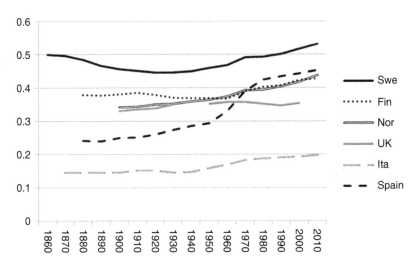

Figure 7.5 Long-run Adjusted Geographic Concentration (AGC) index of population in European countries.

Sources: Authors' calculations based on data on population across comparable regional units from Crafts (2005) for Britain; Felice (2011) for Italy; Rosés *et al.* (2010) for Spain; Enflo (2014) for Finland and Modalsli (forthcoming) for Norway.

This U-shaped concentration pattern is remarkable when put into an international context. Figure 7.5 displays the Swedish ASC indexes in comparison with Finland, Norway, Italy, the UK and Spain, and shows that Sweden is the most centralized country in terms of population throughout the period. Comparable nations in terms of geographic prerequisites, such as Finland and Norway, score much lower in terms of population concentration. This is also true in a broader context, as among the OECD countries only Canada, Australia, Iceland, Mexico and Korea have a higher population concentration than Sweden in the present period (Spiezia, 2003). Second, Sweden is the only country that shows a trend towards decentralization during the first two industrial cycles of the economy. It appears that the First and Second Industrial Revolutions took place with fewer accompanying agglomeration tendencies than could be expected from the international literature. The very rural nature of the first waves of industrialization is a feature that makes Sweden unique in comparative terms, and could also explain why, for example, agricultural wage convergence was strong during this phase (see Enflo *et al.*, 2014b).

Figure 7.6 complements these pictures by showing regional GDP per capita indexed to the nation in 1860 (where the nation is 100). The regional differences in GDP per capita are pronounced (ranging from 57 to 219), again suggesting that Sweden was a country with relatively large regional imbalances at the onset of industrialization (for an international comparison, see Enflo and Rosés, 2015). The highest values can be found in the metropolitan regions of Stockholm and Göteborg, followed by regions dominated by early industrialization and the wood and sawmill industries. In 2007, this pattern had changed substantially (Figure 7.7). The regional differences decreased (and we only need to employ three categories in the legend of the figure). The Stockholm and Göteborg regions were still at the top of the GDP per capita league, but closely followed by regions in the south and along the coast in the north.

Figure 7.8 gives a more detailed account and presents the coefficient of variation (CV) of GDP per capita across all the benchmark years. As seen in the graph, inequality dropped rapidly between 1860 and 1910, remained more or less constant up to 1940, declined again up to 1980, and finally increased during the most recent decades.

The CV calculations reveal the general tendencies for regional convergence in the system, but could, of course, obscure movements taking place within the distribution. In Table 7.1, we therefore offer further discussion of regional mobility or ranking instability, by considering Spearman's and Pearson's rank correlation coefficients. Although Spearman's coefficient displays significant values in the shorter-span calculations (but not in the longer-span calculations), both Pearson's and Spearman's coefficients indicate that regional inequality ranks were far from persistent in Sweden (with the exception of the latest period from 1980 to 2000), with typical values ranging between 0.4 and 0.6. Thus, Swedish regions show a rather high degree of mobility in the distribution over time.

Figure 7.9 gives an additional account of the instability of the regional system over time, illustrated by the correlation between the regional distribution of our variables for a given year (on the x-axis) and the distribution of 1860.[1] The lower the coefficient, the lower the correlation between the regional distribution of regional GDPs in the year in which we are interested and the distribution in 1860, and the larger the turbulence in the regional system between the years of comparison. As expected, the first two cycles of industrialization were comparatively turbulent in terms of geographical redistribution of production. The distribution of regional GDPs, and the correlation with the initial 1860 regional distribution,

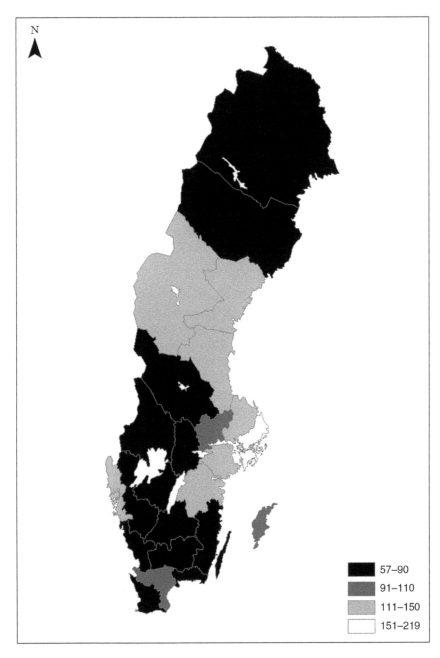

Figure 7.6 GDP per capita in the regions, indexed to the nation (nation=100) in 1860.

70–90
91–110
111–150

Figure 7.7 GDP per capita in the regions, indexed to the nation (nation=100) in 2007.

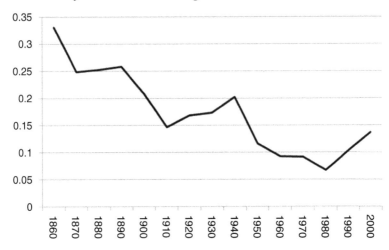

Figure 7.8 Sweden's regional inequality: coefficient of variation of GDP per capita among regions, 1860–2000.

Table 7.1 Rank order correlations across Swedish counties, 1860–2000

	1860–1910	1910–1940	1940–1980	1980–2000	1860–2000
Spearman's coefficient	0.46***	0.52***	0.44***	0.74***	−0.08
Pearson's coefficient	0.58	0.69	0.60	0.82	0.46

Note: The rank order coefficients are computed between the initial and final year of the considered interval. ***Indicates signification at 99 per cent.

declined rapidly until roughly 1900 and stabilized considerably thereafter. The population variable shows smoother developments and indicates that the entire period from the Second Industrial Revolution until the Second World War was turbulent in terms of population redistribution. The regional distribution of GDP per capita is again very different, and is primarily marked by spikes around the population trend. All in all, GDP per capita shows very little of the stability displayed by the other variables. Instead, there seem to have been several turbulent periods of changing GDP per capita distributions over time.

The relative turbulence in regional rankings suggests that the regional Swedish growth experience leaves room for interesting individual stories of regional success and failure. To identify these, we sort the Swedish regions into four groups according to the quartiles in 1890 (the decisive outbreak of the Second Industrial Revolution) and 2000 for regional GDP and regional GDP per capita. Table 8.2 shows such a cross-tabulation. We indicate the number of regions in each size of group (1–4, where 1 indicates the group with the lowest GDP and 4 is the top group). Thirteen of the 24 regions stay on the diagonal (no change of group), while eight regions move only one size of class up or down. One region that shows spectacular upward mobility is the Jönköping region in the south of Sweden. This

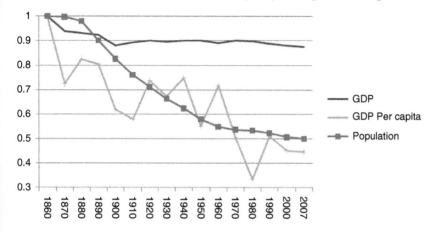

Figure 7.9 Correlations between distributions of regional GDP, regional GDP per capita and population in the regional system between the ten-year benchmark years.

Table 7.2 Transformation matrix of regional GDPs, 1890–2000

		2000			
		1	2	3	4
1890	1	4	2	0	0
	2	1	2	2	1
	3	1	1	3	1
	4	0	1	1	4

region moves from being a poor region with extensive migration to the United States (before the First World War) to a region that was especially successful in the period after the Second World War. On the negative side of transformation, the Kalmar region, which is a region roughly in the same part of the country as the successful Jönköping region, moved from the group of the second largest GDPs to the quartile with the smallest GDPs. The Västernorrland region moved from the group compiled of the largest regions in terms of regional GDP to the group of the second smallest. While the downward journey of Kalmar started early, Västernorrland started its descent primarily after the 1960s.

Table 8.3 is the corresponding regional transformation matrix of GDP per capita. Since this table refers to the mobility of regions in terms of the more volatile per capita figures, we expect a higher mobility than when dealing with absolute figures of GDP only. The table shows a higher number of regional transitions: six regions stay on the diagonal, while seven move only one group up or down. Among the successful up-movers, we find five regions: the Jönköping, Kronoberg, Älvsborg, Skaraborg and Örebro regions. The first two (Jönköping

Table 7.3 Transformation matrix of regional GDP/capita, 1890–2000

		2000			
		1	*2*	*3*	*4*
1890	1	1	1	2	2
	2	2	2	1	1
	3	2	0	2	2
	4	1	3	1	1

and Kronoberg), which were poor regions at the start of our investigation, started to climb up the distribution in the 1960s. Älvsborg and Skaraborg are regions in the west of Sweden that underwent a positive development after the Second World War, peaking in the 1950 to 1970s. The Örebro region had already hurdled to a higher stage in the 1930s. The down-movers in terms of GDP per capita are predominantly peripheral regions, with production that traditionally specialized in natural resources. The Gävleborg, Västernorrland, Jämtland and Norrbotten regions in the northern part of the country started their descent in the 1930s, but the decline of these regions has been especially marked since the Second World War. The peripheral island of Gotland had already started its descent in the early 1900s.

Convergence, divergence and cycles

The empirical evidence presented in this study suggests some distinct tendencies over the last 140 years of spatial economic evolution in Sweden. There are clear tendencies towards increasing regional concentration of economic activities over time. However, this process did not follow a linear pattern. For example, the first two industrial cycles (1860–1930) spread the population more evenly across the country, which resulted in a decreasing population concentration. Comparing Sweden with other countries shows that such a process of industrialization without population concentration is highly unusual. After the Second World War, however, Sweden's regional growth pattern is more in line with international development as growth forces have worked to concentrate the population and production in the core regions of the country, at the clear expense of more peripheral regions. This has resulted in Sweden's population being one of the most concentrated in the whole of the OECD. In terms of GDP per capita, however, we find the opposite tendency. If GDP per capita is a broad measure of the conditions in the regions, the Swedish counties are among the most equal internationally today, and are also considerably more equal than at the beginning of the Industrial Revolution.

All in all, this means that wherever production in the periphery survived the transformation pressures, it became more efficient and employed fewer workers, rendering high incomes for those who maintained their jobs, but unemployment for those that did not. Indeed, this is precisely what we have observed both in the case of agriculture (especially after the Second World War) and in the capital-intensive manufacturing industries in more peripheral areas of Sweden. Notwithstanding these tendencies, the regions that do decline in terms of GDP per capita compared with other regions are almost exclusively peripheral regions in the north of the country. Overall, there are strong longer-term tendencies of increased spatial differentiation between the distant peripheries to the core. The position of the regions in the regional hierarchies is, however, not static in the very long run, but could differ across the industrial cycles. Overall, Sweden's regional system shows a relatively high degree of mobility of rankings in the very long term. The mobility was highest during the first two cycles of industrialization, when exports of natural resources and the creation of internal infrastructure served to create individual regional success stories in previously peripheral locations. This suggests that even though the regional hierarchy is stable within the industrial cycles (Henning *et al.*, this volume), it may very well shift between them. Indeed, this chapter shows that there are eras in which the trend patterns are reversed. These points in time could be referred to as 'criticalities', but they are perhaps not extremely dramatic in themselves. Rather, they form turning points that set off long-term processes of change in the regional system. Using Schön's periodization scheme, a clearer pattern of regional growth emerges.

The first growth regime from 1860 until the Baring crisis of 1890 is clearly an era of increased market integration. Sweden takes full part in the international business cycle, by increasing its exports abroad and importing large amounts of capital. Partly, capital imports financed the building of the railways, which served to further increase the internal market integration. However, overseas migration was also an important feature of this period. Interestingly, market integration did not create a stronger core-periphery pattern, as hypothesized in, for example, the model of Krugman (1991) and found in many other countries (see Williamson, 1965). Instead, Swedish industrialization benefited peripheral regions, which resulted in migration patterns that helped spread the population more evenly and create convergence in wages and incomes. As workers left the areas where labour was abundant and moved to labour-scarce areas, regional wages converged (Enflo and Rosés, 2015; Enflo *et al.*, 2014b). This in turn contributed to the compression of regional income differentials. Overall, the first industrial cycle helped to even out a large part of the regional disparities that marked the agricultural society.

The second industrial cycle (1890–1930) continued to involve the countryside. We see a continued decentralization of the population, albeit at a slower rate. This could possibly be explained by the fact that early export-led growth during the Swedish industrialization process favoured products originating from more traditional knowledge and handicrafts or from agriculture. Therefore, the early industrialization offered economic possibilities outside the main cities and demanded less spatial reallocation of labour or production itself (Schön, 2012). In the last part of this period, however, regional GDP per capita started to diverge. These new tendencies were most probably effects of events related to the Second Industrial Revolution. The new technologies were less intensive in terms of natural resource exploitation, involved a higher degree of human capital and probably benefited more from being closer to the market and major agglomerations. Innovations in the electrical sector, as well as the chemical and machinery industry, formed a new development block that served to accumulate incomes and the population in certain areas (see Enflo *et al.*, 2008 for a further analysis of this development block).

The 1930–1975 cycle saw instead rapid convergence in terms of GDP per capita. This period reversed the trend towards population concentration and was much more stable in terms of regional rankings. It is impossible to overlook the institutional organization of this period as it coincided with the rise of the Swedish model. Two aspects of this might be especially important for the regional orientation towards higher stability. As highlighted by Schön (2012), the Swedish mixed economy model tended to encourage investment in existing firms, but to discourage new firm foundation and investment. Growth patterns were, to a large extent, concentrated around an industry structure established in and after the Second Industrial Revolution, with rationalization investments and efficiency improvements taking place within and reinforcing this established structure. Moreover, the expansion of the public sector tended to obscure and reduce the volatility in the production patterns generated by industries in direct connection with market and consumer demand. Combining the attributes of the growing welfare state with the compressed wage structure resulting from solidaristic wage policy helped Sweden arrive at exceptionally low regional inequality rates. However, the compressed wage structure resulted in unemployment in peripheral areas. The response of the Swedish government was to initiate policies and certain grants to help people move. As less prosperous regions were depopulated, rapid convergence in terms of GDP per capita was followed by increased population concentration. These forces help explain why Sweden, by international standards, became remarkably equal in terms of GDP per capita, yet highly unequal in terms of population per region.

Since 1980, a new era of regional turbulence has emerged, manifesting itself in the divergence of all the variables that we observe. Thus, we observe continuing increases in the concentration of production and people, but also a new tendency for widening regional disparities in terms of income per capita. We are not unique in the geographical literature in suggesting that a new regime of spatial growth was introduced with the Third Industrial Revolution in the late 1970s or early 1980s, breaking the confines of the Fordist production system (see, for example, Lundquist and Olander, 2001). This final industrial cycle is related to the growth of metropolitan areas and coincides with structural change towards an increased importance of the service sector and knowledge-intensive industries. Previous studies have analysed the close connection between economic growth and the resurgence of major urban areas since the 1980s in Sweden (see Lundquist, Olander and Svensson Henning, 2008). Services and telecom industries, mainly located in the three major metropolitan areas of Sweden (the counties of Stockholm, Göteborg and Malmöhus), are the main culprits of this new growth upsurge and regional divergence.

Concluding remarks

The results that we discuss here mark only a first exploration into the long-run development of Swedish regions, and leave a number of caveats and important opportunities for further research. The general background sketched in this chapter provides reason to explore the trajectories of some individual regions further. For example, the Jönköping region experienced strong growth after the Second World War. Tentatively, this can be connected to the expansion of manufacturing and mechanical workshops in the area on the basis of early handicraft traditions, and today the region is one of Sweden's most important centres for small-scale manufacturing. The expansion of this sector in the region was directly connected to the expansion of the electrical power grid and the development of electric motors (Schön, 2012), even if the small-scale manufacturing traditions do have historical origins in the region (Magnusson, 2000). In terms of GDP per capita, the economic expansion of the Jönköping and Kronoberg regions after the Second World War is likely to be connected to the expansion of rather small-scale manufacturing industries. Also, regions in the west of Sweden (Älvsborg and Skaraborg regions), known for their expanding manufacturing industries (for example the expansion of the automotive sector), expanded mainly after the Second World War. On the negative side of transformation, the early demise of the Kalmar region may be connected to the fact that the region suffered from early railway system expansion (see Berger and Enflo, 2015 and Schön, 2012). The state railway lines were stretched inland rather than connecting previously prosperous coastal regions. This promoted the growth of a whole new set of cities and regions. For Kalmar, however, which previously benefited from its position along the coast of the Baltic Sea, railway expansion contributed to a negative shift of growth forces.

Indeed, although we have tried to suggest some tentative explanations for the observed empirical patterns, we can only hint here at their explanatory power rather than provide a fully fledged evaluation of each one of them. In particular, it seems relevant to explore the extent to which structural change in terms of the varying importance of sectors and industries feeds into, or drives, the long-term patterns that we have observed. For this, we need to go into more disaggregated series in terms of geographical units and industry classification. An example of such a study can be found in Henning *et al.* in this book, for the period 1978–2004. A future avenue of research would be to expand data series on detailed industries and for smaller regional units than the counties for the period that we cover in this chapter.

Lastly, the theoretical aspects of long-term regional change need to be further explored and debated. Even though historical perspectives should be especially interesting to evolutionary researchers interested in growth regimes, criticalities and stabilities, relatively little research has been conducted on regional patterns of production in a long-term perspective. To some extent, the evidence we present confirms the discussion of Storper and Walker (1989) where the locational unboundedness of new industries causes dramatic patterns of regional restructuring. This gives an unpredictable process of development of growth and industrial wealth, as criticalities in the system take place on a highly occasional basis. Combining these insights with the logic of Schön's structural model and its geographical implications (Lundquist *et al.*, 2008) could help bring order to what might seem just a cacophony of unrelated regional events.

Note

1   We take $corr(X_t, X_{1860})$ where X is the distribution of the variable in the regions at time t and 1860, respectively.

References

Andersson, Å. E. (1978), 'Demografisk och ekonomisk utveckling'. In *Att forma regional framtid. 13 forskares syn på regionala problem*. Rapport från ERU. Stockholm: Liber.

Berger, T. and Enflo, K. (2015), 'Locomotives of local growth: The short- and long-term impact of railroads in Sweden', *Journal of Urban Economics*, available online at: doi:10.1016/j.jue.2015.09.001.

Boschma, R. and Martin, R. (2007), 'Editorial: Constructing an evolutionary economic geography', *Journal of Economic Geography*, vol. 7(5), pp. 537–48.

Buyst, E. (2010), 'Reversal of fortune in a small, open economy: Regional GDP in Belgium, 1896–2000', *Rivista di Storia Economica*, vol. 26, pp. 75–92.

Crafts, N. (2005), 'Regional GDP in Britain, 1871–1911: some estimates', *Scottish Journal of Political Economy*, vol. 52(1), pp. 54–64.

Ellison, G. and E. L. Glaeser (1997), 'Geographic concentration in U.S. manufacturing industries: a dartboard approach', *Journal of Political Economy*, vol. 105(5), pp. 889–927.

Enflo, K. (2014), 'Finland's regional GDPs 1880–2010: estimates, sources and interpretations', For the analys in *Economic History 135*, Lund University.

Enflo K. and Rosés, J. (2015), 'Coping with regional inequality in Sweden: structural change, migrations, and policy, 1860–2000', *Economic History Review*, vol. 68(1), pp. 191–217.

Enflo, K., Henning, M. and Schön, L. (2014a), 'Swedish regional GDP 1855–2000: estimations and general trends in the Swedish regional system', *Research in Economic History*, vol. 30, pp. 47–89.

Enflo, K., Kander, A. and Schön, L. (2008), 'Identifying development blocks, a new methodology', *Journal of Evolutionary Economics*, vol. 18(1), pp. 57–76.

Enflo, K., Lundh C. and Prado, S. (2014b), 'The role of migration in regional wage convergence: evidence from Sweden 1860–1940', *Explorations in Economic History*, vol. 52, pp. 93–110.

Felice, E. (2011), 'Regional value added in Italy (1891–2001) and the foundation of a long term picture', *Economic History Review*, vol. 64(3), pp. 929–50.

Freeman, C. and Perez, C. (1988), 'Structural crises of adjustment, business cycles and investment behavior'. In Dosi, G., Freeman, C., Nelson R., Silverberg, G. and Soete L. (eds) *Technical Change and Economic Theory*. London: Pinter Publishers.

Geary, F. and Stark, T. (2002), 'Examining Ireland's post-famine economic growth performance', *Economic Journal*, vol. 112(482), pp. 919–935.

Gerschenkron, A. (1962), *Economic Backwardness in Historical Perspective: A Book of Essays*, Harvard University Press.

Henning, M., Enflo, K. and Andersson, F. N. G. (2011), 'Trends and cycles in regional economic growth. How spatial differences formed the Swedish growth experience 1860–2009', *Explorations in Economic History*, vol. 48(4) pp. 538–55.

Krantz, O. and Schön, L. (2007), *Swedish Historical National Accounts 1800–2000*. Lund Studies in Economic History 41. Almqvist & Wiksell International.

Krugman, P. (1991), *Geography and Trade*. Cambridge, MA: MIT Press.

Lundquist, K.-J. and Olander, L.-O. (2001), 'Den glömda strukturcykeln: ny syn på industrins regionala tillväxt och omvandling', *Rapporter och Notiser 161*, Department of Social and Economic Geography, Lund University.

Lundquist, K.-J., Olander, L.-O. and Svensson Henning, M. (2008), 'Decomposing the technology shift: evidence from the Swedish manufacturing sector', *Tijdschrift voor economische en sociale geografie*, vol. 99(2), pp. 145–59.

Magnusson, L. (2000), *An Economic History of Sweden*. Abingdon: Routledge.

Martinez-Galarraga, J. (2010), *Market Integration and Regional Inequality in Spain*. University of Barcelona (diss.).

Modalsli, J. (forthcoming), 'Norway's regional GDP'. In Rosés, J. and Wolf, N. (eds.) *The Economic Development of Europe's Regions*. Abingdon: Routledge.

Monfort, P. (2008), 'Convergence of EU regions. Measures and evolution', *European Union Regional Policy Working Papers 01/2008*.

Roses, J.R., Martínez-Galarraga, J. and Tirado, D.A. (2010), 'The upswing of regional income inequality in Spain (1860–1930)'. *Explorations in Economic History*, vol. 47(2), pp. 244–57.

Rostow, W. W. (1960), *The Stages of Economic Growth: A Non-communist Manifesto*. Cambridge University Press.

Schön, L. (1988), *Historiska nationalräkenskaper för Sverige, Volym 2: Industri och hantverk 1800–1980*. Skrifter utgivna av ekonomisk-historiska föreningen. Vol: LIX, Lund.

Schön, L. (1995), *Historiska nationalräkenskaper för Sverige, Volym 1: Jordbruk med binäringar 1800–1980*. Skrifter utgivna av ekonomisk-historiska föreningen. Vol: LXXIV, Lund.

Schön, L. (2006), *Tankar om cykler – perspektiv på ekonomin, historien och framtiden*. Stockholm: SNS.

Schön, L. (2012), *An Economic History of Modern Sweden*. Oxon: Routledge.

Schön, L. and Krantz, O. (2012a), 'Swedish Historical National Accounts 1560–2010'. *Lund Papers in Economic History 123*, Lund University.

Schön, L. and Krantz, O. (2012b), 'The Swedish economy in the early modern period: constructing historical national accounts', *European Review of Economic History*, vol. 16, pp. 1–21.

Schumpeter, J. A. (1939), *Business Cycles. A Theoretical, Historical, and Statistical Analysis of the Capitalist Process*. New York: McGraw-Hill.

Söderberg, J. and Lundgren N.-G. (1982), *Ekonomisk och geografisk koncentration 1850–1980*. Stockholm: Liber.

Spiezia, V. (2003), 'Measuring regional economies', OECD Statistics Brief, No. 6, October.

Storper, M. and Walker, R. (1989), *The Capitalist Imperative. Territory, Technology, and Industrial Growth*. New York: Blackwell.

Svensson Henning, M. (2009), *Industrial Dynamics and Regional Structural Change. Geographical Perspectives on Economic Evolution*. Meddelanden från Lunds universitets geografiska institution, avhandlingar CLXXXI. (diss.).

Tirado, D., Paluzie, E. and Pons, J. (2002), 'Economic integration and industry location: the case of Spain before World War I', *Journal of Economic Geography*, vol. 11(2), pp. 343–63.

Williamson, J. G. (1965), 'Regional inequality and the process of national development: a description of the patterns', *Economic Development and Cultural Change*, vol. 13(4:2), pp. 1–84.

8 Regional analysis and the process of economic development

Changes in growth, employment and income

Martin Henning, Karl-Johan Lundquist and Lars-Olof Olander

Analyses based on national totals, averages and trends are traditionally the focus of economics and economic history. Even though national aggregates tell us a lot about the processes of economic evolution, national figures are composed of a wide range of regional trajectories. These diverging and converging regional paths not only sum up and compose the national trajectory of economic transformation, but also, to a large extent, define the everyday living conditions of people as well as the daily conditions of the operations of firms in regions across countries. This chapter will show that once national trajectories of economic development are decomposed, industrially as well as geographically, a hierarchical pattern of economic renewal and obsolescence will emerge.

Our understanding of this will build on advances in economic history, economic geography and evolutionary economics. For quite some time now, the early writings by Schumpeter (for example 1934, 1939) have inspired the development of an extensive 'neo-Schumpeterian' literature on innovation, economic change and growth, especially within the various stances of evolutionary economic thinking (Nelson and Winter, 1982; Fagerberg, 2003; Saviotti, 2001; Freeman and Louçã, 2001; Nelson, 2006). The evolutionary framework, broadly defined, has also diffused into the core discussion of other disciplines such as economic geography (Boschma, 2004; Frenken, van Oort and Verburg, 2007; Boschma and Frenken, 2006; Boschma and Martin, 2010). Especially within the non-formalized, 'appreciative' (Nelson and Winter, 1982) stances of evolutionary economics, several scholars have discussed the occurrence of paradigms or structural periods of economic development and change. These eras of economic growth tend to define the main cognitive search area of innovations and innovation implementation in the economy. As these paradigms are often dominated by one or two defining key innovations, some scholars connect this search area to the pervasive impact of general-purpose technologies (Bresnahan and Trajtenberg, 1995), and emphasize that the eras in this way are also accompanied by new relative price structures (Dosi, 1988; Freeman and Perez, 1988; Schön, 2012).

Indeed, in the more encompassing versions of these theories, such as the one developed by Lennart Schön and colleagues, the dominating forces of growth are associated with the co-development of dominant technologies and their complementarities, and institutional as well as organizational structures

(Schön, 2006, 2012). By quantitative analysis of aggregated time series (among other investments, capital/labour quotas and productivity), as well as more qualitatively oriented evidence, Schön and colleagues have identified reoccurring phases of development in the Swedish economy. These reoccurring phases share similar characteristics in terms of investments, technology diffusion, systematic lag effects between industry and institutional structures, forge-ahead and lagging industries, pre- and post-crises behaviour among actors and distribution of wage/profit quotas. Within each reoccurring period ('technology shift') of about 50 years, development is characterized by the stylized sequence of, to put it all too simply, transformation–rationalization–crisis.

In fact, in Swedish economics and economic history, structural research has a long and vibrant tradition, mainly within the structural analysis tradition (Dahmén, 1950; Åkerman, 1970). In particular, Schön's theory relates to concepts such as general purpose-technologies, macro inventions (Mokyr, 1990) and the 'development block' thesis formulated by the Swedish economist Erik Dahmén in the 1940s and 1950s (Dahmén, 1950, 1988). Schön provides explanations for the growth and demise of industries over time in a national production system since the initiation of industrial capitalism, as well as the dynamics of macroeconomic crises.

Yet, the main idea behind the technology shift thesis was not to develop a theory about regional economic change. Using the technology shift thesis as a theoretical backdrop, the objective of this chapter is to empirically investigate systematic time lags between regions in economic transformation and diffusion of growth within specific regional systems. Using an extensive Swedish micro-level data set, which is supplied to us by Statistics Sweden, as well as auxiliary industry price data, we investigate this issue for Sweden during the years 1978/1985 to 2008. By doing so, we sum up about a decade of research into the industrial and geographical details of the current technology shift. The detailed results of these investigations, as well as more detailed method descriptions, can be found in some previous publications (for example Lundquist *et al.*, 2008a, b; Svensson Henning, 2009; Lundquist and Olander, 2011). Compared with these previous works, this chapter, however, improves on three specific points. First, in line with Martynovich and Lundquist (2015), we integrate the analysis of service and manufacturing industries when defining key groups of driving industries. Second, we use updated data, and now expand the time series as long as the classification systems will allow us. Third, we extend previous analyses to ask whether regional economic transformation and growth are associated with increases in economic welfare (employment and household income) at a regional level. Our particular interest in this last question is spurred by the ongoing debate about the divergence in many regional systems in the developed economies, and whether the national transformation process is systematically benefiting some regions at the expense of others, which then 'pay' for the transformation process.

Following this introduction, we give a short summary of the link between the theoretical arguments behind the technology shift and the method that we devise to decompose industrial and regional growth trajectories in Sweden since the late 1970s. Thereafter, we provide the empirical findings, which reveal not only the lead-lag relations between growth in Swedish regions and industries over time, but also how this is correlated with the overall job and wage performance of the regions. We end the chapter with some conclusions.

Empirical issues: from theory to method

One of the core arguments in the technology shift framework is that new general-purpose technologies (GPT) (Bresnahan and Trajtenberg, 1995) define the main characteristics of economic transformation, renewal and growth during the technology shift process. These technologies spur growth in new industries and revitalize older parts of the economy through productivity increases and lower costs. However, the impact on particular industries and sectors are differentiated not only in terms of scale, but also at different points in time.

Table 8.1 sums up the main characteristics of the transformation and rationalization periods, based on Perez (1983), Schön (2006, 2012) and our own research (Lundquist and Olander, 2007, 2011). The spread of GPT and macro inventions leads to investments in new production areas during the *transformation* (20–25 years). Growth increases rapidly in new industries and later spreads to older industries. Thus, economic resources are reallocated between businesses. During this period, productivity increases primarily through the transfer of resources from low-productivity to high-productivity industries. Production increases faster than productivity at the beginning of the transformation because of extended learning periods and limited availability of skills in the new technology. This relationship only changes later in the transformation. The renewal and growth during the period are primarily visible in the increased activity on the supply side of the economy. New technologies lead to falling relative prices and rising relative volumes in new and updated technology-intensive production.

At the beginning of the *rationalization* (15–20 years), services and demand-driven industries expand, while the previous supply-driven industries slow down. The new technology that emerged in the preceding period is standardized, expands into other fields of application and spreads efficiently to older parts of

Table 8.1 Characteristics of transformation and rationalization

Transformation	Rationalization
GPT initiation	Diffusion of competence
New industries	Technological standardization
GPT diffusion	Decomposition
Supply-driven industries	Demand-driven industries
Development blocks	Consumption growth
Slow productivity growth	Rapid productivity growth
Bottlenecks	Credit market expansion
Building investments	Machinery investments

the economy. Investments are primarily focused on cutting costs in production and distribution. At the end of this period, slow growth, recurring recessions and falling profits will eventually lead communities and economies to prepare for opportunities for new paths of growth.

This periodization of the ongoing technology shift, and its characteristics, inspired us to define stylized combinations of growth and productivity trajectories for industries in the Swedish economy from 1978, with different industries assuming different roles in the technology shift process. As an auxiliary variable in this process, we used information on industry price-volume development. Industries producing key inputs for new products associated with new GPT would, for example, show combinations of trajectories and price-volume changes that are differentiated from those of industries with other roles to play. The latter could, for instance, be early or late adopters of the new technologies, industries that serve as demand-driven suppliers to technology-driven industries, consumer goods industries driven by real wage increases, or industries that are directly affected very little by the technology shift.

In essence, we analyse the production volume, productivity and relative price development of Swedish industries from 1978/1985 to 2008. Following the arguments of the technology shift thesis, we make extensive use of subperiodizations, as these mark important variations in the movement from transformation to rationalization during the technology shift process. Four ideal market situations for the different industries emerged from combining relative price and relative volume development on markets over time: *market push* (growth by strong innovation implementation or marketing), *market pressure* (increasing competition from product and process improvements), *market pull* (induced effects from the growth/demise of other industries) and *market contraction* (increasingly obsolete manufacturing). These four market situations, derived from literature in the field (Dahmén, 1950; Josefsson and Örtengren, 1980; Ljungberg, 1990), can be used to determine whether industries have been relatively supply-driven or demand-driven during a specific period.

Also, when it comes to the regional dimensions and the regional welfare aspects of economic long-term transformation, the technology shift thesis is in need of further qualification. Regions are differently equipped with the ability to develop, absorb, implement and commercially translate the growth forces of the technology shift (process and product innovation). In previous research, this ability has been coined the *regional receiver and development competence* (Lundquist and Olander, 2001; Svensson Henning, 2009; see also Karlsson and Nilsson, 2002). This capacity is closely linked to the arguments of New Economic Geography, where regional economic growth builds upon the principle of increasing returns, which in turn is derived from internal and external scale effects, the size of a local market, transaction costs and comparative advantages from production factors (Krugman, 1991; Fujita *et al.*, 1999). Indeed, the idea of increasing returns can also be closely linked to the endogenous capacity of regions to receive and exploit ideas, innovations, technology and market changes from elsewhere, but also to generate innovations (see Jaffe *et al.*, 1993; Boschma and Lambooy, 1999).

The most advanced regional receiver and development competence is found in the large regions, where new technologies can be received and developed because of the big regional markets which give early economies of scale, superior agglomeration advantages and advanced sets of human capital inputs. Increasingly, smaller regions, where the regional receiver and development competence diminishes correspondingly, have, on the other hand, low relative cost structures. This becomes beneficial as new technologies gradually mature, and congestion effects in the bigger regions force a decentralization and relocation of the industries, especially drawing from the new possibilities of the technology shift (Lundquist and Olander, 2011). Indeed, variations in the regional receiver and development competence in different parts of the regional hierarchy should give rise to lead-lag relationships between industries and regions in different stages of the technology shift process.

Method

The four categories of industry market situations enable us to create theoretically informed stylized industry groups, each assumed to have a different role to play during the technology shift process.[1]

Empirically, we sorted 170 Swedish manufacturing industries into one of these groups using consistent time series data for the years 1978 to 2004. The procedure consists of three stages: 1) identification of industry groups exhibiting similarities in their growth of value added over time, 2) dividing these industry groups into subgroups based on similarities in their growth in labour productivity, 3) distinguishing between those industries that could be assumed to be more supply-driven in their development and those that could be assumed to be more demand-driven, based on analysis of their relative price and relative volume development. The final different groups of industries (aggregates) are called *actor industries*, where the different actor industries represent a sliding scale from 'supply-driven' to 'demand-driven' and from 'market expansion' to 'market stagnation'.

The procedure is summed up in Figure 8.1, which also contains the names of the different actor industries. This classification will be used as a guide for selecting those manufacturing industries that could be used as main indicators of the economic transformation, when it comes to estimating the impact on economic welfare (in terms of jobs and wages) later on.

For the service sectors, we had to proceed according to quite a different logic because of data restrictions. First, service industry data created in the effort to construct consistent time series (however, restricted to 1985 to 2004) were sorted into three groups based mainly on service user orientation. Second, we divided these user-oriented groups into two subgroups: 'strong to medium growth' and 'medium to weak growth'. These were based mainly on value added development, but controlling for productivity development. Since no relative price series are available for service industries for such an extensive time period, service industries within the subgroups could not be classified into supply-driven and demand-driven following the price/volume logic. Therefore,

• Hypothetical and stylized growth and productivity trajectories • Insertion of actual industries through growth and productivity characteristics • Final classification through price and volume development	
Supply-driven actor industries	Demand-driven actor industries
Market expansion 1) Renewed 2) Transformed 3) Early followers 4) Late followers	5) Induced I 6) Induced II 7) Contracting 8) Obsolete I 9) Obsolete II *Market stagnation*

Figure 8.1 Classification of actor industries (manufacturing sector).

• Groups of services according to market and user orientation • Division of services groups through growth characteristic • Final classification into supply and demand driven groups based on temporal growth variations.	
Strong to medium growth service industries	**Medium to weak growth service industries**
Producer services	
Supply-driven 1) ICT services 2) Advertising, design and other consultancy 3) R&D laboratories 4) Security services	*Demand-driven* 5) Financial and legal services 6) Technical and engineering consultancy 7) Leasing of man. equipment 8) Industry-related wholesale
Consumer and general services *Mainly demand driven*	
1) Cleaning and sanitation 2) Cons. related wholesale 3) Restaurants and hotels 4) Retail/occasional products 5) Recreation and culturals 6) Food retail	7) Other retail 8) Vehicle trade and maint. 9) Communication, postals. 10) Construction 11) Other consumer services 12) Dept stores/hypermarkets 13) Electricity, gas, water

Figure 8.2 Classification of service industries.

we let the growth rates over time for the service industries, in combination with productivity development, decide, together with product/market characteristics, whether the industry should be classified as supply-driven or demand-driven. This is summed up in Figure 8.2.

A national picture

In general and aggregated terms, the Swedish economy has been characterized by dramatic shifts from severe downswings and crisis to dramatic expansion periods during the last 30 years.

The period studied here, 1978 to 1980, commences with a severe crisis (1975/1980). This crisis in particular is not covered in this paper. However, the late 1970s were not just a time of crisis but also the starting point of the renewal/transformation phase of the new technology shift. Growth rate therefore began to increase during the 1980s, partly due to new technologies and partly to short business cycles favourable to Swedish industries, and was followed by a short but severe crisis (1990/1993) where the last remnants of the former cycle were definitely shaken out. From then on growth increased even more during the 1990s, interrupted by a temporary downswing around the millennium shift. The 2000 downswing could be regarded as the culmination crisis of the first half of the structural cycle. This kind of crisis is the result of hectic growth, in the end causing frivolous entrepreneurship, overinvestment and sometimes bottlenecks in production. Once this crisis was mastered, the economy ran more smoothly for a couple of years when rationalization took over, until faced with the global financial crisis.

For the core of our analysis, we select the most progressive actor industries from manufacturing and services. The public sector is excluded. In this analysis, we mainly focus on industries that have grown faster than the economy as a whole during the period studied. These are selected from both manufacturing and services, and from both the supply- and demand-driven categories. Figure 8.3

Supply-driven (Strong national growth industries)	Demand-driven (Strong national growth industries)
1. Renewed (manufacturing industries) 2. ICT services 3. Advertising, marketing, other consultancy 4. R&D laboratories 5. Security services	1. Induced (I) (manufacturing industries) 2. Financial and legal services 3. Technical and engineering consultancy 4. Leasing of man. equipment 5. Industry-related wholesale 6. Cleaning and sanitation 7. Consumer-related wholesale 8. Retail/occasional products 9. Restaurants and hotels

Figure 8.3 Most salient supply- and demand-driven industries.

displays which industries represent the most progressive development among the supply- and demand-driven industries, respectively (hence called 'most salient supply- and demand-driven industries'). Industries not included in the figure are summarized as 'other industries' during the rest of the chapter. These industries have not been driving the economy, but they are, of course, not unimportant. Despite the fact that their shares have diminished substantially during the period studied, they still account for half of the market-oriented economy.

National growth is summarized in Figure 8.4, using selected industries. The late starting year (1985) is explained by data restrictions for the service industries. The period 1985–1992 is early transformation when old and new technologies are struggling for supremacy in the economy. The period 1992–2000 is late transformation and 2000–2008 is the rationalization period. Despite the simplifications made, the main characteristics of economic growth, as displayed in earlier studies, are still indicated in Figure 8.4. Supply-driven industries were growing very early in the technology shift process. Already in early transformation, growth was increasing faster than for other industries. After the bank and budget crisis at the beginning of the 1990s, growth accelerated further and reached its first peak around the year 2000. Growth was at a standstill during the so-called transformation crisis, but then accelerated again and reached its final peak in 2004, from then on losing its momentum.

The most salient demand-driven industries could not keep up with the technology-driven industries in terms of growth, but grew faster than the rest of the market economy during early transformation. The main effects of the technology shift on demand-driven industries, however, emerge much later. Not until a couple of

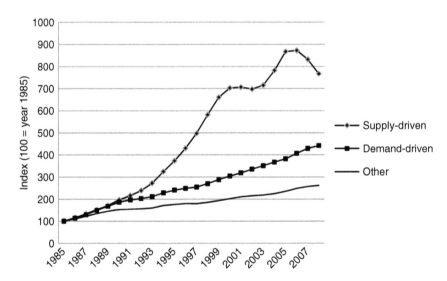

Figure 8.4 Growth indices of most salient supply- and demand-driven industries, and other industries, 1985–2008.

Note: Indices (1985=100) calculated by authors on current value added. Original data from Statistics Sweden.

Table 8.2 Growth in value added in most salient supply-driven, most demand-driven industries, and other industries, 1985–2008

	Growth in value added in per cent				Shares of value added in market economy			
	1985– 1992	1992– 2000	2000– 2008	1985– 2008	1985	1992	2000	2008
Supply-driven industries	128	222	2	650	8.4	11.4	23.1	18.6
Demand-driven industries	100	53	45	346	19.7	23.4	22.5	25.9
Other industries	53	33	28	162	71.8	65.2	54.5	55.5
Total	69	60	26	240	100	100	100	100

Note: Calculated by authors on current value added. Original data from Statistics Sweden.

years before the millennium shift did growth rates slowly begin to increase. Other industries grew at a slow and steady pace, only slightly and indirectly affected by the technology shift process.

Table 8.2 accounts more specifically for the growth of the same industry aggregates during different time periods and for their shares of the market economy at different points in time. Supply-driven industries were already in the lead in early transformation and peaked in full transformation (1992–2000). They have grown almost three times as fast as the aggregate market economy during the period. All in all, the share of the supply-driven industries first tripled in transformation then settled at a doubling in rationalization.

Also, the most salient demand-driven industries grew faster than the economy as a whole. However, their shares increased by only a few percentage units. Other industries grew very slowly and decreased their shares by almost 20 percentage units. Industries that have been leading the transformation, on the supply as well as on the demand side, have thus increased from about a quarter to almost half of the market economy during the technology shift process.

Focusing on employment, Table 8.3 shows that economic growth preceded employment growth on a national level. The most salient supply- as well as the demand-driven industries increased their employment during early transformation when employment development in the whole market economy was rather sluggish. A more visible increase occurred in full transformation and rationalization. Other industries did not contribute to any increase in national employment. The most salient supply- and demand-driven industries therefore accounted for all of the increase in employment in the country during the period that we study.

A systemic approach to regional development

A central issue in this chapter is whether the transformation, growth and employment change that have been analysed on an aggregate national level occurred simultaneously in all regions in the Swedish system. The technology shift approach in fact suggests that due to variations in the receiver and development

Table 8.3 Employment in most salient supply- and demand-driven industries, and other industries, 1985–2008

	Growth in employment in per cent				Shares of employment in market economy			
	1985– 1992	*1992– 2000*	*2000– 2008*	*1985– 2008*	*1985*	*1992*	*2000*	*2008*
Supply-driven industries	32	93	4	166	7.7	11.4	17.9	17.8
Demand-driven industries	18	8	11	41	22.7	23.4	26.3	27.6
Other industries	−4	−8	3	−9	69.6	65.2	55.8	54.6
Total	4	6	5	16	100	100	100	100
Absolute figures	78,675	117,720	109,565	305,960	1,935,022	2,013,697	2,131,417	2,240,982

Note: Original data from Statistics Sweden.

competence, regions will play different roles over time in the economic development of a country. Divergence among regions might therefore prevail during certain time periods, while being counteracted by convergence in later periods. This sequence of systematic lead-lag relationships between regions has formed the bases of *the geographical reference cycle* (Schön, 1998; Lundquist and Olander, 2010), where the economy's adjustment during a technology shift process is far from equally distributed across space. At the beginning of the technology shift, we can expect that the industries making early use of new technological opportunities are mainly located in the bigger regions at the top of a regional hierarchy. These regions provide sufficient economies of scale when transaction costs are high. In these regions, mature businesses, which initially dominate the scene, gradually decrease in size and importance, offering space and resources to newly emerging activities. Regions at lower levels of a regional hierarchy, which lack sufficient receiver and development competence, are not able to attract new industries in the early stages of the technology shift. As the technology shift progresses, transaction costs will gradually fall in the new industries and the larger regional markets become strained on the resource side. In this situation, industries that draw upon new technologies or incorporate them into their core activities start to diffuse regionally. This leads to an accelerated growth in value added, productivity and employment in a much broader set of regions. However, this is not an 'epidemic' diffusion process in the sense that it is the same thing or technologies that diffuse over time (Freeman *et al.*, 1982).

The geographical reference cycle is a stylized depiction of the theoretical expectations of regional lead-lag relationships during a technology shift process. But it stresses that processes of adjustment following the introduction of new general-purpose technologies are inherently determined by complex patterns in the changing roles of various industries and regions. In the

Table 8.4 Population and number of industries within tiers in 2000

Tiers	Population (mean)	No. of industries (index)	Variation coefficient	No. of regions
Stockholm	2,171,700	100	—	1
Gothenburg	898,400	95	—	1
Malmö	635,600	93	—	1
Medium	138,500	67	9	29
Small	29,500	41	17	35
Micro	7,600	22	21	25

Notes: Index relates to the number of industries in Stockholm (index=100). Variation coefficient is within group variation of number of industries. Original data from Statistics Sweden.

following analysis *a systemic approach* will be applied, referring to the notion that a technology shift is spread throughout and affects the whole regional system in which all parts are working together. A similar view is shared by Martin (2015). He suggests that an encompassing evolutionary-historical, geographical understanding of the economy should embrace the manifold of endogenous and institutional approaches to regional development and that we do little such work today. Focus will be set on how regional development at different levels of the regional hierarchy relates to the national development, and to the renewal in other regions.

In the analysis, 92 LA regions (local labour market regions) have been categorized into six groups based on regional size (population). Besides the three metropolitan regions of Stockholm, Gothenburg and Malmö, the rest of the Swedish LA regions are grouped into medium, small and micro regions. As can be seen from Table 8.4, mean population and mean industry diversity in groups are well related. Homogeneity within groups is quite high, as shown by the variation coefficients. The core of the analysis will be the two main forces of the technology shift already discussed: the primary supply and technology effect, and the secondary or induced demand effect.

Drivers of transformation in regions

Table 8.5 gives a first indication that regions on different levels of the regional system have been affected by the technology shift in varying ways. The growth patterns of the most salient supply-driven industries display obvious geographical (hierarchical) and temporal patterns. Growth in these industries was initialized and led primarily by the Stockholm region (first-tier region). One striking feature is the dominant position that the Stockholm region had in 1985. Even more striking is that this position was further strengthened until the millennium shift, when half of the value added (VA) produced in the country in supply-driven industries was located in the region. With a time lag, a diffusion process took place, causing Gothenburg and Malmö to strengthen their positions in supply-driven industries. All groups at lower levels of the regional hierarchy had significantly lower growth

Table 8.5 Regional growth rates and shares of value added in most salient supply- and demand-driven industries, and other industries, 1985–2008

	Growth in value added (%)				Regional shares of total VA in the industries			
	1985–1992	1992–2000	2000–2008	1985–2008	1985	1992	2000	2008
Stockholm								
Supply-driven	178	239	−4	805	39.0	42.4	50.0	47.1
Demand-driven	93	58	41	331	34.0	32.9	33.8	32.9
Other industries	70	31	41	212	19.6	19.8	21.3	23.3
Total	*91*	*80*	*24*	*326*	*24.1*	*25.0*	*30.8*	*30.2*
Gothenburg								
Supply-driven	130	328	16	1043	7.8	9.4	10.5	11.9
Demand-driven	92	57	60	381	12.1	12.0	11.9	13.1
Other industries	46	31	50	188	10.5	11.2	9.9	11.5
Total	*62*	*65*	*45*	*285*	*10.6*	*11.2*	*10.5*	*12.0*
Malmö								
Supply-driven	150	227	45	1081	4.7	5.1	5.2	7.3
Demand-driven	100	60	58	406	7.8	7.7	8.2	8.8
Other industries	61	9	34	135	6.8	6.6	5.8	6.1
Total	*75*	*40*	*43*	*251*	*6.8*	*6.7*	*6.2*	*7.0*
Medium								
Supply-driven	86	195	−4	428	39.4	34.4	29.4	27.7
Demand-driven	109	50	41	344	37.0	38.2	37.8	36.9
Other industries	51	36	21	146	47.5	47.3	47.5	44.6
Total	*63*	*52*	*21*	*199*	*44.7*	*44.0*	*41.1*	*39.4*
Small								
Supply-driven	82	108	23	367	8.6	8.0	4.4	5.4
Demand-driven	101	37	47	304	8.1	8.1	7.3	7.3
Other industries	41	46	18	144	13.1	12.8	13.2	12.2
Total	*52*	*49*	*24*	*179*	*11.7*	*11.3*	*9.9*	*9.7*
Micro								
Supply-driven	99	258	25	789	0.5	0.7	0.5	0.6
Demand-driven	117	37	44	326	1.0	1.1	1.0	1.0
Other industries	37	32	34	143	2.5	2.4	2.3	2.4
Total	*46*	*39*	*35*	*174*	*2.1*	*1.9*	*1.6*	*1.7*

Note: Original data from Statistics Sweden.

rates during the early (1985–1992) and late transformation (1992–2000). The renewal impulses induced by the technology shift have thus primarily generated strong growth effects in the top three levels of the regional hierarchy. This results in a strong divergence in the regional system during the transformation phase of the growth cycle. However, in the following rationalization period (2000–2008), the difference in growth rates between different levels in the regional hierarchy diminished. This indicates the start of a 'catch-up period' for regions just below the top of the regional hierarchy. This is shown by the fact that the Stockholm region displays decreasing growth rates and falling shares in the most salient supply-driven industries while Malmö and Gothenburg still exhibit strong growth rates and increase their share of these industries. Small and micro regions recover slightly during the rationalization. However, both small and medium-sized regions are very far from regaining their positions from the mid-1980s in terms of shares of the country's supply-driven industries.

It is also apparent from Table 8.5 that the regional variation in growth rates is more extensive in the supply-driven part of the economy than in the demand-driven part. Stockholm and Gothenburg show lower growth rates during early transformation in demand-driven industries than regions at lower levels of the regional system. The reason for this is that the small regions are still very competitive in old production and are not yet being challenged by new demand. It was not until late transformation and rationalization that growth in these industries took off in the metropolitan areas, based on new demand coming from supply-driven industries and increasing household purchasing power. The transformation process at the top of the hierarchy is, with time, increasingly characterized by induced or secondary growth forces. The growth effect coming from demand-driven industries is lagged compared with supply-driven industries. In general, the effect seems to be minor also, demonstrated by the fact that the shares of industries in the different groups of regions are quite stable over time.

Finally, a closer look at the development of other industries over time and space further confirms the national picture that these industries are not the core target of technology shift or important drivers of regional transformation. The growth rates, compared with supply- and demand-driven industries, are considerably lower and more evenly spread between regional groups. This is particularly the case in the transformation phases. In early transformation the growth rates are quite similar in all regional tiers, although slightly higher in Stockholm and the other metropolitan regions compared with the lower levels of the regional system. Late transformation shows the opposite pattern and the metropolitan regions, in particular Malmö, are lagging behind. For other industries the net effect of 15 years of transformation is stability; the regional groups' shares of these industries are very stable. After the millennium shift the pattern reverses when growth rates accelerate in the metropolitan regions leading to these regions gaining shares of the total VA produced in other industries. This development is clearly at the expense of all other types of regions, but particularly of medium-sized regions. Even though other industries exhibit a 'passive' or indirect and late role in the technology shift, their development is important for the understanding of the outcome of long-term regional growth and transformation. Although strongly decreasing in size over time, it is still by far the largest industry group in the country. In many respects they constitute the backbone of the economy in medium, small, and micro regions and have acted as a stabilizing factor in this part of the regional system. However, a problematic situation or a paradox for medium, small and micro regions is that over the whole period 1985–2008 they lose rather considerable shares of VA from this declining industry group, at the same time as they become increasingly specialized in these industries.

Drivers of economic growth in regions

An issue of great concern is how the different trajectories of supply-driven and demand-driven transformation are linked to total regional growth. Table 8.6 displays the value added growth rates of the most salient supply-driven industries and the total market economy for the different regional groups during early transformation (1985–1992), late transformation (1992–2000) and the beginning of rationalization (2000–2008). Tables 8.7 and 8.8 show the corresponding information for the most salient demand-driven industries and other industries, respectively.

During early transformation, supply-driven industries in the metropolitan regions (Stockholm, Gothenburg and Malmö) were the predominant drivers of growth, together with demand-driven industries to a lesser extent. Especially in Stockholm, the strong growth was based on a superior supply-driven development during early transformation. For medium and small regions, the picture is reversed. These were primarily dependent on growth in demand-driven production in ageing industries, with supply-driven industries playing a secondary role. In fact, in most of the regional system, supply-driven growth was strong enough to compensate for the phasing out of older activities in the wake of the technology shift. Other industries did not play an important role for total growth in any of the regional groups during early transformation.

Table 8.6 Regional growth rates of value added: most salient supply-driven industries and total market economy, 1985–2008

	1985–1992		1992–2000		2000–2008		1985–2008	
	Supply-driven	*Total*	*Supply-driven*	*Total*	*Supply-driven*	*Total*	*Supply-driven*	*Total*
Stockholm	178	91	239	80	−4	24	805	326
Gothenburg	130	62	328	65	16	45	1043	285
Malmö	150	75	227	40	45	43	1081	251
Medium	86	63	195	52	−4	21	428	199
Small	82	52	108	49	23	24	367	179
Micro	99	46	258	39	25	35	789	174
Sweden	*128*	*69*	*222*	*60*	*2*	*26*	*650*	*240*

Notes: Original data from Statistics Sweden. Change over periods in per cent.

Table 8.7 Regional growth rates in value added: most salient demand-driven industries and total market economy, 1985–2008

	1985–1992		1992–2000		2000–2008		1985–2008	
	Demand-driven	Total	Demand-driven	Total	Demand-driven	Total	Demand-driven	Total
Stockholm	93	91	58	80	41	24	331	326
Gothenburg	92	62	57	65	60	45	381	285
Malmö	100	75	60	40	58	43	406	251
Medium	109	63	50	52	41	21	344	199
Small	101	52	37	49	47	24	304	179
Micro	117	46	37	39	44	35	326	174
Sweden	100	69	53	60	45	26	346	240

Notes: Original data from Statistics Sweden. Change over periods in per cent.

Table 8.8 Regional growth rates in value added: other industries and total market economy, 1985–2008

	1985–1992		1992–2000		2000–2008		1985–2008	
	Other industries	Total	Other industries	Total	Other industries	Total	Other industries	Total
Stockholm	70	91	31	80	41	24	212	326
Gothenburg	46	62	31	65	50	45	188	285
Malmö	61	75	9	40	34	43	135	251
Medium	51	63	36	52	21	21	146	199
Small	41	52	46	49	18	24	144	179
Micro	37	46	32	39	34	35	142	174
Sweden	53	69	33	60	28	26	166	240

Notes: Original data from Statistics Sweden. Change over periods in per cent.

During late transformation, supply-driven growth became much more diffused in the regional system, and the most important driver of growth in all regional groups. However, Gothenburg replaced Stockholm as the most important regional growth engine for these industries. Only in the middle of the regional hierarchy, in Malmö and the medium-sized regions, were the demand-driven industries already contributing to the total regional growth. Other industries did not have an important role for total growth in this period either. Only in the smallest regions (small and micro) did other industries grow at a rate reasonably in line with average regional growth.

Overall, the positive effects of the technology shift initially mainly benefited regions at the top of the hierarchy. Towards rationalization, this picture gradually changed, and all top-level regions except Malmö, including the medium-sized regions, lost the growth power of their supply-driven industries. Instead, they needed to rely on the growth of demand-driven industries. Only in Malmö and in the very small regions did some supply-driven growth still remain in late-developed niches of these industries during rationalization. Growth in the smaller regions was still very reliant on the growth in demand-driven industries during rationalization. Also, during rationalization, for the first time in this technology shift, other industries played a more leading role for regional growth. During this period, these 'wealth- and consumption-driven' industries contributed to the general growth at the top of the regional hierarchy (Stockholm and Gothenburg). In the smaller regions, however, these industries were much less able to sustain regional growth.

The regional growth evidence reveals obvious hierarchical patterns in growth over time, as well as lead-lag relationships between the regional groups and industries during the technology shift. The investigated period as a whole (1985–2008) revealed yet another hierarchical pattern in the regional system. In general, the top-tier regions did benefit from both very strong growth in the most salient supply-driven industries, and growth in total value added. Even with a diffusing growth pattern following the beginning of rationalization after 2000, the first parts of the technology shift process induced divergence in the regional system. This strong divergence accrued from the growth of a particular set of supply-driven industries. In contrast, the growth effects of the demand-driven industries were much more evenly distributed in the regional system than that of the supply-driven industries. During the technology shift, the driving forces of growth seem to start in the supply-oriented part of the economy, and are subsequently supplemented by and shifted towards the demand-driven industries. In rationalization, other industries become important for the growth of the top-hierarchy regions.

Overall, regions further down the hierarchy are characterized by a substantially weaker economic development during the time that we study. This is the case not only in terms of much more humble average growth, but also in the fact that the growth of the most progressive industries of the technology shift never really seems to take off in the smaller regions. They are, in this sense, also left with increasingly vulnerable economic structures. An exception is the comparatively strong growth that supply-driven industries in the micro regions display during rationalization. However, this growth takes off from very low numbers, and it remains to be seen to what extent this could be sustained in the longer run.

Growth and employment

With the identified hierarchical patterns of growth and lead-lag relations between industries and regions in mind, we now expand the analysis by looking at the relations between total regional growth and job creation. During the whole period more than 300,000 new jobs were created. The question is: to what extent have the different regional groups gained from this strong increase in employment? Table 8.9 compares total value added (VA) growth rates with employment change for the different regional groups during the different subperiods of the technology shift.

Early transformation (1985–1992) is a period characterized by a battle between new emerging industries and old remnants from the former cycle. During this

Table 8.9 Regional growth rates of employment and value added of total market economy, 1985–2008

	1985–1992		1992–2000		2000–2008		1985–2008	
	Employment	*VA*	*Employment*	*VA*	*Employment*	*VA*	*Employment*	*VA*
Stockholm	11.1	91	16.1	80	4.8	24	35.2	326
Gothenburg	6.4	62	10.2	65	12.4	45	31.8	285
Malmö	9.3	75	5.6	40	10.0	43	26.9	251
Medium	1.2	63	0.3	52	3.0	21	4.5	199
Small	−3.4	52	0.2	49	4.4	24	1.0	179
Micro	−5.6	46	−0.4	39	1.5	35	−4.6	174
Sweden	*4.1*	*69*	*5.8*	*60*	*5.1*	*26*	*15.8*	*240*

Notes: Original data from Statistics Sweden. Change over periods in per cent.

turbulent phase of the technology shift, 78,000 new jobs were created; however, they were very unequally distributed in the regional system. Only the metropolitan areas create strong growth in VA in combination with increasing employment. This is, as discussed earlier, a result of strong growth mainly based on supply-driven, and to some extent demand-driven, industries creating new jobs at a rate that clearly exceeds the ones lost in other parts of the economy. Medium-sized regions are more or less on a par when it comes to growth rate and employment development. During the same period, small and micro regions also generate growth in VA, but display a strong decrease in employment. Of course, this depends on lower growth rates in general, but more importantly on the character of growth. These regions rely to a great extent on surviving industries from the rationalization phase of the former technology shift working with price competition, rationalization and a decreasing number of jobs. The weak growth that takes place in supply-driven industries in small and micro regions is very far from compensating for the job losses in other parts of the economy.

In late transformation (1992–2000) the job creation increases at an even stronger pace, particularly at the absolute top of the regional hierarchy. The combined forces of supply- and demand-driven growth go hand in hand with an explosion of new jobs in Stockholm and Gothenburg, counting for more than 80 per cent of the total of 117,000 new jobs generated during the period in the country. Malmö and medium-sized regions are falling behind but still combine growth in production with increased employment, although on a considerably lower level than the two other metropolitan areas. For small and micro regions that suffered seriously during the early transformation, the situation improves in late transformation. Small regions have a slight increase in employment and micro regions are more or less on a par again. This means that in general all regional groups contribute to the strong increase of employment during late transformation. Although the situation for many regions down the hierarchy gradually becomes more favourable in absolute numbers, the period is, in relative terms, very much characterized by a strong divergence in the regional system, to the benefit of the top levels of the hierarchy.

The strong trend of divergence observed during transformation is partly halted in the rationalization phase (2000–2008). Stockholm, which during this period displayed lower growth rates in general but particularly in supply- and demand-driven industries (see Tables 8.6 and 8.7), has lost momentum when it comes to job creation. The role as the country's most important employment engine is now shifting to Gothenburg, which outperforms the Stockholm region, and Malmö, not only in relative terms but also in absolute numbers. Also, medium, small and micro regions increase their employment when the growth impulses from the technological shift gradually start filtering down the hierarchy, although at rather modest growth rates. However, this has not compensated for the severe losses in earlier phases of the technology shift.

Figure 8.5 summarizes the relation between regional growth and employment. National average growth rates are set to zero. Regional values for the two variables are deviations from these national values. For our entire investigated period, there is a very strong descriptive connection between regional economic growth, measured in VA, and changes in the number of employees. However, a closer inspection of the graph shows that there are differences in returns to total VA growth in different parts of the regional system. The lowest layers of the regional system (micro and small regions) exhibit increasing returns to total VA growth while the middle part (small, medium and Malmö) displays an almost constant

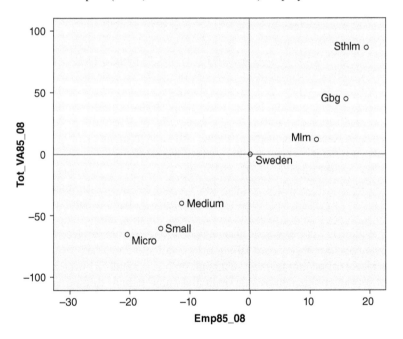

Figure 8.5 Growth of value added in total market economy versus growth of employment in different tiers of regions, 1985–2008: deviation in percentage units from the national growth rate.

Note: Original data from Statistics Sweden.

return. The top level (Stockholm and Gothenburg) demonstrates decreasing returns, implying that the economic growth is generated with a higher labour productivity per capita.

Twenty-five years of growth and transformation have immensely strengthened the labour market at the top level of the regional hierarchy in Sweden (Table 8.9 and Figure 8.5). These regions, mainly based on strong supply-oriented growth, account for 87 per cent of the 305,000 new jobs created in the country. Medium-sized regions consolidate their position in absolute number of jobs but losses in relative terms. Small and particularly micro regions suffer more from the technology shift and the following structural transformation. Only in the most favourable exceptions did the growth force in these regions manage to sustain a growth level compensating for the jobs that are phased out. This problem is related to the tricky dilemma discussed by Martynovich and Lundquist (2015), where regions lower down the hierarchy tend to increase the inflow of labour through increased specialization, and this generates even higher outflows of labour leading to a negative cumulative process of shrinking local labour markets, increasing specialization and leading to fewer opportunities to diversify into related industries. In summary, 60 out of 92 labour market regions have not been able to benefit from the jobs created during the last three decades of transformation and growth in the wake of the current technology shift in Sweden.

Growth and regional income

We now expand the analysis once more by looking at the relation between regional growth and regional incomes. In doing so, two income concepts will be used. One of these concepts is gross market income, which is wages coming from employment and private business activities in the market economy. Public sector wages are, however, included in market income. The other concept is gross total income, comprising market income as mentioned, plus basic pensions, and social transfer payments. Thus, gross total income includes political efforts to influence the outcome of market forces.

In early transformation it was primarily medium and small regions still operating within the older economy that managed to change total VA growth into increasing market income (Table 8.10). For Stockholm and Malmö it was the other way around. Growth was increasing more than market income, probably because new expanding industries still had an abundant supply of young yet well-educated people that kept wages down. In late transformation market income increased, but much less than total VA growth. Not in one single group of regions did income even grow on a par with total VA growth. This is a surprising outcome for late transformation when new industries were expected to absorb huge amounts of adequately skilled labour, even facing bottleneck situations in labour markets. One probable explanation might be a strong governmental budget discipline in these years combined with a fierce fight against inflation, which kept wage demands down. All this said about late transformation, however, turned round completely in rationalization. All regional groups saw their market incomes

Table 8.10 Regional growth rates of market income and total market economy value added, 1985–2008

	1985–1992		1992–2000		2000–2008		1985–2008	
	Market income	*Total VA*	*Market income*	*Total VA*	*Market income*	*Total VA*	*Market income*	*Total VA*
Stockholm	79	91	53	80	43	24	292	326
Gothenburg	71	62	47	65	50	45	276	285
Malmö	73	75	39	40	49	43	258	251
Medium	68	63	32	52	41	21	213	199
Small	62	52	26	49	38	24	181	179
Micro	53	46	19	39	33	35	141	174
Sweden	*71*	*69*	*39*	*60*	*43*	*26*	*238*	*240*

Notes: Original data from Statistics Sweden. Change over periods in per cent.

increasing faster than their total VA growth. Growth rates for market incomes were also converging in the regional system in this time period. Seen across the whole time period, market income development was quite hierarchical, with metropolitan regions having growth rates double those of small regions. Metropolitan regions increased their total share of market income in the country by 6.2 percentage units after 1985. Thus, regional disparity in market incomes widened.

Figure 8.6 makes more visible the relation between total VA growth and market income growth between 1985 and 2008. National average growth rates are set to zero. Regional values for the two variables are deviations from these national values. At the bottom of the regional hierarchy there is increasing returns to total VA growth. A small difference in growth rates between micro regions and small regions corresponds to a much bigger difference in market income rates. At the top of the hierarchy there is, in contrast, decreasing returns to total VA growth. Between Malmö and Gothenburg and between Gothenburg and Stockholm, the total VA growth rates were increasing more than the corresponding market income rates. The explanations for this are probably labour productivity differences in combination with increasing competition between capital rents and market incomes.

Basic pensions and social transfer payments could be expected to level out differences in market income development between regions. This is actually what happened between 1985 and 2008 but to a rather small extent (Figure 8.7). In early transformation there was a distinct 'Robin Hood effect' creating a redistribution of incomes from metropolitan regions to small and micro regions when these regions were still working in the old economy and suffering from severe unemployment during the 'shake out' crises at the very beginning of the 1990s. In late transformation there was a weak and smooth levelling out of income differences between regions. Nothing more seems to have been called for in this time period when the whole regional system began to come into full swing. Finally, in rationalization an inverted 'Robin Hood effect' became noticeable, with Stockholm receiving increased shares of pensions and social transfer payments and small regions

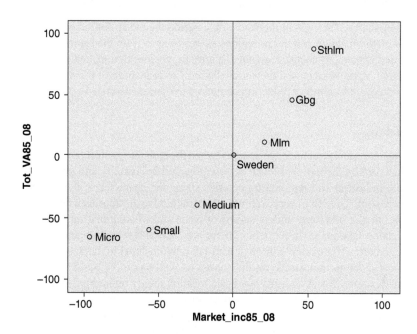

Figure 8.6 Growth of value added in total market economy versus growth of total market income in different tiers of regions, 1985–2008: deviation in percentage units from the national growth rate.

Note: Original data from Statistics Sweden.

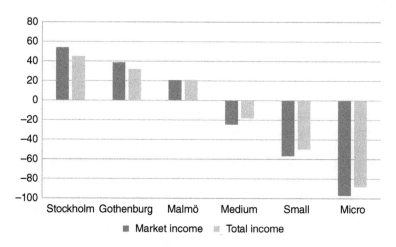

Figure 8.7 Regional growth rates in market income and total income, 1985–2008: deviations in percentage units from the national growth rate.

Note: Original data from Statistics Sweden.

losing their shares. Throughout the whole time period the redistribution of incomes favoured medium, small and micro regions as can be seen from the figure, but to a very limited extent. In general, regional disparity in incomes diminished very little. Metropolitan regions increased their total share of total income in the country by 4.7 percentage units, a minor reduction compared to market income.

Conclusions

Interesting empirical structures are revealed when the technology shift process, normally analysed on the national level, is disaggregated industrially and geographically. The industrial and regional trajectories shape the character of the national technology shift. They fit in very well with the structural cycle approach developed by Schön but also add more understanding of when and where transformation and rationalization take place. In particular, there are clear and systemic general geographical patterns (for example through lead-lag relationships) in the development of the most dynamic industries, on the supply as well as on the demand side of industrial development. As it turns out, basic location theory on internal and external scale economies, factor endowments and transaction costs works very well with the technology shift thesis in understanding its general spatial outcome. Growth during the period that we study reinforces the already present hierarchy of regions in the Swedish regional system. So far, the gains and most progressive dynamics of the technology shift have been to the advantage of the metropolitan regions at the top of the hierarchy. This is evident in all our investigated variables – value added, employment and income. There are some tendencies of spatial diffusion of growth in the leading industries, but the main tendency is still that the effects of the technology shifts seem to diffuse to a broader range of industries at the top of the hierarchy, rather than further down the hierarchy to peripheral regions.

The systemic approach that we propose to specifically analyse growth and transformation over the medium term is very different from the dominant theoretical perspectives on these matters in economic geography and the regional sciences today. Theories about clusters, agglomerations and innovation systems have, in many cases, provided excellent understanding of the prerequisites of growth and transformation in individual regions. However, this has, to some extent, been at the expense of an understanding of how regions are affected by each other, and by developments elsewhere in the economy. Our approach does not at all rule out the existence or importance of clusters, agglomeration externalities or regional institutions promoting growth. Indeed, these factors form vital aspects of the regional receiver and development competence. But rather than emphasizing the uniqueness of each region and its economic trajectory, we chose the systemic approach to emphasize the traits that regions on the same level in the hierarchy share, rather than what makes them distinct. And they seem to share quite a lot. Overall, in this chapter we have not stressed the competitive aspect between regions, but that complementarity between regions is equally important.

So far, our findings have not been good news for regions in the middle and lower parts of the regional hierarchy. At the same time as these regions lose relative national shares of other industries, they still tend to become more specialized in these industries. This could be characterized as an 'anorectic' process of specialization where these regions cannot expect to gain enough weight from strong growing supply- and demand-driven industries, but only from specialization in mainly decreasing and stagnating industries with fewer prospects for the future. If the diffusion tendencies of previous technology shifts (Enflo and Henning, this volume) do not reach the lower parts of the hierarchy, many of these regions will face problems in sustaining high-productivity activities in the future.

The hierarchical growth patterns, though of course interesting in themselves, also have consequences for job creation, and for the development of regional income. The revitalization during the current technology shift has thus far been a top-hierarchy phenomenon that correlates strongly with overall regional growth rates. The metropolitan regions are very clear drivers and winners of this 40-year development. They constitute 80 per cent of total employment growth in the private sector during the period that we investigate. Some catch-up by smaller regions does take place at the end of the cycle, but this far from compensates earlier losses in value added and employment. We suspect that the main tendencies identified in this chapter can be found in other countries as well. However, if a systemic approach is used to analyse the transformation of other economies in the future, we believe that this has great potential to enrich the current debate in economic geography.

Our suggested approach echoes the classic arguments by Christaller (1966) and Lösch (1954). However, this way of seeing regions as parts of economic hierarchies has left little trace in contemporary economic geography. We find this unfortunate, because it limits our understanding about the prerequisites for growth. Regional size, hierarchy and distances in combination with cyclic impulses seem to put strong restrictions on what can be achieved by individual regions, although this will not determine the future trajectory of each region. Of course, all regional tiers have their outliers, i.e. regions performing better or worse than their colleagues in the tier. Identifying which ones they are and why they are performing in different ways, perhaps due to unique local growth incentives, is an important future research field, opening the way for multi-theoretical approaches within the suggested structural framework.

Note

1 A thorough exposition of methods and data used for manufacturing industries is given in Svensson Henning (2009) and Lundquist et al. (2008a). For service industries a similar account is given in Lundquist et al. (2008b).

References

Åkerman, J. (1970), 'De långa vågornas gåta'. In *Internationell politik och samhällse-konomi*. Lund: Studentlitteratur.
Boschma, R. A. (2004), 'Competitiveness of Regions from an Evolutionary Perspective', *Regional Studies*, vol. 38, pp. 1001–14.

Boschma, R. A. and Lambooy, J. G. (1999), 'Evolutionary Economics and Economic Geography', *Journal of Evolutionary Economics*, vol. 9, pp. 411–29.

Boschma, R. A. and Frenken, K. (2006), 'Why is Economic Geography not an Evolutionary Science? Towards an Evolutionary Economic Geography', *Journal of Economic Geography*, vol. 6, pp. 273–302.

Boschma, R. and Martin, R. (eds) (2010), *The Handbook of Evolutionary Economic Geography*. Cheltenham: Edward Elgar Publishing.

Bresnahan, T. F. and Trajtenberg, M. (1995), 'General Purpose Technologies: Engines of Growth?' *Journal of Econometrics*, vol. 65, pp. 83–109.

Christaller, W. (1966), *Central Places in Southern Germany* (translated by C. W. Baskins). Englewood Cliffs, NJ: Prentice Hall.

Dahmén, E. (1950), *Svensk industriell företagarverksamhet. Kausalanalys av den industriella utvecklingen 1919–1939*. Stockholm: IUI.

Dahmén, E. (1988), '"Development Blocks" in Industrial Economics', *Scandinavian Economic History Review*, vol. 36, pp. 3–14.

Dosi, G. (1988), 'Sources, Procedures, and Microeconomic Effects of Innovation', *Journal of Economic Literature*, vol. 26, pp. 1120–71.

Fagerberg, J. (2003), 'Schumpeter and the Revival of Evolutionary Economics: An Appraisal of the Literature', *Journal of Evolutionary Economics*, vol. 13, pp. 125–59.

Freeman, C. and Perez, C. (1988), 'Structural Crises of Adjustment, Business Cycles and Investment Behaviour'. In Dosi G., Freeman C., Nelson R., Silverberg G. and Soete L. (eds) *Technical Change and Economic Theory*. London: Pinter Publishers.

Freeman, C. and Louçã, F. (2001), *As Time Goes By. From the Industrial Revolutions to the Information Revolution*. Oxford: Oxford University Press.

Freeman, C., Clark, J. and Soete, L. (1982), *Unemployment and Technical Innovation: a Study of Long Waves and Economic Development*. London: Frances Pinter.

Frenken, K., van Oort, F. G. and Verburg, T. (2007), 'Related Variety, Unrelated Variety and Regional Economic Growth', *Regional Studies*, vol. 41, pp. 685–97.

Fujita, M., Krugman, P. and Mori, T. (1999), 'On the Evolution of Hierarchical Urban Systems', *European Economic Review*, vol. 43, pp. 209–251.

Jaffe, A. B., Trajtenberg, M. and Henderson, R. (1993), 'Geographic Localization of Knowledge Spillovers as Evidenced by Patent Citations', *Quarterly Journal of Economics*, vol. 108, pp. 577–98.

Josefsson, M. and Örtengren, J. (1980), 'Priser och omvandling i svensk industri'. In Dahmén, E. and Eliasson, G. (eds) *Industriell utveckling i Sverige. Teori och verklighet under ett sekel*. Stockholm: IUI.

Karlsson, C. and Nilsson, R. (2002), 'Agglomeration, Economies of Scale and Dynamic Specialisation in a Central Place System'. In Johansson, B., Karlsson, C. and Stough, R. (eds) *Regional Policies and Comparative Advantage*. Cheltenham: Edward Elgar Publishing.

Krugman, P. (1991), *Geography and Trade*. Cambridge, MA: MIT Press.

Lösch, A. (1954), *The Economics of Location* (translated by W. H. Woglom). New Haven, CT: Yale University Press.

Ljungberg, J. (1990), *Priser och marknadskrafter i Sverige 1885–1969. En prishistorisk studie*. Lund: Ekonomisk-historiska föreningen (diss.).

Lundquist, K.-J. and Olander, L.-O. (2001), 'Den glömda strukturcykeln. Ny syn på industrins regionala tillväxt och omvandling', *Rapporter och notiser*. Lund: Department of Social and Economic Geography.

Lundquist, K.-J., and Olander, L.-O. (2007), *Omvandlingens geografi. En studie i svensk ekonomi och regioners roller genom tre decennier*. Malmö stad, Lunds universitet, Region Skåne.

Lundquist, K.-J. and Olander, L.-O. (2010), 'Growth Cycles. Transformation and Regional Development', *SRE-DISC2010/04*, Institut für Regional- und Umweltwirtschaft, Wirtschaftsuniversität, Wien.

Lundquist, K.-J. and Olander, L.-O. (2011), 'Tillväxtens cykler – nationell omvandling och regional utveckling. Storstäder och tillväxt'. In Lindell, J. (ed.) *Storstäder och tillväxt: om storstadsregioners roll, betydelse och utmaningar för hållbar ekonomisk utveckling.* Uppsala: Department of Social and Economic Geography.

Lundquist, K.-J., Olander, L.-O. and Svensson Henning, M. (2008a), 'Decomposing the Technology Shift: Evidence from the Swedish Manufacturing Sector', *Tijdschrift voor Economische en Sociale Geografie*, vol. 99, pp. 145–59.

Lundquist, K.-J., Olander L.-O. and Svensson Henning, M. (2008b), 'Producer Services. Growth and Roles in Long Term Economic Development', *Service Industries Journal*, vol. 28, pp. 463–77.

Martin, R. (2015), 'Rebalancing the Spatial Economy: The Challenge for Regional Theory', *Territory, Politics, Governance*, vol. 3, pp. 235–72.

Martynovich, M. and Lundquist, K.-J. (2015), 'Technological Change and Geographical Reallocation of Labour: On the Role of Leading Industries', *Regional Studies*, vol. 45, (forthcoming) DOI: 10.1080/00343404.2015.1052062.

Mokyr, J. (1990), *The Lever of Riches. Technological Creativity and Economic Progress.* Oxford: Oxford University Press.

Nelson, R. (2006), 'Evolutionary Social Science and Universal Darwinism', *Journal of Evolutionary Economics*, pp. 16, pp. 491–510.

Nelson, R. R. and Winter, S. G. (1982), *An Evolutionary Theory of Economic Change.* Cambridge, MA: Belknap Press of Harvard University Press.

Perez, C. (1983), 'Structural Change and Assimilation of New Technologies in the Economic and Social Systems', *Futures*, vol. 15, pp. 357–76.

Saviotti, P. P. (2001), 'Variety, Growth and Demand.' *Journal of Evolutionary Economics*, vol. 11(1), pp. 119–42.

Schumpeter, J. A. (1934), *The Theory of Economic Development. An Inquiry into Profits, Capital, Credit, Interest and the Business Cycle.* Cambridge, MA: Harvard University Press.

Schumpeter, J. A. (1939), *Business Cycles. A Theoretical, Historical, and Statistical Analysis of the Capitalist Process.* New York: McGraw-Hill.

Schön, L. (1998), 'Industrial Crises in a Model of Long Cycles: Sweden in an International Perspective'. In T. Myllyntaus (ed.) *Economic Crises and Restructuring in History. Experiences of Small Countries.* Katharinen: Scripta Mercaturae.

Schön L. (2006), Tankar om cykler. Stockholm: SNS Förlag.

Schön, L. (2012), *An Economic History of Modern Sweden.* Oxon: Routledge.

Svensson Henning, M. (2009), *Industrial Dynamics and Regional Structural Change.* Lund: Department of Social and Economic Geography (diss.).

9 Economic environmental history

Anything new under the sun?

Astrid Kander

Sometimes a reflection upon one's own scholarly work can be useful. To what degree is one simply standing on the shoulders of giants and adding small pieces to the scientific mountain, and to what degree is one truly being novel and twisting the research agenda?

I belong to a new generation of professors at the Department of Economic History at Lund University. I wrote my PhD thesis under the supervision of Lennart Schön, completed it in 2002 and became full professor in 2010, which is fast by Swedish standards. Probably one reason for my success is that I managed to strike a balance between continuing research traditions in the discipline of economic history, and introducing new elements and broadening the research into entirely new areas.

This short essay will provide some thoughts on how my economic historical heritage has influenced my own research and more specifically how the methods and ideas in the research group around Lennart Schön at Lund University have been beneficial to my work on past and future energy transitions and their environmental implications. This work was first developed in my PhD thesis (2002), in subsequent articles and more recently in the book *Power to the People* (2013). Here, I will provide some research highlights with an emphasis on the methods and concepts developed and used. Basically, I would say that I inherited a set of ideas and analytical tools that had been employed at Lund. I developed these along my own lines to a new research agenda in the discipline – that of economic environmental history. First I did this for Sweden, later together with other researchers for a broader setting of Western Europe, and in some respects even for the globe.

Environmental history is a field that has expanded greatly over the last few decades. Economic environmental history could be considered a subdiscipline in this broad field, which focuses on the interaction of economies and their environmental impacts. On the macro level, this field of study deals with structural change in a broad sense, which may be completely unrelated to cycles of economic growth. Structural change occurs when sectors (such as industry, agriculture and services) grow at different rates. Structures can also change as a consequence of shifts in foreign trade, if countries import goods that they used to produce themselves. On the micro level, economic environmental history has typically dealt with how companies have affected their environment over time (Bergquist, 2007; Söderholm and Bergquist, 2013; Bergquist *et al.*, 2013) and how this has changed with institutional changes.

My main aspiration with this essay is to inspire young scholars, searching for their own path in research, to reflect upon their own intellectual heritage and what they could contribute. Further, that they should consider which new research questions they could pose and which possible novel combinations they could contribute with. Hopefully the essay will also be enjoyable reading for many scholars, both inside and outside our department, who have influenced my thinking over the years.

In addition, the essay will provide a brief history of the emergence of a new research area in the department and in economic history more broadly, one that is lively and expanding today. While I am writing these lines, several external research grants at our department employ about ten people in environmental history and there are still many fruitful research paths that may be taken by entrepreneurial young scholars.

My economic-historical heritage

The first thing you could ask yourself as a researcher is how and why you picked the topics you did. The world view of economic historians in the research group around Lennart Schön is basically materialistic and positivistic. Real economy factors influence ideas, as Marx suggested, rather than the other way around, as Hegel proposed. This materialistic world view is not outspoken, but clear from the research focus that mainly centres on measurable factors of production such as GDP, labour force and capital stocks, and not so much on the history of ideas or the importance of individual persons in history. The world is considered real and as scientists we can speak of it fairly objectively and argue over who is right and who is wrong. The debate is not all a matter of interpretations and competing world views, where the most powerful one will win the discussion, as postmodernists propose. Nevertheless, even with these positivistic features of the research tradition in Lund, there is a strong recognition that social science and history are not the same thing as natural science, and that creating a narrative is necessary for a good historian. Hermeneutics certainly does have a place in our discipline. We need to be able to tell a good story with a red thread and catch the interest of the audience. This narrative should be continuously tested and assessed in a critical manner, through empirical evidence, as far as is possible.

The Lund structural research tradition can therefore be categorized as an appreciative kind of history writing. The order of historical events matters for the appreciation, but also the heuristic devices and key concepts play a critical role. This is a strong tradition among historians: 'Theorizing the social process via narrative is a deep tradition in both history and sociology' (Abbott, 1991, p. 227). 'Narratives are not just sequences of events, but are tied together by a central theme' (Pedriana, 2005, p. 357).[1]

Yet, for economic historians to conduct analysis of single events or create a narrative is not always deemed sufficient. We prefer to get an idea of the magnitude of things and, if possible, directly assess the effect of one change upon another, in so-called 'decomposition analysis', where the relative importance of different factors is given in percentages. And, when we cannot assess direct impacts and are left with regression models, we find it important to look at the economic significance and not just the statistical significance. As famous economic historian McCloskey succinctly put it: 'Tell me the oomph of your coefficient; and do not confuse it with merely statistical significance' (Ziliak and McCloskey, 2004, p. 527). Size matters and this makes quantification and data collection necessary.

One of the more important things I learnt from Lennart Schön is that historical reconstruction and long time series of strategic variables can be useful for assessing our contemporary world. Putting numbers on things for which there were initially no statistics is a challenging task for the economic historian. This requires a combination of ingenuity with knowledge about facts and available numbers to create an image of the size of past phenomena, such as GDP or energy consumption. Such time series can allow us to look at our present societal problems in the historical rear-view mirror. We may take our point of departure from today's significant problems and see how strategic trends and trend breaks behaved in the past. This might shed light on whether recent developments are truly new or rather a repetition or even an enforcement of the past. In addition, such time series can be combined in relevant ways as ratios (energy/GDP, or 'energy intensity', for instance), and the long-term evolution can be used to question established ideas or stylized facts that are often based on much shorter time horizons or cross-sectional analysis, for example the environmental Kuznets curve or the idea about environmental relief through the transition to the service economy.

Questioning established facts is typical for famous economic historians like Robert Fogel, Nobel laureate in 1993, who launched counterfactual thinking (Fogel, 1964). Counterfactual thinking in history means that you ask the question: how would things have developed if a particular event or process in history had not taken place at all or had ended differently? One question asked by Fogel is: what if the railroads had never been invented? Would our economies have been greatly hampered or only moderately affected? If there had not been any railways, how would transport have been organized instead and how costly would that alternative have been in terms of foregone benefits to society? The method developed by Fogel is called the 'social savings approach', and is a growth accounting technique for the assessment of the historical implications of new technology on economic growth. In social savings calculations, the cost of the second-best alternative is estimated, and the difference between this (larger) cost and the actual cost of the better alternative is the social savings – what society saved in terms of cost in adopting the better alternative. While this approach is stimulating and aims to assess the magnitude of impacts, the drawback is that it has difficulty capturing the dynamic, positive benefits of a new technology, such as the spillover effects the railroads had for the capital market or corporate management. Fogel himself missed the time savings involved in using railways instead of canals for personal travel, but other scholars have since improved upon that particular aspect (Leunig, 2006). Although interesting, social savings misses out on some benefits and especially dynamic and reinforcing effects that create synergies and boost development.

In the economic history department at Lund, synergies around new major technologies, such as steam engines, internal combustion engines, electricity or the microprocessor, are considered to form the core of so-called development blocks. The development block is a concept introduced by Erik Dahmén (Dahmén 1950, 1988), and has, in Lennart Schön's research, been used in a wider macroeconomic sense for analysing technology shifts in economic growth (Schön, 1994, 1998, 2000, 2004, 2007, 2012). In the Lund structural change analysis, some related concepts that are more commonly used to study technology shifts are also important, such as three industrial revolutions (rather than just one big one starting in eighteenth-century England), and general-purpose technologies (GPTs), (Bresnahan and Trajtenberg, 1995). The first industrial revolution was centred on the iron-steam-coal development block, the second industrial revolution had two major development blocks, one around oil and the internal combustion engine and the other one around the electric engine and generator, and the third industrial revolution centres on the development block around the microprocessor and information and communication technology (ICT). The growth impact from GPTs is considered to be so wide that a full quantification along counterfactual thinking is deemed impossible. But in a more limited sense, counterfactual reasoning is the foundation for a method used to analyse these new structures: shift-share analysis. Shift-share analysis estimates how much of a particular change, for instance a productivity increase, is due to changes within sectors (technical change) and between sectors (structural change). It does so by asking the counterfactual question: what would productivity in the economy have been if there had only been the productivity increases within the sectors, and no structural change (change of employment between sectors)? Holding one variable constant, pretending it had not changed, allows the effect of the other variable to be estimated. Shift-share analysis has been frequently used for analysis of Swedish productivity and economic growth, and is a generally accepted method in international economic history.

Another line of thinking in economic history to which I am deeply indebted is related to structural change, and can be described as phases of economic development. This view refers to the idea that all countries may broadly develop naturally along a course, where they start as agricultural economies, later industrialize and in a later phase again make a transition to the service economy. Every country could logically go through both these transitions. With an enabling institutional framework, and access to physical capital (machines and buildings), natural and human capital and social trust, countries are able to embark on a development journey that will bring them through these phases of economic development. They are not seriously held back by more powerful nations, which allegedly should force them to play a less developed role in the world economy, according to the strand of thought of World-System theory or Dependency tradition. The argument of these theories holds that the emergence of global trading empires and colonial economies introduced fundamental inequalities into world trade, with a division between 'core' countries (often using coercive power) and 'peripheries'. Core countries specialized in more skilled and profitable activities while the peripheries became specialized providers of resource-intense goods and raw materials, permanently shaping their economic paths (for example Barbier, 2005, 2011; Wallerstein, 1974). Thinking about development as phases of growth, but with certain variations among countries, is in contrast optimistic, and is also part of my economic-historical heritage.

The last important influence from economic history that I rely firmly on in my own research is that prices matter (Jörberg, 1972; Schön, 1979; Ljungberg, 1990). Who would think that price history could be exciting? You will find out that it is if you start digging into it. One price compared with another price – the relative price – matters for development. It determines the direction for economic growth and the environmental stress, through the replacement of one (more expensive) factor with another (cheaper), which sets countries on a capital deepening path (more machinery per worker), or on a modern energy path (fossil energy replacing traditional renewable energy carriers).

Relative prices may also create intriguing price illusions when developments over longer time periods are assessed. Economic development can in fact look very different depending on whether things are portrayed in current or constant prices. A sector with increasing relative prices grows much faster in current prices than in constant prices, compared with one with decreasing relative prices. And the choice of year for the price level, which is used for the estimation in constant prices, also matters for how large economic sectors seem to be (i.e. agriculture, industry, services). A sector with increasing relative prices will look larger than others if a late price level year is chosen than if an early one is chosen. Famous economist William Baumol (1967) stressed price illusions when he discussed the cost disease of the service sector. Different productivity developments in the progressive sector (largely industry) and the less technical progressive sector (largely service), where human labour time is an intrinsic part of production, in combination with an integrated labour market that keeps wage development fairly equal in the two sectors, means that over time prices of services will go up compared with industrial goods. In Baumol's view, this explained why cities could not afford to send children to swimming classes even though society had become richer. A necessary qualification of this internal price development logic is that not all services have unchanging or slow-growing productivity. Some service sectors are technically progressive, for example banking and retail trade, in which computers take over many tasks. It is mainly personal services that are of the low-productivity kind. The dual character of the service sector led Baumol to the conclusion that it is asymptotically stagnant. Economic historian Steve Broadberry empirically measures the idea that part of the service sector is highly productive. He assesses the industrialization of certain services (Broadberry, 2006), which in fact levels out the productivity levels and growth of certain business-related services to those of industry.

Economic environmental history

Let us move on to some research in the field of economic environmental history that I have produced alone or together with others. In what sense and to what extent is this research new or similar to the economic historical heritage described earlier in this chapter. I will focus this section on the new questions that I have asked and on the combination of existing and new data, methods and concepts used and elaborated upon in order to answer them, and only briefly touch upon the results.

Economic growth, energy consumption and CO_2 emissions in Sweden 1800–2000

I could not have written my PhD thesis without access to data from a project aimed at developing Swedish historical national accounts carried out by Lennart Schön and Olle Krantz. This established GDP data back to 1800 for Sweden and was divided into the main sectors of agriculture, services and industry, which enabled structural studies (Krantz, 1986, 1987a,b, 1991; Schön, 1988, 1995; Ljungberg, 1988; Pettersson, 1987; Krantz and Schön, 2007; Schön and Krantz, 2012). This offered a golden opportunity for two new PhD students, myself in Lund, with Lennart Schön as supervisor, and Magnus Lindmark in Umeå, with Olle Krantz as his supervisor. We realized that this enabled detailed studies of the interaction between economic growth and natural resource use and pollution, and set out to estimate indicators of the environmental aspects of growth, in order to combine them with the GDP data.

I had by then encountered the environmental Kuznets curve (EKC) literature (World Bank, 1992; Selden and Song, 1993; Grossman and Kreuger, 1995; Ekins, 2000). The EKC suggests that industrialization has worsening environmental effects, but with technological development and growth of services the detrimental effects are alleviated. This means that the environmental impact and perhaps even the natural resource use describe an inverted U curve. I wanted to examine whether the inverted U-shape pattern held for energy in relation to GDP, with the inclusion of more careful historical reconstruction of both traditional energy and modern fossil fuels and electricity (Reddy and Goldemberg, 1990). My hypothesis was that the upward trend of the U-shape curve was partly caused by traditional energy carriers being underestimated in previous studies (Martin, 1988). I got a flying start in this work by gaining access to the data that Lennart Schön had prepared on Swedish energy consumption in industry, which were very detailed from 1890 onwards (Schön, 1990, 1992). I expanded the estimates of energy consumption and energy transitions to include the entire Swedish economy, and constructed estimates for agriculture, transportation, services and households. Further, I directed attention to the environmental consequences of modern energy use, in terms of CO_2 emissions. This was not very difficult for the fossil fuels that were imported to Sweden and available in the import statistics, since all carbon in the burnt fuels eventually end up as CO_2 and there are specific CO_2 factors for different fuels (Levander, 1991). For firewood the picture was much more complicated, both because the quantities of burnt firewood were more difficult to assess and because there is only a net contribution of CO_2 to the atmosphere if the forests are not allowed to recover after harvesting. Otherwise the CO_2 uptake by the forest is equally large when trees grow, as the emissions are when trees are burnt. So I devoted a couple of years to exploring the evolution of the standing timber volumes in Swedish forests and the changes in land use in general, on which I wrote a licentiate thesis. Climate change had already been put on the political agenda when I started my PhD studies in 1995, but the debate was more advanced in 2002 when I finished the book. So it was a fortunate choice of topic in retrospect, which probably eased access to publication options and external funds. My thesis is available online and is still my most cited work.

Energy, capital and identifying development blocks

Lennart Schön and I continued some fruitful collaboration after my PhD thesis. One result was the paper 'The Capital-Energy Ratio in Sweden 1870–2000', which was published in *Structural Change and Economic Dynamics* in 2007. The question was concerned with whether capital and energy had acted as substitutes or as complements. We observed an increase in the capital/energy (K/E) ratio over the period 1870–2000, which means that the capital stock has persistently grown at a higher rate than energy use, both at the GDP level and in industry, indicating an energy-saving bias in capital accumulation, or that more quality has been added to the capital stock in relation to a given amount of the energy utilized by this capital. An increase in the K/E ratio could be caused by both substitution and so-called 'biased technical change'. We employed short-term price analyses as well as long-term trend analysis to discuss this increase in the K/E ratio. In the long term, the price of energy has risen in relation to machinery, and we examined the short-term effects of price increases on substitution. We approached the question of biased technical change (the notion that more technology is embodied in the capital stock) by constructing an alternative indicator, energy services (useful energy such as light, motion, electricity and heat), to capital. Here we could rely on the conversion factors between energy and energy services for the US economy constructed by Ayres and Warr (2005). We found that capital and energy services were highly complementary in the long run. This study has inspired younger scholars, such as Rick Hölsgens in Groningen, to write on the issue of capital, energy and growth.

In our collaboration, we soon involved a highly talented young PhD student called Kerstin Enflo. We acted as co-supervisors of her PhD thesis, which consisted of a collection of articles, some of which were co-authored among the three of us. Kerstin is very skilled in econometrics and could conduct more advanced statistical analysis than we were able to. We set out to empirically identify development blocks among the industrial branches in Sweden. By operationalizing development blocks as consisting of mutually reinforcing links, because of complementarity, rather than unidirectional impacts, we could use cointegration of the growth patterns of sectors to study their interdependencies. The results identified two partly overlapping development blocks, both centred on electricity. Our joint paper, 'Identifying Development Blocks: A New Methodology', was published in the *Journal of Evolutionary Economics* in 2008.

The three of us collaborated on another task: assessing the importance of electrification in the productivity of energy in Swedish industry. Through an innovative counterfactual construction of the electricity variable, we were able to assess spillover effects from electricity on productivity that go beyond the fact that electricity is a secondary energy carrier, produced by primary energy carriers such as coal, nuclear or hydropower. We found that in sectors where electricity has multiple uses, for instance heating, lighting and motion, there was a positive effect from electrification on energy productivity. This was published under the title 'Electrification and Energy Productivity' in *Ecological Economics* in 2009.

Environmental history of Sweden

At roughly the same time as I wrote my thesis, Magnus Lindmark in Umeå estimated several other negative environmental effects of economic growth (Lindmark, 1998), and in 2004 we joined forces to publish an article about the economic environmental history of Sweden over 200 years (Kander and Lindmark, 2004). In the following year we combined our competences again to analyse the history of energy embodied in Swedish international trade during the twentieth century (Kander and Lindmark, 2006). This questioned the gloomy displacement hypothesis – that advanced countries have only managed to lower their own energy consumption and carbon emissions by importing more and exporting fewer energy-demanding goods. We applied a counterfactual analysis and found that, on the contrary, Sweden had always been a large net exporter of energy embodied in traded commodities. Nevertheless, this had not changed since 1970, when Swedish energy intensity went down and carbon emissions declined in absolute terms. Sweden had, therefore, managed to improve its technology and consumption patterns to lower CO_2 emissions after 1970, which, however, is not to say that achievements to date are sufficient for sustainability. Today Swedish emission levels are about 6 tons CO_2 per capita and to reach sustainability it should not exceed 1 ton. But Sweden still constitutes one positive example: that it is possible to lower CO_2 emissions and still maintain welfare. Real progress can take place and does not need to be a consequence of moving the problems elsewhere through trade, which of course is no solution at all for a global problem like climate change.

Soon after my thesis was completed, I expanded the land use change studies to encompass the full agricultural sector and all greenhouse gases, not just CO_2.

I had the chance to publish 'Is it Simply Getting Worse? Agriculture and Swedish Greenhouse Gas Emissions over 200 Years' in *Economic History Review* in 2008. This has been considered an interesting piece of environmental history and has been used for teaching purposes by, for instance, Professor Christine MacLeod at Bristol University, but so far it has neither received many citations nor initiated any follow-up studies for other countries. My guess is that this is mainly because of time demands and the complexity of the study with all of the variables that need to be taken into account and quantified. This work was in fact very time-consuming and challenging in terms of methods and data.

Power to the people – energy in Europe over the last five centuries

Something that was very beneficial to my intellectual development was attending an international summer school in economic history for PhD students, where I met Professor Paolo Malanima from Italy, who had long taken an interest in pre-industrial economies and their use of traditional energy carriers. He invited me to present a paper in Italy in 2002, a few months before I defended my PhD thesis, and there I met Professor Tony Wrigley and his younger colleague Paul Warde for the first time. I dared to send my PhD book to Tony Wrigley, and a week before my defence I got one of the nicest letters I have ever received back, where he praised the study and invited me to give a seminar at Cambridge. That seminar took place the following spring and became the start of a network of scholars working over several years to produce consistent time series of energy and CO_2 emissions over the last 200 years for several European countries.

Some of us in the network (Ben Gales, Paolo Malanima, Mar Rubio and myself) wrote a comparative paper, 'North versus South: Energy Transition and Energy Intensity in Europe over 200 Years', published in the *European Review of Economic History* in 2007, which has received over 100 citations and is one of their most cited papers.

The book *Power to the People*: *Energy in Europe over the Last Five Centuries*, which I wrote together with Paul Warde and Paolo Malanima, was based on extensive data collection by this group of scholars. When I attended a conference about energy transitions in Eindhoven in 2009, one of the most famous professors of our discipline, Joel Mokyr, was there and very politely asked if he could interest us in publishing our planned book in his Princeton book series. We were very honoured, of course, and worked hard over several years on the 500-page manuscript. I had the privilege of setting the overall framework for the study based on one of Schön's favourite pictures: how three industrial revolutions were helpful in making a historical generalization of the trends in the long-run data series and their interrelations. The book is about innovations that enabled entirely new transformations of energy, which saved on the scarce land resource and increased power to the people, both physically and metaphorically. Innovations changed the relative prices of modern compared with traditional energy, and lowered the price of machinery compared with labour. This enabled capital deepening and economic growth.

The main puzzle we set out to solve in the book is why some important time series showed distinct trend breaks in the 1970s. Why was it that energy per capita in Europe stabilized after a long period of rapid growth after the first industrial revolution? And why did CO_2 emissions in Europe stagnate after the 1970s? Of course, the oil crises played some part in this, especially in households' propensity to save energy and better insulate their homes etc., and in the expansion of nuclear power, natural gas and domestic fuels. Our main argument for the stabilization of energy consumption is that economy structures changed after 1970 with more light industries and more service activities, consuming less energy. The lighter industrial structure was mainly related to the development block around ICT and due to internally changing patterns of consumption. Outsourcing of heavy industrial manufacturing production to less developed countries did not largely drive it, at least not for all countries. So here the optimistic interpretation of phases of economic development is clear, even though it gives a warning: the rapidly growing economies today, such as China and India, take the second and third industrial revolution in one big leap, and thus tend to increase their energy consumption. And climate change is far from solved. The third industrial revolution with ICT is never going to do the entire job of combating climate change through energy savings. There is a need for a rapid decoupling of carbon to energy, so-called 'decarbonization', by making the transition from fossil fuels. That change needs political determination.

In *Power to the People*, I have elaborated the development block concept, and adapted it to fit the energy transition discussion. My main new contribution is the periodization of the two concomitant forces in a development block: those of market suction (demand pull) and market widening (supply push). While Ljungberg and Schön do not make any periodization of which force is stronger in which periods, I argue that energy transitions are initially driven by a market suction period and later by a market-widening phase. The market-widening phase occurs when the new energy carrier (first coal and later oil) is used to transport itself out to the customers, via railways, steamships and oil tankers, so the price of it falls so drastically it stimulates the transition.

The second novel conceptual contribution is distinguishing between primary energy-saving development blocks and those that are energy expanding. While the major development block of the first industrial revolution (coal-steam-iron block) was largely energy expanding, the second industrial revolution had two major blocks: one around oil and internal combustion engines, which was also largely energy expanding, and another around electricity, which was to a great degree also energy saving. The third industrial revolution had one major development block, which is largely energy saving, by saving energy in old traditional industries through fine-tuning of material and energy flows, and stimulating the growth of lighter industries, even though the picture is complex because computers need electricity to run and the inputs for making computers can demand a lot of energy and material.

Service transition and the environment

Questioning established truths can be very stimulating. I was intrigued by the insights that Baumol had gained on the reasons for the growth of the service sector in modern societies. His idea of the cost disease of services stimulated the hypothesis that the service transition is perhaps a mere price illusion when measured in constant prices. If so, it could not logically be the reason why energy consumption stabilized in many countries after 1970. A shift-share analysis based on the sectors' shares in constant prices would then show that the decline in energy intensity was caused by what happened within the sectors, and was not due to any relative growth in the size of the service sector, if the polluting transport sector is treated separately. It turned out that the suspicion was correct for Sweden, and the argument and results were presented in 'Baumol's disease and dematerialization of the economy', published in *Ecological Economics* in 2005. I sent the draft to Professor William Baumol, and received a very nice and encouraging letter back, in which he said he found it interesting how his ideas had been used in another context and thought the argument was compelling and clear. I told my nine-year-old daughter Amanda about this letter the same day and she became really interested and wanted to know: what are you working with, Mummy? What is it called? If ever she becomes a researcher this will count as the start of her career.

Nevertheless, Sweden is only one country, and it would be interesting to see what the results were like for several other countries. Together with Sofia Henriques, who was my PhD candidate, I wrote a follow-up paper called 'The Modest Environmental Relief Resulting from the Transition to the Service Economy', published in *Ecological Economics* in 2010. As the title indicates, there was for some countries, unlike Sweden, a real (but modest) increase of the service sector in constant prices, and a full decomposition analysis, along the lines of Ang (2005), still confirmed that the most important driver were changes in the industrial sector and among households, as in the case of Sweden.

Energy and growth

Another scholar that had caught my early interest was David Stern, who had published extensively on energy and growth and on the environmental Kuznets curve (EKC), for instance 'The Rise and Fall of the Environmental Kuznets Curve' (Stern, 1998; Stern and Common, 2001; Stern, 2004). Encouraged by the friendly response by Professor Tony Wrigley, I took a chance and sent my dissertation to David Stern, too. This was the start of friendship and collaboration. David taught me to send manuscripts to top journals and in the case of refusal try the next, rather than becoming depressed. This was not how things were done yet in Sweden. Rather, people would put their manuscripts in drawers after they had presented them at some conference and in many cases never really complete or publish them at all. This has all changed now, but I learnt the American style early.

David's skills in economic modelling and econometrics were fruitfully used for economic environmental history. Together we wrote two articles that model industrialization where energy is an important factor of production: 'The Role of Energy in the Industrial Revolution and Modern Economic Growth' (2012) and 'Economic Growth and the Transition from Traditional to Modern Energy in Sweden' (2014).

How to account for consumption-based emissions?

In 2011 the picture that was frequently figuring in Swedish media was that Swedes had increased their carbon footprints substantially and that all the apparent gains from reduced emissions that had taken place when measured as territorial emissions were arguably due to outsourcing dirty production abroad. It was suggested that while we live in the service economy our industrial goods are produced elsewhere, in less developed countries (Hermele, 2002). Glen Peters, from Cicero Research Institute in Norway, accusingly said in Swedish media that Sweden was a country that cleaned its own backyard and threw the garbage over to their neighbours (*Dagens Nyheter*, 2011). Was this a fair way of depicting Swedish emissions? It was not the image Lindmark and I had of what was going on: Sweden was a country that had always relied firmly on her natural resources and exported a lot of energy-demanding iron and steel, and pulp and paper (Kander and Lindmark, 2006). And Sweden did this on the basis of an almost carbon-neutral technology, with an electricity supply that was based half on hydropower and half on nuclear power. Consequently, there is a strange imbalance in the way that conventional carbon footprints are calculated. While clean countries that import goods must take responsibility for both the amount and the structure of the goods they import, they are 'punished' for the dirty technology of the countries they buy things from also, by receiving higher national emission figures. But if they export things with clean technology, they do not receive any recognition for that. So cleaner countries always look worse in the carbon footprint account, even if they specialize in exporting goods that by necessity are energy demanding to produce, like steel. The easiest way to explain this is perhaps to consider a case where a country with low carbon emissions in their energy mix exchanges a certain amount of the same good, say steel, with a country that has coal as their dominant source of energy. This will make the cleaner country's carbon footprint increase, and the dirtier country's emissions decline, even if their consumption has not increased and no global emissions (apart from those involved in the transport of the goods) have increased. The more a cleaner country becomes involved in trade, the more their carbon footprint will increase. But this does not have to be mainly related to what you really want to measure with the carbon footprints: the amount and structure of consumption. It can at least partly be due to technology differences in what is exchanged in trade (Jacob and Marschinski, 2013).

What, then, is a suitable method for allocating carbon emissions among countries that trade with each other? Here counterfactual thinking was necessary and helpful. Together with Magnus Jiborn, a philosopher whom I recruited to an interdisciplinary project and who got really hooked on the idea of constructing the ideal method, we designed a method called the 'technology-adjusted carbon footprint'. This is in essence an improved carbon footprint, where countries also have to take responsibility for the technologies in their exports. We ask the counterfactual question: what if a certain export had not taken place from a country, what would have happened then? The most plausible assumption in our view is that some other producer would have provided it. Since we do not know who that producer would be, the least demanding assumption is that it would be provided at a weighted average technology for that product group on the world market. In practice, this means that a country like China that acts as a workshop for the world will receive lower emissions than the territorial emissions that they report to the UN, but they will not be able to fully deduct all the emissions in their export sector as in the conventional carbon footprint, but must resume responsibility for the share of export emissions that are surpassing the global average technology. A country like Sweden, on the other hand, will receive recognition for their relative cleanliness, and their contribution to lowering global emissions through their exports, by being able to deduct more emissions than they actually use in their export sector. This measure fulfils three reasonable principles: 1) it should be responsive to factors that nations can influence, such as level and composition of consumption and domestic carbon efficiency; 2) countries should not be able to reduce their national carbon footprints by acting in ways that contribute to increased global carbon emissions; and 3) the sum of emissions for all countries should equal global emissions. Together with Magnus Jiborn, Dan Moran (Norway) and Tommy Wiedmann (Sydney), whom I got into contact with through David Stern, we managed to recalculate the map of global CO_2 emissions. The method and the results were published in the May issue of *Nature Climate Change* in 2015. We have already been invited to speak about this method at several meetings, including the Swedish parliament. We also have a follow-up project, including new collaborators in Japan and from the field of political science in Sweden, which will start late this year, funded by the Swedish Energy Agency.

In another international project, funded by the Swedish Research Council, historical trade and the robustness of national energy histories to the consumption-based approach are studied. The project, along with several papers and a new database, TEG (Trade, Energy, Growth), is currently being completed by Paul Warde, Sofia Henriques, Hana Nielsen, Viktoras Kulionis, Dimitrios Theodoridis, Silvana Bartoletto and myself.

Conclusion

A strong research agenda, like that of structural analysis, carries the seeds of variety and internal development. Lennart Schön established such a strong research tradition at our department and his work has inspired mine. Lennart created an open atmosphere in his research group, where new ideas could thrive. As supervisor he was always acccessible, encouraging and helpful and never scared that we would get lost in the new bold tasks that we set out to accomplish. He never demanded full control over anything, which was very good.

The emerging field of economic environmental history is the product of the contribution of many scholars together, often in interdisciplinary projects. It has also shown that the new research topic is founded in the structural economic history tradition in Lund, where Lennart Schön has been the leader for many years. Together with Magnus Lindmark, I have been prominent in establishing this new research path within our discipline in Sweden and Europe. Schön and Krantz, our supervisors, of course influenced our way of thinking and approaching problems, and we both gained access to critical data sets, such as the newly constructed Swedish historical GDP. Conceptual ideas much used by Schön, such as those concerning three industrial revolutions and development blocks, have formed our own economic environmental narrative. And structural analysis and counterfactual thinking in our discipline have been critical in the novel approaches we have applied to our new research topic: the interrelations between the economy and the environment.

What would then be the response to the initial question in this essay about how innovative one is as a researcher and the extent to which one stands on the shoulders of giants? Here in the conclusion I would like to rephrase the allegory using a tree. Maybe the important question we should ask ourselves is rather: are we strong new branches on a tree trunk that flourish and give rewards to the entire tree?

This text was written with the aim of providing some guidance to younger scholars, who want to pursue a career in academia. So what practical advice could be given to this readership?

1   Things take time. Do not despair if you experience periods when not much happens, especially if you wrote a monograph and need to adjust it to the format and style of international journal articles.
2   Collaboration is very important for achieving success in research. This is because of complementarity in the competence, knowledge and personality of different scholars.
3   Counterfactual thinking and new methods based thereupon can be very useful for the analysis of new topics.
4   Do not take established ideas for granted! Be critical and challenge established ideas.
5   Be novel in new combinations! Be novel in the small bits and parts, try to modify concepts and ask new socially relevant questions.
6   Go to international conferences and workshops. Search for new contacts in your field of interest. Be bold and send your papers to people you admire and whose work has inspired you.

Note

1 Both these quotations are provided in Geels, 2011, p. 35.

References

Abbott, A. (1991), 'History and Sociology: The Lost Synthesis', *Social Science History*, vol. 15, pp. 201–38.

Ang, B. W. (2005), 'The LMDI Approach to Decomposition Analysis. A Practical Guide', *Energy Policy*, vol. 33, pp. 867–71.

Ayres, R. and Warr, B. (2005), 'Accounting for Growth: The Role of Physical Work', *Structural Change and Economic Dynamics*, vol. 16(2), pp. 181–209.

Barbier, E. (2005), *Natural Resources and Economic Development*. Cambridge: Cambridge University Press.

Barbier, E. (2011), *Scarcity and Frontiers: How Economies Have Developed through Natural Resource Exploitation*. Cambridge: Cambridge University Press.

Baumol, W. J. (1967), 'Macroeconomics of Unbalanced Growth: The Anatomy of Urban Crisis', *American Economic Review*, vol. 57, pp. 415–26.

Bergquist, A.-K. (2007), 'Guld och Gröna Skogar? Miljöanpassningen av Rönnskärsverken 1960–2000', *Umeå Studies in Economic History*, No. 36/2007 (diss.).

Bergquist, A.-K., Söderholm, K., Kinneryd, H., Lindmark, M. and Söderholm, P. (2013), 'Command-and-Control Revisited. Environmental Compliance and Technical Change in Swedish Industry 1970–1990', *Ecological Economics*, vol. 85, pp. 6–19.

Bresnahan, T. F. and Trajtenberg, M. (1995), 'General Purpose Technologies: "Engines of Growth"?' *Journal of Econometrics*, vol. 65, pp. 83–108.

Broadberry, S. (2006), *Market Services and the Productivity Race 1850–2000: British Performance in International Perspective*. Cambridge Studies in Economic History. Cambridge: Cambridge University Press.

Dagens Nyheter (2011), 6 August. Available online at: www.dn.se/ekonomi/import-ger-fina-egna-utslappssiffror/.

Dahmén, E. (1950), *Svensk industriell företagarverksamhet. Kausalanalys av den industriella utvecklingen 1919–1939*. Part I–II. Stockholm: IUI.

Dahmén, E. (1988), 'Development Blocks in Industrial Economics', *Scandinavian Economic History Review*, vol. 36, pp. 3–14.

Ekins, P. (2000), *Economic Growth and Environmental Sustainability: The Prospects of Green Growth*. London: Routledge.

Enflo, K., Kander, A. and Schön, L. (2008), 'Identifying Development Blocks: A New Methodology', *Journal of Evolutionary Economics*, vol. 18, pp. 57–76.

Enflo, K., Kander, A. and Schön, L. (2009), 'Electrification and Energy Productivity', *Ecological Economics*, vol. 68, pp. 2808–17.

Fogel, R. (1964), *Railroads and American Economic Growth: Essays in Econometric History*. Baltimore: Johns Hopkins Press.

Gales, B., Kander, A., Malanima, P. and Rubio, M. (2007), 'North versus South: Energy Transition and Energy Intensity in Europe over 200 Years', *European Review of Economic History*, vol. 11, pp. 219–53.

Geels, F. W. (2011), 'The Multi-level Perspective on Sustainability Transitions: Responses to Seven Criticisms', *Environmental Innovation and Societal Transitions*, vol. 1, pp. 24–40.

Grossman, G. M. and Kreuger, A. B. (1995), 'Economic Growth and the Environment', *Quarterly Journal of Economics*, vol. 110, pp. 353–77.

Henriques, S. and Kander, A. (2010), 'The Modest Environmental Relief Resulting from the Transition to the Service Economy', *Ecological Economics*, vol. 70, pp. 271–82.

Hermele, K. (2002), *Vad kostar framtiden? Globaliseringen, miljön och Sverige*. Stockholm: Ordfront.

Jacob, M. and R. Marschinski (2013), 'Interpreting Trade-related CO_2 Emission Transfers', *Nature Climate Change*, vol. 3, pp. 19–23.

Jörberg, L. (1972), *A History of Prices in Sweden, 1732–1914*. 2 vols. Lund: Gleerups.

Kander, A. (2002), *Economic Growth, Energy Consumption and CO_2 Emissions in Sweden 1800–2000*. Lund Studies in Economic History 19. Lund: Almqvist & Wiksell International.

Kander, A. (2005), 'Baumol's Disease and Dematerialization of the Economy', *Ecological Economics*, vol. 55, pp. 119–30.

Kander, A. (2008), 'Is it Simply Getting Worse? Agriculture and Swedish Greenhouse Gas Emissions over 200 Years', *Economic History Review*, vol. 61(4), pp. 773–97.

Kander, A. and Lindmark, M. (2004), 'Energy Consumption, Pollutant Emissions and Growth in the Long Run: Sweden through 200 Years', *European Review of Economic History*, vol. 8, pp. 297–335.

Kander, A. and Lindmark, M. (2006), 'Foreign Trade and Declining Pollution in Sweden: A Decomposition Analysis of Long-term Structural and Technological Effects', *Energy Policy*, vol. 34, pp. 1590–9.

Kander, A. and Schön, L. (2007), 'The Capital-Energy Ratio in Sweden 1870–2000', *Structural Change and Economic Dynamics*, vol. 18(3), pp. 291–305.

Kander, A. and Stern, D. I. (2014), 'Economic Growth and the Transition from Traditional to Modern Energy in Sweden', *Energy Economics*, vol. 46, pp. 56–65.

Kander, A., Malanima, P. and Warde, P. (2013), *Power to the People: Energy in Europe over the Last Five Centuries*. Princeton: Princeton University Press.

Kander, A., Jiborn, M., Moran, D. and Wiedmann, T. (2015), 'National Greenhouse-Gas Accounting for Effective Climate Policy on International Trade', *Nature Climate Change*, vol. 5(5), pp. 431–5.

Krantz, O. (1986), *Transporter och kommunikationer 1800–1980*. Lund: Studentlitteratur.

Krantz, O. (1987a), *Husligt arbete 1800–1980*. Lund: Studentlitteratur.

Krantz, O. (1987b), *Offentlig verksamhet 1800–1980*. Lund: Studentlitteratur.

Krantz, O. (1991), *Privata tjänster och bostadsutnyttjande 1800–1980*. Lund: Studentlitteratur.

Krantz, O. and Schön, L. (2007), *Swedish Historical Accounts 1800–2000*. Lund Studies in Economic History 41. Lund: Almqvist and Wiksell International.

Leunig, T. (2006), 'Time is Money: A Re-Assessment of the Passenger Social Savings from Victorian British Railways', *Journal of Economic History*, vol. 66, pp. 635–73.

Levander, T. (1991), 'Koldioxid – Utsläpp och beräkningsmetodik', *Nutek Rapport 12*.

Lindmark, M. (1998), *Towards Environmental Historical National Accounts for Sweden*. Umeå Studies in Economic History 21 (diss.).

Ljungberg, J. (1988), *Deflatorer för industriproduktionen 1800–1955*. Lund: Studentlitteratur.

Ljungberg, J. (1990), *Priser och marknadskrafter 1885–1969. En prishistorisk studie*. Lund: Ekonomisk historiska föreningen (diss.).

Martin, J.-M. (1988), 'L'íntensité energetique de l'activite economique dans les pays industrialises. Les evolutions de tres longue periode livrent-elles des enseignements utiles?' *Économies et Sociétés*, vol. 4, pp. 9–27.

Pedriana, N. (2005), 'Rational Choice, Structural Context and Increasing Returns: A Strategy for Analytic Narrative in Historical Sociology', *Sociological Methods & Research*, vol. 33, pp. 349–82.

Pettersson, L. (1987), *Byggnads och anläggningsverksamhet 1800–1980*. Lund: Studentlitteratur.

Reddy, A. K. N. and Goldemberg, J. (1990), 'Energy for the Developing World', *Scientific American*, vol. 263, pp. 111–18.

Schön, L. (1979), *Från hantverk till fabriksindustri. Svensk textiltillverkning 1820–1870*. Kristianstad: Arkiv (diss.).

Schön, L. (1988), *Industri och hantverk 1800–1980*. Lund: Ekonomisk-historiska föreningen.

Schön, L. (1990), *Elektricitetens betydelse för svensk industriell utveckling*. Stockholm: Vattenfall.

Schön, L. (1992), *Trädbränslen i Sverige 1800–1990 – användning och prisutveckling*. Stockholm: Vattenfall.

Schön, L. (1994), *Omvandling och obalans. Mönster i svensk ekonomisk utveckling*. Bilaga 3 till Långtidsutredningen 1994. Stockholm: Finansdepartementet.

Schön, L. (1995), *Jordbruk med bināringar 1800–1980*. Lund: Studentlitteratur.

Schön, L. (1998), 'Industrial Crises in a Model of Long Cycles. Sweden in an International Perspective'. In Myllyntaus, T. (ed.) *Economic Crises and Restructuring in History. Experiences of Small Countries*. Katharinen: Scripta Meracaturae.

Schön, L. (2000), *En modern svensk ekonomisk historia. Tillväxt och omvandling under två sekel*. Stockholm: SNS.

Schön, L. (2004), 'Total Factor Productivity in Swedish Manufacturing in the Period 1870–2000.' In Heikkinen, S. and van Zanden, J. L. (eds), *Explorations in Economic Growth*. Amsterdam: Aksant.

Schön, L. (2007), 'Technological Shifts and Convergence in a European Perspective since 1950', *Scandinavian Economic History Review*, vol. 55, pp. 222–43.

Schön, L. (2012), *An Economic History of Modern Sweden*. Oxon: Routledge.

Schön, L. and Krantz, O. (2012), 'Swedish Historical National Accounts 1560–2010', *Lund Papers in Economic History 123*. Lund: Lund University. Annual updates available online at: www.ekh.lu.se/en/research/economic_history_data/shna1560-2010.

Selden, T. and Song, D. (1993), 'Environmental Quality and Development: Is there a Kuznets Curve for Air Pollution Emissions', *Journal of Environmental Economics and Management*, vol. 27, pp. 147–62.

Söderholm, K. and Bergquist, A.-K. (2013), 'Environmental Adaptation and Industrial Competitiveness: Experiences from the Swedish Pulp Industry', *Sustainability*, vol. 5, pp. 1789–805.

Stern, D. I. (1998), 'Progress on the Environmental Kuznets Curve?' *Environment and Development Economics*, vol. 3, pp. 173–96.

Stern, D. I. (2004), 'The Rise and Fall of the Environmental Kuznets Curve.' *World Development*, vol. 32(8), pp. 1419–39.

Stern, D. I. and Common, M. S. (2001), 'Is there an Environmental Kuznets Curve for Sulfur?' *Journal of Environmental Economics and Management*, vol. 41, pp. 162–78.

Stern, D. I. and Kander, A. (2012), 'The Role of Energy in the Industrial Revolution and Modern Economic Growth', *Energy Journal*, vol. 33(3), pp. 127–54.

Wallerstein, I. (1974), *The Modern World-System I. Capitalist Agriculture and the Origins of the European World-Economy in the Sixteenth Century*. London: Academic Press.

World Bank (1992), *World Development Report 1992: Development and the Environment*. New York: Oxford University Press.

Ziliak, S. T. and McCloskey, D. N. (2004), 'Size Matters: The Standard Error of Regressions in the American Economic Review', *Journal of Socio-Economics*, vol. 33, pp. 527–46.

Index

actor industries 153, 154, 155
adjusted geographic concentration index (AGC) 132, 136
advancing industries 80
ARIMA models 35

band spectrum regressions 44–52; how to estimate a model 44–6; inflation and economic growth 48–52; ordinary least-squares estimator 44; regression results inflation model 50, 51; simulations 46
bank: central 105; commercial 104; -created money 112; currency operations 115; deposits 117; investment 4; national 108
banking crisis 100
biased technical change 180
bill jobbing 117
bottleneck situation 167
branch banks 114
bullionist controversy 112
business cycle theory, weakest point of 59

calculus models 25
capital imports 103–5, 122
capitalism: description of 57–8; industrial 150
carrier industries 71
causal analysis 21
climate change 13, 180
Cliometrics 19
coefficient of variation (CV) 131, 137
commercial banks 104
Cow Deal 90
creative destruction see Gerschenkron effect, creative destruction and structural analysis
criticalities 143
currency principle 114, 115

cycles and long waves in economic time series, identifying and modelling of 34–55; ARIMA models 35; band spectrum regressions 44–52; cycles in economic activity 38–44; discrete wavelet transform 36; GDP growth 39; inflation and economic growth 48–52; maximal overlap discrete wavelet transform 36; multiresolution analysis 37–44; ordinary least-squares estimator 44; orthogonality property 37; regression results inflation model 50, 51; total factor productivity growth 38, 40; transform matrix 37; wavelet analysis 35–52; wavelet transform 36–37

decarbonization 183
decomposition analysis 176
deflation 28, 106
demand-driven industries 157
demand-pull manufacturing 80, 97
demand-reduction manufacturing 80, 97
Dependency tradition 178
development blocks and structural analysis 56–77; boundaries and composition of development blocks 68–72; business cycle theory, weakest point of 59; carrier industries 71; creative response 61; development blocks in comparative perspective 67–8; development blocks and techno-economic interdependencies 58–9; dilemma 167; evolution of development blocks 62; gap filling innovations 60; general-purpose technologies 63–5; geographical innovation clusters 61; historical approaches 65–7; imbalances that spurred innovation activity 70; induced industries 65;

innovations 62, 63; location theory 60; lock-in 63; major technology shifts and technological systems 63–7; modularity 71; network communities 70; network phase 62; notion of development blocks and its genesis 59–63; rationalization and efficiency 62; reverse salients 66; Schumpeter-type disequilibrating innovations 60; second industrial revolution 64; sequence of widening imbalances 62; structure and interdependence in economic thought 57–8; system goal 66; techno-economic paradigms 64–5; transformation pressure 61
discrete wavelet transform (DWT) 36

economic environmental history 174–90; accounting for consumption-based emissions 185–6; biased technical change 180; capital/energy ratio 180; climate change 180; decarbonization 183; decomposition analysis 176; development blocks 177; economic environmental history 179–80; economic-historical heritage 175–9; energy, capital and identifying development blocks 180–1; energy in Europe over the last five centuries 182–3; energy and growth 184–5; environmental history of Sweden 181–2; environmental Kuznets curve 179, 184; hermeneutics 175; information and communication technology 177; international project 186; materialistic world view 175; outsourcing of heavy industrial manufacturing production 183; price illusions 178; questioning of established facts 176; service transition and the environment 184; social savings approach 176; spillover effects from electricity on productivity 181; stabilization of energy consumption 183; structural change 177; World-System theory 178
economic growth and inequality among Swedish regions (1860–2010) development of 126–48; adjusted geographic concentration index 132, 136; benchmarks 131; coefficient of variation 131, 137; convergence, divergence and cycles 142–4; creative destruction, stability following 126; criticalities 143; data and measurement

130–2; empirical patterns 145; era of increased market integration 143; GDP per capita 138, 139; "great spurt" 127; industrial cycles 143; location and names of the Swedish regions 133; long-run regional inequality 128; long-term development of regional inequality 132–42; New Economic Geography 128; operationalization and measurement techniques 131–2; post-industrial era 129; regional concentration index 131; regional GDP 130; regional shares of total national GDP in 1860 and 2007 134; regional shares of total national population in 1860 and 2007 135; regional transformation matrix 141; solidaristic wage policy 129; structural cycle 129; Swedish growth experience from a regional perspective 127–30; Swedish model of economic organization 129; technology shift model 128; Third Industrial Revolution 129, 144
economic history 19–33; calculus models 25; causal analysis 21; Cliometrics 19; deflation periods 28; index number problem 20; Keynesian theory 25; Krantz and Nilsson (1978) 23; Marxist theory 19; periodization 21; structural limits in the Swedish economy (1861–1975) 24–30; sub-aggregates 28; Swedish historical national accounts 22–3; theory of technical change 20
economic theory prices 78
economic time series, cycles and long waves in 34–55; ARIMA models 35; band spectrum regressions 44–52; cycles in economic activity 38–44; discrete wavelet transform 36; GDP growth 39; inflation and economic growth 48–52; maximal overlap discrete wavelet transform 36; multiresolution analysis 37–44; ordinary least-squares estimator 44; orthogonality property 37; regression results inflation model 50, 51; total factor productivity growth 38, 40; transform matrix 37; wavelet analysis 35–52; wavelet transform 36–37
energy-saving bias in capital accumulation 180
entrepreneur 2
environmental Kuznets curve (EKC) 179, 184

failed innovation 86
foreign borrowing 118
fund theory 112

gap filling innovations 60
GDP: growth, wavelet analysis 39;
    regional 130; Swedish regional 127
general-purpose technologies (GPT) 63,
    149, 151
geographical innovation clusters 61
geographical reference cycle 158
Gerschenkron effect, creative destruction
    and structural analysis 78–102;
    advancing industries 80; agricultural
    machinery 88; banking crisis 100;
    branches of manufacturing 80;
    classification of industries according
    to change in relative prices 95–6; Cow
    Deal 90; creative destruction 80, 91;
    data, prices and quality change 82–5;
    economic theory prices 78; electrical
    equipment, relative price of 87;
    Gerschenkron effect 81; hedonic index
    82; HMPI 84; imitating firms 85; index-
    number problem 79; industry innovation
    80; international prices 91; Laspeyres
    price index 79, 83; machinery, relative
    price of 86; mineral goods 90; negative
    Gerschenkron effect 98; Paasche price
    index 79, 83; phenomenon of falling
    prices 78; points of departure 79–81;
    positive and negative transformation
    pressure 91–100; quality change 84;
    rationalization 94; relative prices of
    significant products 85–91; stagnating
    industries 80; textiles 89; typology of
    market forces 99
gold standard and industrial breakthrough
    in Sweden 103–25; bill jobbing 117;
    bill legislation 120; branch banks
    114; bullionist controversy 112; buy-
    backs 113; capital imports 103–5,
    122; convertibility 105, 108; credit
    instruments 117; currency mismatches
    119–20; currency principle 114,
    115; deflation 106; development and
    integration of the payment and banking
    system, foreign borrowing and *Riksbank*
    117–19; development of currency
    policies 112–14; developments after
    the crisis in 1857 114–16; emergency
    loans 114, 122; foreign borrowing 118;
    foreign currency 109, 111; foreign debt
    122; fund theory 112; gold standard

and capital imports 105–6; government
    borrowing 104; Holm disaster 118;
    liquidity buffer 114; Long Depression
    106; monetary tightening 114; mortgage
    associations 104; National Debt Office
    118, 122; Original Sin problem 109;
    paradoxical development 114; price
    specie flow mechanism 107; redemption
    of banknotes, obstruction of 116;
    rules of the gold standard game 107;
    Scandinavian credit market conditions
    120; silver standard 112; sources of gold
    standard stability 106–10; Stockholm-
    Hamburg-London triangle 117
government: agricultural reforms 23; bond
    issues 119; borrowing (Sweden) 104;
    budget discipline 167; currency stability
    109; custom duties 106; labour market
    policies 129; post-war policy 81
Great Depression (Sweden) 106

hedonic index, price quotations and 82
hermeneutics 175
hierarchy (regional analysis) 164
Holm disaster 118

imitating firms 85
index-number problem 20, 79
induced industries 65
industrial capitalism 150
information and communication
    technology (ICT) 177
innovation: alternating current in
    three-phase system 62; clustering
    of 3; cognitive search area of 149;
    complementarities 64; downstream
    68; electrical sector 144; failed 86;
    imbalances that spurred 70; industry
    80; interdependencies of 57; negative
    transformation pressure and 92;
    opportunities for 7, 126; product and
    process 81, 152; secular waves of 6;
    theory of 21; types 60
international prices 91
investment bank 4

job: creation 164, 165, 171; losses 165;
    performance 151

Keynesian theory 25

Laspeyres price index 79, 83
location theory 60, 170
lock-in (development blocks) 63

Long Depression (Sweden) 106
long waves *see* cycles and long waves in economic time series, identifying and modelling of

machinery, relative price of 86
manufacture prices, change of 78
manufacturing, branches of 80
market situations, ideal 152
Marxist theory 19
maximal overlap discrete wavelet transform (MODWT) 36
mineral goods 90
mortgage associations 104
multiresolution analysis 37–44

negative Gerschenkron effect 98
network communities 70
New Economic Geography (NEG) 128

ordinary least-squares (OLS) estimator 44
Original Sin problem 109
outsourcing 183, 185

Paasche price index 79, 83
periodization 21
phenomenon of falling prices 78
post-industrial era 129
price illusions 178
price specie flow mechanism 107

rationalization 94, 151
regional analysis and the process of economic development 149–73; actor industries 153, 154, 155; bottleneck situation 167; catch-up period 161; classification of service industries 154; demand-driven industries 157, 163; drivers of economic growth in regions 162–4; drivers of transformation in regions 159–62; empirical issues 151–5; general-purpose technologies 149, 151; geographical reference cycle 158; growth and employment 164–7; growth indices 156; growth and regional income 167–70; hierarchy 164; ideal market situations 152; increasing returns 152; industrial capitalism 150; job creation 165; labour market 167; location theory 170; most salient supply- and demand-driven industries 155, 156; national picture 155–7; pensions and social transfer payments 168; rationalization 151; regional economic change, theory

about 150; regional receiver and development competence 152; Robin Hood effect 168; structural cycle, culmination crisis of 155; supply-driven industries 157; systemic approach to regional development 157–9; technology shift thesis 150; transformation crisis 156; value added 159, 164
regional concentration index 131
regional economic change, theory about 150
reverse salients 66
Robin Hood effect 168

Schumpeter-type disequilibrating innovations 60
social savings approach 176
structural analysis and the process of economic development 1–18; climate change 13; contributions 10–14; entrepreneur 2; patterns of growth 3–10; secular waves of innovation 6; structural cycles 1–3; systemic approach 13; technology flow matrix 12; total factor productivity 11
structural periods *see* economic history
supply-contraction manufacturing 80, 97
supply-driven industries 156, 157
supply-push manufacturing 80, 97
system goal 66

techno-economic paradigms (TEPs) 64–5
technology-adjusted carbon footprint 186
technology flow matrix 12
Third Industrial Revolution 129, 144
total factor productivity (TFP) 11, 38
transformation pressure 61, 91–100

value added (VA) 159, 164

wavelet analysis 35–52; ARIMA models 35; band spectrum regressions 44–52; cycles in economic activity 38–44; discrete wavelet transform 36; GDP growth 39; inflation and economic growth 48–52; maximal overlap discrete wavelet transform 36; multiresolution analysis 37–44; ordinary least-squares estimator 44; orthogonality property 37; regression results inflation model 50, 51; total factor productivity growth 38, 40; transform matrix 37; wavelet transform 36–37
World-System theory 178

For Product Safety Concerns and Information please contact our EU
representative GPSR@taylorandfrancis.com
Taylor & Francis Verlag GmbH, Kaufingerstraße 24, 80331 München, Germany